THE SELF OBSERVED

THE SELF
OBSERVED

Swift

Johnson

Wordsworth

MORRIS GOLDEN

The Johns Hopkins Press

BALTIMORE AND LONDON

The Johns Hopkins Press, Baltimore, Maryland 21218
The Johns Hopkins Press Ltd., London

Library of Congress Catalog Card Number 70-179137

ISBN 0-8018-1289-5

TO

Hilda, Olivia, Daniel

CONTENTS

PREFACE

WHEN I WAS planning this study, Professors Donald J. Greene, Robert L. Haig, Arthur Sherbo, and the late Edward L. McAdam, Jr., were so good as to recommend it to the John Simon Guggenheim Memorial Foundation, and I hereby thank them and the Foundation for a year of unexpectedly comfortable work. At a stage when I was uncertain which of several related organizing devices to make central, Professor Ronald Paulson commissioned a paper on the author's involvement in his work for an issue of *Eighteenth Century Studies* which he was to edit; writing "The Imagining Self in the Eighteenth Century" (an earlier version of parts of Chapters I, II, and VI, which Professor Robert Hopkins, the editor of *Eighteenth Century Studies*, has kindly granted me permission to use) helped me to settle my approach. In Oxford, where I spent a year reading and writing, I found a particularly cheering welcome from Dr. L. F. Powell, Dr. J. D. Fleeman, Dr. Roger Lonsdale, and Miss Kirstie Morrison; a convenient reading room in the Bodleian; and courteous cooperation from the librarians at the English Faculty Library. At home, I am grateful to the library staffs of the Connecticut Valley colleges, particularly to that of the University of Massachusetts; and I want to thank most warmly my colleague, Professor Richard Noland, whose reading of the first draft prevented at least some of the inaccuracies that I was planning to perpetrate.

I

INTRODUCTION

IN THIS ESSAY, I seek in the works of Swift, Johnson, and Words-worth their distinctive visions of man in the world; and in them and some of their contemporaries, a hint of how the conceptions of individual writers are related to a communal vision. Though such goals loom distressingly vague, in constant danger of blurring into a haze of time spirit and world orientation, at least the first and main one would have had their sanction. Again and again, Swift, Johnson, and Wordsworth tell us to observe their creatures as symbols, archetypes, emblems, allegories, myths, or forms of man acting out his life. And even where they leave such readings implicit, our critical age insists on the presence of large symbols: though we may devastate whole forests to print our quarrels over *Gulliver's Travels*, we agree that like *An Essay on Man, Rasselas, The Prelude*, and *Prometheus Unbound* it undertakes to show us man in the world.

We would agree also, I think, that as great artists and as representatives of their times, Swift, Johnson, and Wordsworth should repay such study with pleasure and with some instruction in the shaping of the literary imagination. They all wrote a great deal, both publicly and privately; they have been the subjects of extensive and sometimes stimulating examination; their careers range over a fascinating and ambiguous span of great changes in every aspect of western life; and they provide rich mixtures of the idiosyncratic, the generic, the topical, and the universal to feed our larger speculations over the distinctions among them.

Such distinctions between the generic and the universally literary on the one hand and the idiosyncrasies of person or period on the other do not immediately strike the reader, for western tradition unites more than the words *classical* and *romantic* can divide. Although the change in literary orientation from Swift's birth to Wordsworth's death has sometimes looked massive and fundamental, the same underlying patterns of psychological and social life informed the imaginative visions of those writers whom we still know. In the narratives of Swift, Johnson, and Wordsworth, for example, the transition from innocence to experience was the staple archetype, as it was in most other fiction of their time. Although writers defined the terms of this transition idiosyncratically and ranged in response from Swift's grim or Johnson's melancholy acceptance through Jane Austen's cheerful preference for adulthood to Blake's and Shelley's intense compensatory faith in transcendence, they generally shared a conception of it as a movement from integrity to division.

Furthermore, all the writers, whether Neoclassical, Post-Augustan, Preromantic, or Romantic, are more or less participants in the great debates over man's lot which have stirred literature from before *The Odyssey*: the claims of subjective and objective, of what is outside and what inside; the value of retirement as against social activity; the surface against the substance; appearance against reality; imaginative delusion against imaginative transcendence; the motives of mind against the body's appetites. All of them reflect the pressure of the social system on the ideal of self-fulfillment and social harmony; all seek to reconcile psychology ("nature") and dreams of moral law, some like Johnson exalting experience, others like Pope and Wordsworth more pleased to contemplate universal schemes. In the process, all grope to reconcile free will and determinism; to ascertain whether order is single and available, continually to be assembled or organically developing; to relate morality, private feelings, and other people; to define and compare civilization and the primitive; to choose between or combine the easy-instinctive and the arduous intellectual or voluntary. And like all writers whatever the era, in attacking chaos or the mechanical, each sees himself as champion of life against death.

But while these authors are representatives of the western humane tradition, they are also distinct personalities expressing themselves during a specific segment of this tradition. Granted that personality is elusive, indeed ultimately undiscoverable, still some of its larger distinguishing characteristics can be defined where a long lifetime of publishing provides massive materials. Borrowing an idea from a letter of Johnson's to Mrs. Thrale, I assume that each writer is an organic being who responds to life and sees his visions in ways special to himself. After a certain period, Johnson wrote on August 2, 1775, the mind, like the body, has reached its maturity and no longer advances: "The mind may be stored with new languages, or new sciences, but its power of thinking remains nearly the same, and unless it attains new subjects of meditation, it commonly produces thoughts of the same force and the same extent, at very distant intervals of life, as the tree unless a foreign fruit be ingrafted gives year after year productions of the same force and the same flavour."[1]

Evidently, if we could know all the essential elements which form the mind of any writer, we could thoroughly understand him and therefore his work. Such certainty, however, even if it were desirable is impossible. Our progress from understanding the writer to examining his books suffers grandly from our uncertainty about both our origin and our destination and in detail from the impossibility of knowing everything that happened to him, deriving meaningful patterns from the knowledge, and confidently applying to the creations of unique artists such general and limiting labels as "guilt complexes," "anxiety neuroses," or "identity crises." If we nerve ourselves to such claims, we may well be substituting a reductive illusion for the rich reality of the poem or novel. But to abandon hope because we cannot be certain, and like the linguists in Swift's Grand Academy of Lagado point wordlessly to avoid thinking about our subject, would be critically evasive, even cowardly. Perhaps we can seek the artist's personality through less precise and technical avenues, and perhaps we can guess at its ties with the imagination through the work of art itself. Instead of delusions of certainty, perhaps we can establish manageable approximations, representative characteristics of the organism, the fruits from which we can infer the species of the tree.

Whatever the imagination's ultimate source, it surely derives much of its force and shape from our reveries; and these reveries—most of our undirected mental activity and much that is voluntary—largely center on ourselves. Since literature is a direct product of the individual imagination at work on the condition of man, a specific writer's creations are likely to take their form from the brooding of his individual imagination on his own condition. This, at any rate, is the approach which I am testing, the element which I hope can give value to this essay: that a writer sees man in the world more or less in ways that reflect his view of himself in the world. My first object, then, is to discover how the writer habitually sees himself. I pursue this northwest passage to the writer's work and his mind mainly in his letters, conversations, and diaries, and I take cautious sightings where necessary against what seem to be the objective circumstances of his life. If I can follow the markings of the self-image (to fly the fashion-

[3]

able colors of our time), I may arrive at a clearer understanding of the shapes that the imagination has taken in its triumphant embodiment in literature.

Throughout, I have tried to be skeptical of easy relationships, whether psychological or social. Large elements immediately visible in the lives of the writers would obviously affect the forms and themes of their work—for example, Pope's abnormal smallness, Thomson's migration across the border, the advanced age of Johnson's parents at his birth, and Wordsworth's loss of his parents in early life. Yet the private and partly unconscious evaluations of reverie are not necessarily proportional to what others see as outward stimuli; none of our authors could anticipate what his biographers two centuries later would call significant experience, even if like Goldsmith he could smell our sort of age, "when the Scaligers and Daciers will vindicate my character, give learned editions of my labours, and bless the times with copious comments on the text."[2] Though Swift's exceptional orphaned birth and his kidnapping in childhood perhaps should have directed his attitudes on everything from authority to the metallurgy of pennies, they have left no clear track in his writings; but his Irish nationality, which he shared with enough people for it to be called normal, formed an important locus of his reveries and a clear influence on his works.

Again, and analogously, I have tried to determine a writer's concerns or fantasies on the basis of his texts and personal writings rather than on the basis of "objective" biographical evidence. Since a writer's works may be scattered over a long period of time (during which his social class and environment often change bewilderingly) and in various circumstances and forms, we can see inconsistencies and contradictions; yet we may also discover the thread of individual identity. Secondary biographical sources are perhaps less trustworthy, for people's reactions to an author are often variable, scattered, haphazardly preserved, biased by their own expectations, and uncertain in language and scope. As often, Johnson has most clearly made this point:

> Nothing but experience could evince the frequency of false information, or enable any man to conceive that so many groundless reports should be propagated, as every man of eminence may hear of himself. Some men relate what they think, as what they know; some men, of confused memories and habitual inaccuracy, ascribe to one man, what belongs to another; and some talk on, without thought or care. A few men are sufficient to broach

falsehoods, which are afterwards innocently diffused by successive relaters.[3]

In short, it is much easier to say precisely what Swift or Johnson or
Wordsworth thought of his England, even allowing for any man's
normal gyrations and posturings, than to determine his place in it.

In arriving at the writer's self-image, I do not assume that his patterns of acting and thinking were set in early childhood or at any
arbitrary age, though it seems to me plausible that very general
responses to the world, such as retreat or eager engagement with challenges, may be formed early. Furthermore, I see no reason to relate
the general patterns and movements of the writings or the writer's
mind to a single touchstone, such as his sexual predilections or his
complexes or syndromes, though our storehouse of reductive labels
tempts me as it tempts my betters. That Thomson's imagination cher-
ishes images and patterns of probing and fertilizing seems to me important not as a clue to his long-vanished lusts, but as a guide to the forms
of his poetry and the nature of his world vision. Very possibly a
sexual drive lurks in such a vision, or in Johnson's pouncing on experience or Wordsworth's worries about purity, and it may even excite
readers; but I cannot see how or why to gauge the unintended effects
of complex poetry on an infinite variety of indeterminable sensibilities.

To arrive at the authors' visions, I had planned to seek no special
techniques or devices aside from thematic analysis and moderately
close reading. Because I have always been puzzled by the postulated
shift from objective to subjective as "Classicism" moved to "Romanticism," I had expected to begin by examining the relations of literary
and actual self in such poems as the *Epistle to Arbuthnot*, *The
Deserted Village*, and *Tintern Abbey*. A good deal of help in this
direction has come from recent discussions, to which I refer in Chapter II, of persona and autobiography. But in the midst of my work,
I realized that my writers were splitting their reveries of the self into
an observed, struggling, idiosyncratic element acting in the world
and a reflective self which observed it. Through this device, or habit,
or unconsidered reflex pattern so congenial to the dualisms apparent
then in all areas, writers were able not only to formulate such sub-
sidiary issues as the proper relations between the reason and the
passions, the self and society, and the specific and the general, but
more fundamentally to convey a sense of man's whole career on and
off the stage of the world. As I looked with the consciousness of the

divided self, an approach suggested by contemporary thinking in various fields, I seemed to see more clearly the individual achievements of the writers and the change through the century and a half. If this view is accurate, the relations between projected selves, varying among individual writers and yet responding to the impress of particular times, may open an additional way to the understanding not only of Swift, Johnson, and Wordsworth, but of literature.

II

OBSERVER
AND OBSERVED
IN EIGHTEENTH-
CENTURY LITERATURE

IN THE EIGHTEENTH century as always, poets perceived and imagined
their unique worlds as participants in the life of a certain time and
place, as heirs of history, and as distinct, special selves. Their creating
imaginations, like those of all writers, took impressions and even shape
from their public experience—the theses and explosions and portents of
their time, the genres provided by the past, and the enduring myths
and archetypes—and also from their personal ways of understanding
reality and dealing with it. Often, and particularly I think in the
eighteenth century, this imagination has been directed by a double
sense of the writer as representative man: as a self acting across a
world stage and as an observer evaluating the complex of actor
and world.

To critics and historians defining a writer's imaginative world, the
part contributed by environment has seemed most substantial, perhaps
because it is easiest to substantiate. Dryden's mind and his poems, for
example, were evidently stamped by the Stuart problem of royal suc-
cession, and Fielding, Goldsmith, and Cowper came upon the moral
poles of London and Somerset-Auburn-Olney-Eden amidst the social
upheavals of urbanization. Such outward events and conditions as

British adventures on the European continent and empire-building on the others, domestic Whig-Tory or Catholic-Protestant antagonisms, the rise of Methodism, the bustle of the Royal Society and the discoveries by Newton and Boyle, economic booms and bubbles, the slave trade, increased dealings with the Orient and the Caribbean, the revolutions of 1715, 1745, 1776, and especially 1789, all provide masses of phenomena from which to fashion the literature of an age. Though not the constituents of the imagination, these are its materials, stimuli, and casual guides.

Other themes and images which modify poetic worlds are too deeply implicated in the culture for huge or sudden changes, and yet they may be insistent at one time and subdued at another. The conflicting calls of the contemplative and active life or of the individual and society sound throughout literature, but the first pair are heard more often before the seventeenth century and the second since. Medical and architectural images, a fundamental part of the "conservative myth" when studied in Dryden,[1] proliferate whenever a traditional vision of world order is in danger, as in Jacobean and Victorian literature and in our own evangelical campaign rhetoric ("America the sick society" or "a continent of falling dominoes"). If harmony is thought of as imitating nature's unity in variety, then gardening images crowd on the writer's soul: pruning excrescences, enjoying profusion, or trying carefully to combine the bold and regular can provide models of the best way for ordering the mind, a political organization, art, education, athletics, sex, or any other experience which can be conceived of as characteristic.

Like themes and tropes, the various genres wax and wane in their ascendancy over the creative effort. We cannot doubt the importance of the generic stance of the satirist in Pope's *Epistle to Arbuthnot*, though we recognize in him the idiosyncratic poet as well.[2] Aside from such ancient genres as pastoral elegy, Roman elegy, pindaric ode, Horatian ode, georgic, formal satire, comedy, epic, and tragedy, the eighteenth century was profuse if not rich in elaborations or inventions of its own: the great ode addressed to a personified abstraction, the topographical poem, the country-house poem, the picaresque novel, the prose allegory, the romance, the comic epic poem in prose, the opened packet of mail which could become *Pamela*, the travel description which led to *Humphry Clinker*, the confessional spiritual autobiography such as *Robinson Crusoe*, the utopian fiction, the protean oriental tale, the rogue biography, the Rabelaisan miscellany, the series of essays fictionally connected in a *Spectator* or a *Citizen of the*

World, the quarreling epilogue, the imitation of a classical poem, and so on. Yet usable genres change with time and need; a current list would discard some of these forms (for example, the great ode) and add at least the lyric in free verse (our universal pickle), the epiphanic short story, the absurdist play.

Less enslaved by time and place are, by definition, the archetypal figures or conditions or myths—the patterns that seem to be available to us all, presumably because of the recurrence of the forms of psychological energy or of social interaction, for Swift and Fielding the eternal identity of Nature. Among the archetypes of reverie are the fantasies of sexual or social dominance, of the Oedipus complex, of children dying to reproach their parents' inhumanity, of guarded virgins and marauding strangers, of the ideal community or the heavenly city or the garden of Eden, of recollections of innocence idealized and destroyed, of ugly ducklings becoming swans, beauties mating with beasts, deadened selves revived by the kiss of love, and heroes (Roderick Random) or villains (Vathek) tearing their ways through the world against all odds. Such archetypes seem more congenial to some periods than to others, but as genuine aspects of the human condition they are always at least latent: Prometheus flourishes among the romantics, but we can also find him in Gray's Bard and Richardson's Lovelace.[3]

In a world arranged to discourage critical arrogance, none of the social or psychological forces can be precisely defined as an influence on any writer or even single work, much less on the literature of an age. Intellectual currents wash over millennia, wars tap undying responses through the viscera, and genre, myth, and the elements of the mind cloudily merge and separate in the caverns of ultimate answers. But if the angels suspect the footing, the best authorities advise hardihood. Without rushing in to settle the claims of all the influences on eighteenth-century English literature, I can try to look freshly at one mildly neglected element in that literature, the author's sense of himself as it affects his vision of life.

In so far as these senses of the self are archetypal and recurrent, they are parts of man's universal vision, uniting Virgil with Milton over seventeen hundred years, and Horace with Herrick. But though the dreams of perfect omnipotence and perfect passivity, of perfect love and perfect hate, of serene heaven and restless hell, of passionate heaven and frozen hell, inform the contending myths of mankind, when incorporated in specific works of art, which flow from the individual imagination engaging man's career and fate, they project the private special worlds of the writer's reveries. Writers who see themselves as separated from society, as subject to attack or eminent above attack, as eagerly seeking adventure or domestically secure, as fearing disorder or delighted with haphazard variety or profusion, or as gloomy with guilt or innocently radiant, would seem likely to create worlds containing characters in similar conditions. If, for example, a writer conceives of himself as a sensible man surrounded by malign chaos, he may recurrently create figures, like Gulliver, who teeter on the edge of madness and sometimes fall.

Where the artistic world is viable, its private vision has universal allies. While the pattern of hope and disappointment partially emanates from Swift's or Johnson's views of the self, it may also be an inevitable aspect of satire or of all art, an archetype of man's ultimate defeat by death.[4] What individuates an artist would be the positions he assumes and the myths he most intensely projects; what individuates his period may well be not only its favorite myths but how its artists resolve the conflicts and divisions in themselves and in the myths that they find congenial.

Unlike Swift in *A Tale of a Tub*, a mere critic cannot assert the vision of a period; but it seems reasonable to seek a possible unity in the private visions of its most sensitive people, its literary artists. Our conception of the European renaissance or of the expansive American spirit of the nineteenth century is surely based on the exuberant visions of Ariosto, Rabelais, and Marlowe, of Twain, Whitman, and even Emerson, though there is more to it, as there is more to these writers. If a similar connection exists between the private and the public, between the idiosyncratic in the poet and the character of his culture in eighteenth-century England, perhaps we can find it in a fundamental element in significant imagined worlds, the conception of the self striving in the world.

In the eighteenth century particularly, the vision of man projected against the world, which is always part of the artist's imagination, seems characteristically to reflect the author's private cheering or admonishing sense of himself. Eighteenth-century writers consistently advertise universal intentions in their idiosyncratic portraits, which they often copy from a mirror as in *Tristram Shandy* or Pope's *Epistle to Arbuthnot*. Wherever we look in the period, we are reminded that its guiding epistemological concept is Locke's divided mind, one part operating on signals from without and one observing these operations. The image, or rather the sense, of a separated observing self is a shaping element of the century's consciousness, a part of its literary attitude and expectation which could enter into Boswell's stance as diarist, a critic's normal assumptions about the psychological condition of theatergoers, a Richardsonian heroine's writing "to the moment" of sexual turmoil, and an essay series or a poem by the Spectator, the Wanderer, the Rambler, the Connoisseur, the Citizen of the World, the Hermit in Town, or the Traveller.[5] Almost every eighteenth-century writer presents ironic epitomes of himself, which he persuades us are the visions of what is in us. When Gulliver the hero-butt looks at a Yahoo and recognizes himself, he enacts his author's discovery and anticipates ours.

Since full proof of the tie between the private and the public visions, based on a complete examination of everything asserted to be imaginative in the century, is impossible, one must select. I begin with three poets—two unquestioned in their time as both representative and distinguished, and one high in current esteem. While Pope, Thomson, and Smart do not touch all aspects of the eighteenth century, they ranged widely enough in genres and techniques and differed in enough ways as persons in specific situations to provide useful clues to its visions. Their careers stretched from "neoclassicism" to the nameless and frenzied 1760s, they were all learned in the past traditions and curious to examine new techniques and ideas, and they all saw themselves as fundamentally writers and therefore as man intensified. They are certifiably typical of their literary times; if we cannot distill the total spirit of the age from them, we can at least be sure of working with genuine ingredients. Although they do not necessarily lead us in right directions, they cannot take us far out of our way.

Pope everywhere conveys a consciousness of doubleness: his urbane, observing self is continually amused, or touched, or morally heartened, and always fascinated, by his own nature and appearance before the world. In his letters, he characteristically observes himself as a partially ostracized figure who had "been born both a papist and a poet" and was become almost a freak. No doubt he casually borrowed some of this self-pity from the traditional woes of the *poeta*, but he did suffer from serious physical and religious disadvantages.[6] Among other consequences of such alienation was complexity of attitude toward himself and others. His condition abnormally limited the range of his active satisfactions and therefore sharpened his sense of injustice; it also provided a stance and a subject for ironic observation, a mocked and thwarted struggling self that could ironically savor the joys of renunciation.

[11]

Concentrated and purified through the artistic imagination, these dominant conceptions of himself among his fellows find expression in the patterns and themes of his poems. They help shape, for example, *Eloisa to Abelard.* Although the letters of the medieval lovers were of special current interest and although the heroine's stance is to a certain extent determined by Ovid, the very congeniality of the genre suggests that Eloisa manifests universal psychological qualities strongly developed in Pope.[7] Even when Pope complains about his sexual deprivations, mainly in writing to the Blount girls or to Lady Mary, his tone invites not sexual responsiveness but pity and admiration—Eloisa's central motive. As she appears before us thinking her letter to Abelard, she is unnaturally cheated of fulfillment, shielded from bodily sin against her will, alien in a unified community, painfully and unwillingly aware that she cannot be helped. At the end she wants her story to be sung by a poet (preferably passionate and deprived too). As with all of Pope's poetic strategies, the heroine's wish for remembrance was traditionally and generically appropriate; but he used such a wish so regularly that it seems a special yearning for the esteem of posterity, his society with its prejudices removed. Standing in his place before the observing and judging world, Eloisa has won this approval.

When he saw himself in the world, Pope was constantly aware of the interaction of his two roles as ambitious author and moral human being. At first view they seemed to doom him to a division which is reflected in much of his work. Through literary power he could be publicly eminent, a reforming force, perhaps one of those great men who have transcended their societies. But only private life offered to satisfy his yearnings for warm and sensitive friendship, piety, and horticulture. As he says in an early letter, as a public author he ran the constant danger of being, like a whore, at everyone's disposal; and while he affirmed his independence he sought praise even from the idle and vain great whom he saw himself doomed as a "poetical fiddler" to amuse. Hoping to imitate God in a pure union of aesthetics and morality but sensitive to human weakness, Pope saw as early as the *Essay on Criticism* that art requires the distance of the observer, yet that the moralist must rush into the confusion to destroy evil. In developing one ideal of the *Essay on Criticism*—a "well proportioned dome," a whole which "at once is bold, and regular"—he also advocates art as strategy, as a device for winning one's aesthetic way: a view which neatly follows from his picture of himself as a delicate child among normal human beings, an Ariel or Umbriel who moves

people by infiltrating their thoughts. But the specific ideal figure in the poem is the critic, the judge who should rule because he is morally blameless.

At times, these two distinct tendencies are deliberately embodied in Pope's later works. The *Essay on Man*, for example, becomes a detached effort to re-create the symmetry of God's universe, while *The Dunciad* leads into the cluttered, knavish, lunatic vision in the brain of a sleeping hack (following Swift's Grubaean into his dreams, rather like Joyce exploring Earwicker). Pope's aim within each exploration is to reconcile extremes, to mold shape from the whirlwind of involvement, and to bring intense involvement to harmony.[8]

Pope's sense of duality and synthesis, which is reflected in the aesthetic and moral structure of his poems, in his preferences among genres, and in the heroic couplet, governs not only the didactic poems and formal satires but also the apparently freer art of *The Rape of the Lock*.[9] In addition to its thematic ambiguities and polarities— the implied contrasts in societies, in moral positions, and in man's passional nature[10]—the early masterpiece also balances and reconciles parallel symbols. Belinda is surely a symbol of her society as well as the object and expression of moral and aesthetic judgments; this is also true of the Lock. In the girl are concentrated the delicate, selfish, fragile, mercurial, and unavoidably superficial aspects of beauty; the Lock is, in one sense, art, the most powerful defense that man can provide for that beauty against its inevitable ruin by time, but a defense which is itself a ravishment away, a removal through abstraction and idealization. A vision of the refined, ephemeral, idiosyncratic self is balanced against a symbol—and a poem—created by an observing self which is ironically aware of its own and mankind's brief life. Early, before he has accepted a major role as didactic poet, Pope in *The Rape of the Lock* can pose Belinda and the Lock as alternative possibilities, the goods of involvement and detachment which can both be had only in a poem, poles like those which Johnson's Imlac warned we would lose if we attempted compromise. Later, as a public teacher in *The Dunciad*, Pope tries to choose one element as the good and to repudiate serious identification with what is now wholly evil. Although he still shows us the alternatives, he renounces one, the idiosyncratic collection of foolish, mad, and impotent literary selves, as unavoidably poisoned by the times; he retains only the universal self as norm.

In the contemporaneous *Epistle to Arbuthnot*, Pope most directly and satisfactorily examines his roles as poet and man, making himself not merely a witty lecturer like the speaker in his *Second Epistle of the Second Book of Horace* but a complex ideal or archetype, the universal self transcending its mild local attributes of twisted shoulder or Horatian cough. The opening picture of chaos warring with the good man Alexander Pope, of lunatics swarming upon his decent privacy and permitting him no peace because of his poetic eminence, assumes more and more meaning as the poem develops. Throughout, Pope's responses to chaos are compared with those of other actors before the world, from the helpless slaves of poverty and folly to the rulers of society and the models of probity and good taste. Centrally, this warm, impetuous dupe of his good nature is patterned against a triptych of hollow idols, beginning with the frozen, selfish literary exhibit Atticus. After Bufo, a symbolic nullity (like the gaseous Poet set up as a prize for *The Dunciad*'s booksellers), Sporus is a formal moral contrast to Pope—man acting in the world, political and social adviser to a nation—as Atticus had been the competing literary eminence. By his nonhuman ambivalence, Sporus sets off the positiveness, the erectness, the vigor of Pope—the suffering, trusting, affectionate, and dutiful son and citizen. In their hopeless sterility, Addison and Hervey are merely aspects of Bufo, subordinate idols worshipped without reward by the dunces and everywhere countered by Pope's passionate responsibility as man and artist. He has been raised to ideality by his contrast with them, having become not only a poet but harmonious man serving society with the talent that God gave him. He is for once a synthesis of public and private selves, a figure of assured significance in a coherent world. With the friendly *adversarius* Arbuthnot, and with Pope's evaluating self, we nod approval.

As an expression of Pope's sense of his dualism, a vision of lurking dissolution and evanescence menaces the ordered world of his poetry, whether the formal statement is cheerful or pessimistic.[11] The poems are suffused with intimations of the mortality of human ambitions and structures, whether these structures are material or systems of social or philosophic ideas. Even in the pensive, quietly patriotic, affirmative *Windsor Forest*, England's beauty consists of unstable reflections on the surface of the flowing river, equivalents in nature of man's brief striving. Amidst the cocky high spirits of *An Essay on Criticism*, the young poet stops to deplore a world where glorious paints and noble words nourish the seeds of their mortal illness. *The Rape of the Lock* is an acknowledged triumph of tone at least partly because it is that oddity, a tickling elegy: a lament for the loss of beauty, movement, youth, and life itself, for which art offers only

ironic consolation. Achieving its heroine's wish to waste her bloom in the desert rather than be stained by sexual attack, Pope's next heroine, Eloisa, appears as an emblem of human futility: a nun yearning from the convent toward the dream of her impotent lover. The much later *Essay on Man*, summing up the argument to be detailed in the Moral Essays and satires, avowedly grounds its wisdom in man's evanescence:

> Let us (since Life can little more supply
> Than just to look about us and to die)
> Expatiate free o'er all this scene of Man. . . .
> (ll. 3–5)

Let us wander and learn what we can before we dissolve like bubbles on the sea of time.

But though he knows that nothing human can last, Pope ties his own hopes to the classical affirmation that spirit must triumph over chaos. Observing humanity, he tends to focus on the difference between the one right way and the jumble of wrong ways, between the shaped bubble which rises into prominence and the nonhuman sea around it, between the valuable and the worthless, the civilized and the barbarous, the organically distinct and the dead. Yearning to achieve the significant and yet fearful that his gifts will be lost in the uncreating darkness of his times, he tends to conceive of friendship as alliance and is recurrently attracted to the image of the redeeming spark of light or life. Even in the *Essay on Criticism*, a defense of the literary attitudes held in common by educated men, the whole world seems provided for the extraordinary to exercise their talents, as chaos was essential for God's harmonious creativity. The altar of the greatest ancients, decorated with bays, rises for centuries above the sacrilegious, and Pope himself yearns to join them, to be inspired by them to teach vain wits the truth. He exalts individual judgments as against "the spreading notions of the town," the contagion of mass movements which was to poison civilization in *The Dunciad*. Provoking attacks from his own small circle of Catholics, he praises Erasmus for having "stemmed the wild torrent of a barbarous age," driving off the "holy Vandals." While such an attitude was no doubt frequent among Tories in Pope's day and is permanently attractive to the satirist, it peculiarly fits a poet who saw himself as debarred from the common animalism of sex and as one of the few elect in a generally heathen nation.

Similarly, Pope's narratives often follow the recurring archetype of the ambitious journey into the world of confusing experience, which is especially congenial to his combination of determination and difficulty in storming the world. From Belinda to Dulness and the persona of the satires and Moral Essays, whether the figures in his fables are divinely chaotic females or ordinary uncertain men, they set off to seek eminence among their fellows. Although Belinda ends lost in ambiguities, newly tasting her mortality, the gleams left from her radiant embarkation on the Thames, the move from her shallow self into the active outer world, shine the more richly as Umbriel, another representative traveler, sinks through obscurities and phantasms into the stagnant mind. *An Essay on Man*, written by a chronic invalid in middle age, still argues that the journey can be happy: even though man is in a maze or on an ocean, he can control his direction and velocity if he finds and follows truth. In *The Dunciad*, the central journey becomes a projection of the fantasies of the vain, mad, contemporary mind, where Dulness in her lengthy triumph prefers her devotees for the same arts which win rewards in this our actual England.[12] Belinda's mild Cave of Spleen, a coquette's mind in a pet, has been replaced by a sterile waste at the center of the whole society. The journeys of the duncus come to a dead stop at their essential self, the Goddess Dulness, who abolishes all eminence but her own and substitutes mists, fogs, clouds, vapors, and finally vast uncreating night for the social marks of spiritual distinction. Under her sway, which God has visited on man's folly, all journeys end in death. In the middle and end of Pope's career, she rises in cloudy opposition to the sunny Belinda of his youth.

Through the mutual reflections within what he once mentioned to Spence as a unified body of poetry, Pope seems to imply that the precise but tenuous image of the early poem is all the beauty that the artist can now create, the nearest to a pure reflection of a tainted human self. A society that worships idols offers to the poet's vision the materials of vanity and frivolity, elements which he can shape only into Belinda's selfish delicate beauty or Dulness' amorphous, lumpy ugliness. In the body of his work they stand, with Eloisa and his Horatian spokesman of the satires and Moral Essays, as representatives of man's striving self, as they are patent echoes of Pope's own admittedly irrational wishes. Positive grandeur, of the sort he hopes for in the *Essay on Criticism* and finds in the world of Homer, must for him be limited, if not twisted, by contact with the surface evil of his time, so that his largest self-image is not the hero but the embattled satirist. More or less, the figures in his works who yield to the mindless, mechanical, selfish evil of the world, or represent it, or fight it, or transcend it, are recognizable projections of his special self. Either directly or by implication, they are always judged by Pope's other self, the reflective spokesman for universal values.

While James Thomson shares with Pope such contemporary aspirations as synthesis, civilization, and universal harmony, he necessarily shaped them into a different vision. Thomson seems to have been neither alienated nor overtly idiosyncratic. Aside from a line in *Winter* about his boyhood joys in storms and a stanza or two in *The Castle of Indolence* on his poetic ambitions, he did not break the generic limitations of the poeta to speak of his own career or condition. He left few letters or documents, and these reveal no more about obvious mental patterns than we can gather from the anecdotes of his friends about his laziness, his mild sensuality, or his eager good nature. For us, the idiosyncratic elements in his poetic imagination must be derived mainly from the poems themselves. In his two main poems, *The Seasons* and *The Castle of Indolence*, those personal characteristics become, I think, major principles of organization; and Thomson can be evidence that we do not need oddities verging on neurosis to provide critically useful patterns of self-vision in the poetry.

Perhaps because Thomson is much less pressed than Pope by reveries of aggression, eminence, and opposition, he can more directly use fiction to convey the peculiar tensions which characterized the life of the poet, and therefore the life of the self. In the "allegory" of *The Castle of Indolence*, Thomson develops two competing roles of the poet, Magician and Knight, between whom the narrative persona must choose.[13] Their opposition takes place both in the mind of the poet-everyman and in society, as Thomson's projection of the self separates into self-indulgent dreamer and adventuring doer, sensualist and craftsman, hedonist and social reformer. Like Fielding in *Tom Jones*, Thomson tries to synthesize those divisions by urging the artist to send his fancies out in shaped art to show mankind its proper study and, in the process, to improve the health of his own mind. In opposing reverie and social reality, Thomson maintains his extraordinary representativeness. Almost all eighteenth-century English literature implies that the public and private are equivalents or parallels of the real outer world and the world of fantasy, and only in the greatest works—*The Rape of the Lock*, *Tom Jones*, *Songs of Innocence and Experience*, *Emma*—does fusion occur. More usually, as in other periods, its art suffers from the didactic fission of Thomson's Canto II, of Gray's *Progress of Poesy*, or of Goldsmith's *Vicar of Wakefield*.

In his letters, in the formal lecture of Canto II, and in general where he speaks as a moral observer, Thomson endorses the vision of man assuming social obligations rather than withdrawing into dreams, of didactic art and not selfish reverie. But as a poet and pilgrim in a painful world, the acting self finds the pleasures of the imagination seductive. In *The Castle of Indolence*, the setting and the castle itself serve as the seed ground for the imagination, which provides its own appurtenances: the silent shadowy forms which move about the valley, cousins of Pope's shimmering sylphs and uncles of Gray's bards, here as elsewhere Thomson's suggestions of poetic inspiration; the visions that come before half-closed eyes; the sanctum itself, "Close-hid ... mid embowering Trees" (st. vii), the retired and dreaming mind which draws struggling mankind into pilgrimage. Since the Poet-Magician openly feeds man's secret wish, indolent reverie, he affects the pilgrims compulsively (st. xxii); he plays on them, our substitutes, like a hot seducer on a half-reluctant girl (st. xxiii), to melt her to his will and her own pleasurable loss.

Beginning with stanza xxviii, the self-conscious author uses the castle, a refuge in the mind for the indulgence of fantasies, as a device by which to maintain his control over alternative selves and worlds, to move back and forth between fantasy and actuality. The Hebridean shepherd (st. xxx), a figure in the persona's imagination like the other surrounding images of withdrawal into the self, has visions like the persona's, even refining the filminess of reverie. Pinched by his responsible universal self (sts. xxxi and xxxii), the persona promises to resume his social obligations as a poet, but he is drawn back by the castle's seductions, which include tapestries, music, cushions, even a fleeting tickle of sexuality in the reference to the harem bard. The culminating symbol of this sequence, a response to the sound effects of sublimely titillating storms (st. xliii), neatly and ironically contrasts with similar scenes at the center of *Winter*: the warm poet feeding on his imagination indoors, refusing to deal with insistent reality outside. Lulled to sleep by the noise of the storm, the mind has withdrawn to voluptuous, incoherent dreams beyond the power of poetry to follow (st. xlv); in the figure of man before us, activity in the world has been abandoned along with the capacity to evaluate the world.

But the persona has only been speculating on his sleeping condition and observing a contingency that he can still choose to avoid. Immediately (sts. xlvi–xlviii), the world of moral responsibility warns him that the reveries stirred by art, except for elegiac and pastoral memories, are hollow. They waste life as thoroughly, though not as obviously, as the busy mindlessness that repudiates imagination and therefore make us insects. From stanzas xlix to lv, Thomson uses the mirror of folly to satirize the activities repellent to any form of poetic temperament: the self-seeking routine of affairs which provides neither beauty nor improvement, the extreme practicality that balances the sterile imaginings of sleep. As a reminder of these last, and a return to the choices actually open to the persona, the blocked *poeta* of stanzas lvii–lx is a case study of the inability to break from visions to their expression, an artist who suffers awake from dreams that he cannot objectify. The same impotence appears in the last two stanzas in the canto by Thomson (lxxii and lxxiii), which show a further sense of the real dangers of indolence: the gangrene in the secret mind, where self-indulgence has eroded the will and the reason. As most of Thomson's contemporaries would have agreed, the final horror is the self-imprisoned mind.

In Canto II the poet chooses the preeminently social self, dedicated from birth to labor for civilization, improvement, and fruitfulness, as his representative. The Knight of Arts and Industry, whose celebration is to constitute the return to vigor of the persona's imagination (st. iv), grew up close to nature, but under the rigorous tutelage of Minerva and the muses he learned to practice all the arts and sciences. Like a poet from Scotland facing the challenge of England,

> Accomplish'd thus he from the Woods issu'd,
> Full of great Aims, and bent on bold Emprize....
> To-wit, a barbarous World to civilize.
>
> (st. xiv)

Naturally, the Knight makes his seat in Britain, the symbol and ideal vision of a human society that opposes the Magician's castle of solipsism. As the Magician lures the active energies to languish and fester inwards, so the Knight (with the help of his bard Philomelus) brings them out to healthy involvement. In a major attack (sts. xlvii–lxiii), the old bard balances the Magician's song in the first canto, by calling for light, air, nature, and adventure; by repudiating the alternative as capitulating to death; and by advocating a great spurt from one's central will to overcome inertia. On another front, the Knight waves his wand to show the confirmed indolent the delusiveness of their happiness, the rottenness of their private withdrawal, and the inevitability of destruction unless they reform immediately. The last stanzas, lxxviii–lxxxi, show the hell that awaits the incurable, a vision of the true Castle of Indolence: a wasteland ruled by Beggary and Scorn, the bogeys of the conscientious bourgeoisie. The wavering self—the persona, the pilgrims, all those not totally drugged by routine activities—must renounce fruitless reverie and seek social art if it is to save itself, do its duty, and please the observing self which stands for the judgment of universal man.

Thomson's sympathy with the archetypal adventure into the world and the corollary pattern of release of energies—at least a parallel of his movement from Scotland to poetic achievement in England, if not its direct image—is central also in *The Seasons* (particularly in *Spring*) and notable in *Liberty* and the less ambitious poems. His good consists in the principle of expansion, excursion, flowing out into the world.[14] As in *The Castle of Indolence* he conceives the imagination as containing treasures deep within the self, so he everywhere senses potentialities, hidden possibilities awaiting light and flower, and he therefore affirms the value of piercing into the essence, leading it out, allowing it to radiate and create. Any agent for bringing it out, for fructifying or civilizing, imitates the sun or God. In *Spring*, for example, Thomson implies a fertile cycle, a hope of the future to come from the present, in his parallel of the hidden flower manifesting its energies as it blooms and the poet, "me," leaving the town for the country, where

> the raptured eye
> Hurries from joy to joy, and, hid beneath
> The fair profusion, yellow Autumn spies. . . .
> (ll. 111–13)

Heaven "sheds" various plants on nature, and "Swift fancy fired anticipates their growth" (l. 183), the seed within the mind responding to the hidden potentiality outside. The sun is the prototype of those who seize hidden truths (ll. 394–95); a fisherman brings treasures out of the depths (l. 396 ff.); a beloved girl has "looks demure that deeply pierce the soul" (l. 486), awakening its vital responses. From line 578 to the concluding domestic ideal, a number of images of drawing out, pouring in, and gripping the core convey the surge to life and growth in spring, within men as in external nature.

[20]

The complex of piercing into and leading out, of hidden value and treasure (and sometimes mystery or danger) is too fundamental in Thomson's imaginative vision of the world, too congenial for his mind in its attempts to grasp phenomena, to be limited to one season, and we find many examples of it elsewhere. In *Summer*, the dominating sun appears fully, after having been covered, a treasure released to man's and nature's benefit (l. 81 ff.). Its "quickening glance" brings the planets to life (l. 105), causes the vegetable world to ripen, and even, as its vital energy penetrates deep, impregnates rocks to fill diamonds with light (ll. 140–44). When the secret recess of one lover evokes and responds to messages from the other, man participates in the divinely Shaftesburian attributes of union, as in a central episode of *Summer*, a story in which a girl is revealed in awesome nudity to a boy who loves her (ll. 1269–1370). In *Autumn*, the emergence of pastoral love develops as myth, the story of Palemon and Lavinia hinting of Ceres and Persephone as well as its more direct model in the Book of Ruth (ll. 177–310). Cycles, implied in these myths, are central to Thomson's presentation of Winter as part of a hopeful world, and so in the last part of *The Seasons*

> The front-concocted glebe
> Draws in abundant vegetable soul,
> And gathers vigour for the coming year.
> (ll. 706–8)

Near the seat of Winter, Peter the Great adventured forth like Thomson and the Knight of Arts and Industry, found the needed knowledge, and out of mingled love, courage, and duty nurtured the seeds of civilization in his subjects.

At the center of *Spring*, as at the center of the world's living activities, is the impelling force, the eager excursive energy, of love, a form taken by the divine Adventurer which can provide worthy man with the core of motivation. When tracing "Nature's great command" (l. 634) to increase and multiply, Thomson presents the elements of this force that man can comprehend, a complex latent in the whole poem: all creation is driven by Spring, which connects fertility, adventurous explorations, even the sex and warfare of raging bulls (direct from a similar engagement in Virgil's third *Georgic*), and indescribably violent sea monsters, to show that all movement feeds life. Though not so extensively as *Spring* (the poem of birth), the other *Seasons* and the lesser poems also reflect a universe of fertility, movement, and variety.[15] Even *Winter* shows life everywhere but at the seat of the god, with birds in all the skies, peasants on Dutch canals, and wolves and bears prowling across polar regions. As against Pope's universe of careful shadings, Thomson's is a harmony of profusion and bold contrasts. Though he shares with Pope a perfectly artistic universe, he adores not the subtle Manipulator of light and shade but the brave, spectacular Impresario.

Thomson's social and psychological corollary of his vision of a universe harmonized by love is fruitful and serene civilization: both for him and for Pope, civilization is imaged as an eminence constantly endangered by barbarism. In *Summer*, as in *The Castle of Indolence* and *Liberty*, England is the hope and nourishment of the world, an emblem of the divinely fruitful (ll. 1400 ff., 1440), an island which sheds benevolence and humanity through encircling storms (ll. 1595–1601). In the middle of *Autumn* (l. 480 ff.), idyllically busy peasants at harvest, awakened Scottish industry, poets in their inspiring groves, and the learned man superior to superstition and folly (l. 1135), all must replace the preceding vision of the brutal days and sordid nights of hunters. *Winter*, like Canto II of *The Castle*, celebrates the civilizers who can bring warmth to the frozen soul: natural philosophers like Newton, social scientists humanely investigating prisons, Lords Wilmington and Chesterfield, Peter the Great, and the central roll call of the great cultural heroes of history, all hoping to draw truth and harmony out of the mixed confusion of phenomena. The Knight of Arts and Industry may not be our ideal, but in the vision of progress, in Thomson's lecture to himself to assume his social obligations, he is Thomson's. Ranging the world for visions of man acting in it, Thomson's warm-hearted and open-natured observer in *The Seasons*, as in *The Castle of Indolence*, chooses the acting, outgoing, social self.

As might be expected, evil for Thomson is everywhere the perversion or negation of the good, the *Castle*'s poles of the sleeping mind and the barbarous aggressions in the mirror of folly. The images are similar to those of civilizing adventure but carry opposing implications, Thomson's mind apprehending the pattern of a darting force (analogous perhaps to gravity) in the moral universe. In *Spring*, Thomson shows that while God educes harmony from nature, the fallen human mind is the seat of chaos, which activates a series of painful passions (l. 272 ff.). Decay is now erosion, "inward-eating change," as against creative piercing to the core (l. 334). *Summer*, celebrating a "sublime" season when God's might is more visible than his love, manifests brutality in man and nature. After barbarous man, the hidden snake, and the roar of the lion, the sublimity of Africa culminates in the archetypal horror of the shipwrecked solitary (l. 939), a horror sharpened for Thomson because it subverts adventurous hopes. Moving out of the self, out of the protected past, one may reap expressiveness, discovery, and social usefulness, but one may also founder in bitter isolation. *Winter* shrouds the last agonies of death as *Summer* heated the passions of barbarism, and man's own core suffers superlative agony:

> The soul of man dies in him, loathing life,
> And black with more than melancholy views.
> (ll. 61–62)

From its lair, "Then issues forth the storm with sudden burst" (l. 154), mocking the loving movement of the springtime sun, or the latent seeds of life, or the hidden truth, or the poet's vision. Horrible ghosts howl out of groves (l. 192), which in earlier sections had been inspiring shades. From the east and north,

> Thick clouds ascend, in whose capacious womb
> A vapoury deluge lies, to snow congealed.
> (l. 225)

The heart of winter's domain shoots out wolves to perpetrate a series of horrors, which culminate in their digging up and eating the most sublime of forbidden treasure, recently buried corpses (l. 410). At the North Pole itself, the god holds his court of death (l. 895)—an absolute zero of activity, in contrast with the divine center, the world's source of energy and intensity.

Although Thomson usually seeks the hearts of moral nature and of social man, he at times raises his search to the divine, which he characteristically apprehends as a creative point. In *Spring*, for example, the apostrophe to God conceives of Him as a secret element in the center of being:

> Hail, Source of Being! Universal Soul
> Of heaven and earth! Essential Presence, hail!
> (ll. 556–57)

Summer ends in a vision of Philosophy darting through the universe, ranging from matter to the idea of God, to the "ideal kingdom," through the imagination to "notion quite abstract," finally to the indefinable mystery. *A Hymn on the Seasons*, like the end of *Summer*, conceives the highest sense as silent rapture: contemplating God,

> I lose
> Myself in him, in light ineffable!

In *A Poem Sacred to the Memory of Sir Isaac Newton*, Thomson is equally at home with the sublimity appropriate to visions of the earth and heavens. He reveres Newton, he says, because it was he

> whose well-purg'd penetrating Eye,
> The mystic Veil transpiercing, inly scan'd
> The rising, moving, wide-establish'd Frame.

His soul transcended the human; it surveyed the universe at large, reached toward its source (l. 130), and imitated God's position as observer and motivator above and beyond the local. As *Spring* (ll. 210–12) and *Summer* (l. 805 ff.) also suggest, such adventuring over space and time is parallel to the divine, particularly in piercing, discovering, and showing forth the millennially obscured;[16] and in *Autumn*, Thomson asks where "the vast eternal springs" are hidden, "like creating Nature" from the mortal eye, and he wants the answer provided by

> the pervading genius, given to man
> To trace the secrets of the dark abyss.
> (ll. 777–79)

Using what has been brought back, on the other hand, is the province of the ambiguously human arts and industry. While purging man of the brutal and the indolent, the civilizing process also endangers the innocent, the personal, and the imaginative.

Since the step before the Fall, the setting out from within the self to seek the divinely hidden core, is free of such destructive tendencies, for Thomson it constitutes the purest movement of which man is capable: fusing the scientific and the artistic in the imaginative in imitation of God. Both alternative motives that he sensed in his nature—the pulls to imaginative withdrawal and to adventurous involvement—can draw together in the divine art of civilizing. In this very process of uniting the imaginative and the practical, the civilizer (every man's Knight of Arts and Industry) must moderate the divine for a fallen world. Bringing the earthly into his view, man becomes a judge not only of it but also of the divine within himself.

Although Christopher Smart was an Englishman and an Anglican, he seems to have considered himself an outsider, a small and helpless orphan in need of patronage, protection, special consideration. Reflecting his origin as the learned son of a steward, his role at Cambridge, and his later mixed domestic-professional life when he was both dependent and prizewinner, his narrative poems regularly tend to project fantasies in which the humble overcome the grand. In such moralized fantasies as *The Tea Pot and the Scrubbing Brush, The Bag-Wig and the Tobacco-Pipe, The Brocaded Gown and Linen Rag, Mrs. Abigail and the Dumb Waiter, The Country Squire and the Mandrake, The Blockhead and Beehive, The Herald and Husband-Man,* and *Munificence and Modesty,* the pretentious figure scolds the lower one, like a Fielding lady's maid hectoring a footman, but the humble triumphs. The reasons for such consistency seem largely personal, though they are also generic: partly, the writer of fables needs to show clear preferences and distinctions, as against Pope's attempt at harmonious synthesis and Thomson's ranging over choices; partly, Smart, like Pope, seeks identification with the dominant because he knows his own weakness; and partly, one suspects, he chooses the unequivocally manly out of fear that he will fall completely into the role of the small, elegant, entertaining, and dependent—the womanly.

With a resentful upper servant's view of society Smart combines down-to-earth "realism," particularly in evaluating women, as opposed to the fantasy which the century called romantic. Smart's attitude, a vulgarization of Fielding's, mixes sexual delight and intellectual contempt. When he writes to individual women, he can be vividly responsive, as in the poems to Harriot or to his wife, or mildly ribald, as in *The Distressed Damsel* or *On a Woman Who Was Singing Ballads.* But in his narratives, he tends to see women as shrill, extravagant, and in need of control lest they destroy themselves and those around them. After Generosity impoverishes herself (*Care and Generosity*), old Care offers marriage, and they prosper frugally under his rule. Wooed by beautiful Imagination, the recluse Reason (*Reason and Imagination*) refuses marriage because he cannot bear restriction, but he courteously offers friendship and supervision. Almost all the foolish or scolding figures in the fables are female, and they are usually defeated by males. Although Smart revealingly adopted a feminine pseudonym at times, he repeatedly and sometimes explicitly affirms male superiority.

In the unguarded *Jubilate Agno*, the connection between Smart's sexual bias and his sense of weakness is overt, and his fear of identification with the sex created weaker is barely hidden. From his confinement for madness, he writes, "For I prophecy that there will be less mischief concerning women. For I prophecy that they will be cooped up and kept under due controul." Because of the loss of the horn which grew naturally in David's day, man—patently a generalized version of Smart—has shrunk in domestic dignity: "For it is instrumental in subjecting the woman. For the insolence of the woman has increased over since Man has been crest-fallen. . . . For Man and Earth suffer together. For when Man was amerced of his horn, earth lost part of her fertility."[17] When women forget their proper place, they depreciate their lords, thereby throwing the domestic and psychological worlds into chaos. As Smart's great danger is identification with the mocking dependent, so the one great danger to the world is mockery of the divinely real, the genuinely heroic; in seeking and bestowing praise, Smart both affirms manliness and sounds the one note which sustains universal harmony.

In the same way, Smart regularly adores figures of extraordinary grandeur, heroes whom he can celebrate from a child's standpoint. In his most famous poem, *A Song to David*, he delights in David's manly qualities: military daring, protectiveness, zeal for civilizing, mercy, cool-headedness, imagination, passionate warmth. (Characteristically, it is by Michal's loving depreciation that Smart ties David to mere husbandly humanity [ll. 172–74].) Smart eagerly praises his heroes, from Admiral Pocock to King David, ranging over General Draper, the Earl of Northumberland, Henry Fielding, young Master Newbery, various Kentishmen and their opponents (among them Caesar and William the Conqueror), John Sheratt, large numbers of acquaintances or celebrities in *Jubilate Agno*, and, above all and everywhere, his heroic God. If his heroes are fantasies of an active self, the divorce between it and the childlike observing self is almost complete: perhaps here is one key to Smart's mental difficulties.

Smart's casual dismissal of women, like his response to all nature as dazzlingly material, again suggests that he lingers relatively little in conscious reveries centering on the self that he conceives of as weak and dependent. If my guess that he feared introspection as dangerously feminine is right, that would go far to explain his focus on outward sensations; and where fantasy attempts to deny the ordinary data of sensation or society, he wields its own weapon—mockery—to destroy it in an instant. His amused contempt for the conventionally fanciful—here clearly associated with the feminine—animates one extended subversion of the poeta, his trio of poems on the part of the day. The first, *A Morning Piece*, substitutes generic pastoral figures for contemporary English peasants, in an effortless imitation that only its companion poems reveal to be parody. In *A Noon-Piece*, the poeta can either sit with a beloved girl on a shady river bank and fish, thereby changing from the traditional lone dreamer to a courting youth, or outrageously act out with her the amorous passages in Sidney's romances. By the third poem, *A Night-Piece, or, Modern Philosophy*, Smart openly subverts the poeta: Sophron the Wise congratulates himself on aloofness from the bustle of business and then, recollecting his betrothal to one girl, knocks on the door of another and spends the night with her. As in *Reason and Imagination*, Smart insists that our sphere is material reality, the world around us, not the abstractions or reveries of the poeta. To judge by his own sad fate, he insists too much.

This world of matter registers upon him as joyous individual sensations, distinct from each other and from everything else.[18] In his art, in his cosmology, and in his general view of world relationships, Smart emphasizes individual sensations, in contrast with Pope's stress on the harmoniously woven work or Thomson's on contrasts. Toward the latter part of his career, Smart thought that the special distinction of the finest poetry was the literary equivalent of this effect on the reader—"the beauty, force, and vehemence of *Impression*" or "punching, that when the reader casts his eye upon [the words], he takes up the image from the mould."[19] Indeed, in its sharpness of impression as well as in the almost total lack of repetition, *Jubilate Agno* is a monument to the immensity and variety of the stock of specific facts, observations, and sense data in Smart's mind. Everywhere in this poem, as often in his others, Smart emphasizes the separateness of each element which sends up a thread of adoration to God. Although Smart accepts the chain of being, order, and subordination, he perceives a movement directly from the stones to God and from the angels to God, the Focus of the rays singly emitted from every created thing.

As is fitting in a world of elements morally indiscriminate (however distinct to the senses), Smart shows very little awareness of evil beyond what relates to feminine negation.[20] The sentimental evils—ingratitude, which Smart called the sin against the Holy Ghost, and those mocking qualities which he attacked in *Ill Nature*—sum up the opposition to the divine will. Smart's universe is not a moral stage, since creation intuitively fulfills its sole duty to praise. In Thomson's anthropomorphic *Seasons*, if a bird's song is sad 'to our ears, he has lost his wife, and wolves and sharks have human, evil motives; for Smart, all things call on man to share their pure wish to adore God. The greatest and manliest man, untainted by the destructive human-feminine-Smartian ability to mock, is the most intense spokesman for creation, different from an oyster or a mountain only in his power of impression. Such a hero looks up an immense distance when he praises his God; similarly, Smart looks confidently to the hero as one capable of acting, of protecting him against his own and the world's mockery. Although such a sense of intensely real matter uniting to affirm a distant ideal of male grandeur need not derive from Smart's background and self-view, they are obviously congenial.

The division into two selves, so prevalent in the period, shows itself in one form in Smart's fables, where his spokesmen sneer at the usually feminine alternative self. It also appears in his complementary recurrent stance, the poet looking up like a child to its hero–older brother–father. In the praising poems which we still admire, Smart thus tends (perhaps atypically) to adore a projected acting self, but that self is idealized and hugely magnified over the ordinary. It is a distant possibility, like the giants of Macpherson and Blake, not a version of his current self. The active self in Smart's serious poems thus embodies his aspirations, what someone other than himself or an idealized version of himself might have achieved. It takes on the single dimension of mythic grandeur in place of typicality or idiosyncrasy, as the observer has the single dimension of admiration. In his comic poems, his fables, the large body of verse which seems to most of us routinely typical of his time, Smart's less attractive self—the mocker, the selfish, the womanly—tends to be posed for conquest by a version of his attractive self. For Smart, a kind of primitive artist despite his learning and experience, observer and observed, like hero and villain, exist most simply in the poems.

One of Smart's lesser performances as praiser of a servant of the Lord may help us return from his idiosyncratic sensations to a common ground for his contemporaries and us, the idea of art as emotional machinery. In his *Ode on Saint Cecilia's Day*, an exercise in the ornate-sublime-Cowleyan Pindaric, various elements combine to illustrate and praise music's power to sway its hearers. Representative in its very mediocrity, the poem reflects the wish through the century—supported by Lockean psychology if not rooted in it—for a way to turn Mr. Shandy's ass of passion into the gentle and tractable feelings. Art in this view becomes a psychological instrument to be exercised not merely as a demonstration of skill (as by Timotheus in Dryden's *Alexander's Feast*) but for the emotional stimulation and therefore the ultimate improvement of Richardson's, Smollett's, and Sterne's creatures and their readers. In poetry, Dennis, recalling an accepted tie of rhetoric and aesthetics, ticked off the different passions and suggested which genres were to deal with them; equivalent guides were also available for painting.[21] Thomson's *Seasons* deliberately played over the whole range of passions, from the sublime to the gentle, from awe or love to mockery, and Burke's essay on the sublime and beautiful showed later poets how to achieve the grandest effects. The artist and his creatures became halves of a unified consciousness, another aspect of Locke's mind observing its own operations: a reflective self alert to direct the striving, apprehending, passionate self; an ironic self, as in Sterne or Goldsmith, registering both the worth and the absurdity of the acting and feeling self.

Throughout the literature of the eighteenth century, this doubleness of self opposed the real and the fanciful, a fundamental division which shades into the oppositions of the public and the private, responsibility and self-indulgence, Locke's and Sterne's judgment and wit, practicality and imagination, art and nature, civilization and barbarism. As an uneasy awareness of division, this doubleness of self stimulated the attempts in the eighteenth century to seek those elements of identity which can help the self to assimilate the impact of phenomena, understand them, and act outward to them: to tie the outer to the inner through sympathetic communication. Where the pastoral seemed more and more a cowardly escape into the mind, the sentimental ideal of communication—the century's other edenic vision—despite its absurdities and deficiencies still demanded engagement with the world. Perfect bores though they are, Steele's Bevil, Jr., and Richardson's Grandison seemed admirable because—unlike the equally idealistic Don Quixote or Parson Adams—they could feel effective contact with a flawed world. Fielding's most "realistic" and amelioristic novel is also his most sentimental.

Like the techniques of sentimentalism, the figure of the poeta attempts to fuse the private with the public, though by the more austere and symbolic nexus of literary tradition. Even Thomson's rudimentary poeta is separated from other people not only that he may encourage private reveries (though that is one purpose) but also that he may dream and brood for mankind. In Gray's works, the figure who mourns the doomed little boys at Eton or the dead in the church and churchyard, or pleads with Adversity for a feeling heart, or watches youth waste its spring, has become far more than a rhetorical device. By seeing himself, the declassed survivor of twelve children, in the persona traditionally set off from a watchful society, Gray can fit into his vision poetry, art, social justice, and human fulfillment—the whole duty of man.

In the poetry of Gray and even his model Milton, such a solitary figure shows a strain of guilt which allies him to archetypal itinerant outcasts, like Savage's Bastard and Wanderer, Goldsmith's deserted traveler, and Cowper's recognizable daily self. Adding the expulsion from Eden, Goldsmith makes the poet a wandering observer of societies, as Gray's poeta judges life within a society. But where Gray, at his best, perfectly balances the visions in his mind and the external reality so that the dead peasants, aristocrats, and village poet animate the churchyard, church, and village around him at evening, Goldsmith's mournful, alienated, sensitive, imaginative ideal self mixes fantasies of seduced maidens and grotesque tyrants with distracting lectures on demography. In Gray's best poems—*Ode on a Distant Prospect of Eton College*, *Elegy Written in a Country Churchyard*, or *The Bard*—he achieves the fusion of the species in the individual; in *The Deserted Village*, we ourselves must raise the elements to the same symbolic level, transmuting squires and tenants into figures expressive of the archetypal Fall of the poeta into experience. Where Goldsmith succeeds, he succeeds through the poeta's emotional response to his vision of himself and a world fallen together, not through the richness of interplay of poeta and world. In his poetry, but not his prose, Goldsmith abandons the universal judge or merges it with the striving archetype.[22] He does not, like Smart, wholly admire the figures at the center; he merely provides no other consciousness.

Fearful of the doom to which his fantasies always led, Cowper tends to divest the poeta of its public attributes and shape it for the specific, phenomena-connected daily personality which he presented to the citizens of Olney and Weston. Without repudiating the traditional figure, he allows it only the minimal function of introducing him to the reader, after which he provides details exclusively about himself. That is, he wanders like the poeta in the shade and reflects on the meaning of nature, on the futility of human bustle, on God's power and glory. But he is accompanied by a middle-aged lady in walking shoes, and he remains outwardly decorous whatever his agony over man's condition. In him, the poeta becomes as submerged in the actual poet as he is to be in Wordsworth.

If the triumph of outer reality in Cowper reminds us of the eighteenth-century novel, this is still the world of which I have been speaking. Beneath the easy lustiness which has so attracted movie-makers are a complexity of theme and vision as great as in the poetry and similar fashions of imagining them. Moll Flanders, Tom Jones, Clarissa Harlowe, Roderick Random, even Tristram Shandy seek integrity but wander in a world of planned mazes, heirs of the picaresque outsider acting out their authors' fantasies before the shared judging self of author and reader. Seeing himself as a social adventurer, Richardson, like Thomson, inhabits a probing, projecting world of intense energies and deep recesses, of opposed alternative echoes of himself. Sterne's persona, isolated, abandoned, and mocking in a world where all distinctions are man-made and untrustworthy, registers an immensity of discrete sensations as Smart does; but hugging and juggling his impressions of people enclosed in bubbles around him, unlike Smart he has the confidence of typicality and seeks to prick through by sensation, not lead from each upward. Fielding, Smollett, and Goldsmith, all gentlemen decayed from an ideal of aristocratic status and nostalgic for it, affirm an original order which can be reinstated if man cooperates. Amidst the bleakness of current society, they are likely to see such order as emblematic visions within the mind: a noble couple radiating goodness over a country estate, like Tom and Sophia or the pairs at the end of Thomson's *Spring* and in Smart's *Epithalamium*; Auburn, long dead with the poet's innocent childhood; Loch Lomand, an inaccessible paradise. And if this individually motivated ideal is congenial to conservatives in the eighteenth century, it also touches universal man: *The Odyssey*, *The Tempest*, *The Cherry Orchard*, and *Wild Strawberries* suggest that it is more private than politics and as public as mankind.

The characteristic narrative pattern of the century is the journey, from innocent Eden into action and confusion, Johnson's Cairo of the mind; with some notable exceptions (Smart, Macpherson, Blake), the characteristic central figures are posed before us with the ambiguous limitations which their creators knew only too well. Everywhere in the period, this sense of selves acting and observed helps form the vision that unites through their art writers of widely varying backgrounds and self-conceptions. Pope in his sylphs, ambitious authors, and protean idols; Thomson in his mildly burlesque opposing champions; Cowper in the wanderings of his sufferer before God;

Gray weighing the importance of his solitary against the solidity of mankind; Smart even in the hosannahs of his heroes; all those from Pope to Burns affirming the central virtue of sympathy and yet alert to its inherent excesses; all suggest an ironic vision of the self in the world, idiosyncratically varied but representative of the mankind in which it is to live.

Although the notion or sensation of the two selves, one observing the other acting, seems to derive from man's permanent condition, it is particularly suitable to the act of writing, more especially when the writer seeks to emphasize social and psychological representativeness. If the earlier reduction of hybris to self-improvement—in the lovable oddity of Quixote, the ambivalence of Alceste's yearnings, the forgivability of Adam's—cost the eighteenth century high tragedy, it allowed a new tie among author and reader and character. Jane Austen may have caused the reader to "become Emma's helpless conscience," as Lionel Trilling wrote, but that is because Emma acts out the observing reader's discoveries. Throughout the century leading up to her, the observing self wonders how much of the world which its acting complement imagines does in reality exist, how much is delusion, how much should be imagined, how much pain should be expended to make these imaginings useful to other selves (assuming their existence), and how much of the whole business is simple self-indulgence. In reflecting the private visions of the writers of the eighteenth century, the struggles of the idiosyncratic self under the eye of the universal self especially stamp the century's public literature. Through the natures of these selves and the often conscious and ironic relations between them, the writers' psychological patterns and the period's concerns cooperate in an imaginative vision that can be called characteristic.

III

SWIFT

1. Self Views: Priest, Poet, and Humane Observer

OUR ACKNOWLEDGED MASTER of the literary alter ego, Swift builds his visions of the world upon blown-up fragments of himself photographed from misleading angles and framed to deceive the eye. From *A Tale of a Tub* to *Directions to Servants*, his ironic writings usually convey meaning through the mutual illumination of two selves, a grotesquely acting persona and an implied general self who is the common ground shared with the decent, genteel, educated reader of all times and every place. If the two selves were wholly distinct from each other, the distorted elements wholly alien to the norm as in *Absalom and Achitophel* or *The Dunciad*, they would constitute the antitheses of traditional satire and illustrate a clear morality. But to judge by critical diversity, the relations between Swift's generally mad personae and his sane norm have been much more obscure.[1] Even if competent readers no longer confuse him with his manifestly mad characters (Swift as coprophilic Hack or cannibal projector), his occasional comments on what he is writing, as in the letters on *Gulliver's Travels* or the hints to Stella on his political pamphlets, refute any theory of nail-paring aloofness. Once he even provided a subversive persona with a history recognizably analogous to his own: "I served my Apprenticeship in *London*, and there set up for my self with good Success; until by the *Death of some Friends, and the Misfortunes of others*, I returned into this Kingdom; and began to employ my Thoughts in cultivating the *Woollen-Manufacture* through all its Branches. . . ."[2] In this sketch of the Drapier's career, Swift invites his readers to join him observing his idiosyncratic journey with an ironic pity derived from their shared English history. Implicitly, this is the system of relationships among himself, his creations, and his readers that he elects throughout his career.

The complexity of Swift's personae owes a great deal to his choice of genres and to circumstance, but it also depends on his imaginative conception of himself as representative even in his idiosyncrasies. With his contemporaries in the classical-Christian tradition, he held the harmonious Christian as his ideal: but he was well aware that no man can always be his highest self. Striving and flawed in a corrupt world, a man cannot help playing different roles, and in each role he is only a fragment. In letters and autobiographical memoranda, in the relatively unguarded *Journal to Stella*, and even in published poems, like the *Verses on the Death of Dr. Swift* or the more traditional *Part of the Seventh Epistle of the First Book of Horace Imitated* and *The Author upon Himself*, Swift judicially observed himself as an acting figure like any other, an example of man caught in certain situations. Knowing that each dominant humor and each partial role diminishes the whole man to a proper butt of irony, Swift sees himself as proud, isolated, persecuted; as Irishman, priest, teacher, politician, friend, poet, dignitary. Some of his roles, such as lover or economic speculator, he sees as occasional, the lot of most men in certain situations, and therefore not essentially identified with him. Yet when he writes of Irishmen, priests, or poets, social designations that transcend specific periods or situations in his life, he accepts membership in the faulty genus even while he opposes to it his larger sensitivity.

Among the most notable and persisting elements in Swift's view of himself is his awareness of ambition, which he sometimes condemns as pride and sometimes sees as legitimately flowing from his talents. Yet at the same time that he identified himself with those who had achieved eminence through effort and ability, he affirmed the aristocratic stance attractive to the society from which he sprang and consistently supported the landed gentry against money and upstart intellect alike.[3] One of the lower gentry admiring and aspiring to the aristocracy—and thereby acting the socially striving figure for which he yet felt an intimate and sympathetic scorn—he demanded acknowledgment of his self-sufficiency, and in adversity he was pleased to be surrounded by his inferiors. But his pleasure, as often, was compounded by the ironic awareness of his situation.[4] Even when he affirmed an eagerness for fame in the absurd early *Ode to the Athenian Society*, part of him knew it for swelling egotism:

Pardon *Ye great Unknown*, and far exalted Men,
The wild excursions of a youthful pen;
Forgive a young and (almost) *Virgin-muse* . . . [which]
. . . quits the *narrow Path of Sense*
For a dear Ramble thro' Impertinence.[5]

Writing to Thomas Swift on May 3, 1692, of his joy at the publication of this poem, he admits that "I am wholly in the wrong, but have the same pretence the Baboon had to praise her Children, and indeed I think the love in both is pretty much alike, and their being our own ofspring is what makes me such a blockhead."[6]

Whatever the reason (and speculation has ranged from genteel poverty to sexual impotence), Swift continued to be both proud and amused by the absurdity of his pride, sane despite the shock of the Struldbruggs and the Yahoos. Discounting worldly distinctions, he noted with a smile his zeal in their pursuit. Some years after the fall of the Tory ministry, for example, he described his position in Ireland with characteristic ambivalence: "I give hints how significant a person I have been, and nobody believes me; I pretend to pity them, but am inwardly angry. I lay traps for people to desire I would shew them some things I have written, but cannot succeed; and wreak my spight, in condemning the taste of the people and company where I am. But it is with place, as it is with time. If I boast of having been valued three hundred miles off, it is of no more use than if I told how handsome I was when I was young. The worst of it is, that lying is of no use; for the people here will not believe one half of what is true. If I can prevail on any one to personate a hearer and admirer, you would wonder what a favourite he grows. He is sure to have the first glass out of the bottle, and the best bit I can carve" (*Correspondence*, II, 333–34; cf. letter to Bolingbroke, III, 331). Swift was well on his way to a major creation: the crotchety, fallible, eminent Dean of St. Patrick's, Dublin.

Such undermined assertiveness in a sensitive man easily accompanies fantasies of failure and estrangement, recurrent evidences of sane uncertainty which, uncensored by the obligations of ordinary social intercourse, animate the paranoid fears of the Hack and the later Gulliver. Not only when his future was objectively dark, in Ireland after the fall of the Tory ministry, but even in the midst of power in London from 1712 to 1714, he complained of loneliness and talked of withdrawing from all but the most narrowly personal business.[7] Although his normative self always minimized the effect of environment on man's moral obligations, as a striving man he mistrusted fortune and the self-seeking follies and vices of others. He was confident of his own ability to write political essays or administer a deanery, but he often thought himself under attack, feared ridicule, and felt abandoned by such presumed allies as the Irish bishops, the Tory cabinet, or Queen Anne. As his difficult negotiations for the suspension of the Irish "first fruits" were approaching success, instead of reward he found himself suspected and subverted by the Irish clergy—like Gulliver after his naval victory.[8] Not long after that came the greatest shock to his hopes, the ignominious fall of the ministry with which he was identified—England's grand chance for a just society strangled by Lilliputian quarrels and the death of a trivial woman. Although he was too faithful a churchman and too intensely aware of his psychological deficiencies to play the innocent Job or Oedipus, his own fortunes provided him with exemplary lessons in the uncertainty of man's fate.

As a natural reflection of these visions of himself, his striving substitutes convey both eager ambition and a sense of mistreatment, a kind of anticipation of defeat. William Temple, William III, and Archbishop Sanford in Swift's early odes have to make their heroic way against a mob world, and during the years of Tory power the sympathetic figure in his verses suffers for his prominence. In Swift's exhilarating period of pursuing the remission of the "first fruits," for example, the walking man of *A Description of a City Shower* draws a variety of violent attacks from both nature and man. *Atlas,* addressed to Oxford in 1712, calls up all the mythic associations of single, suffering, and selfless eminence. In *Part of the Seventh Epistle of the First Book of Horace Imitated,* the observing Swift shows us his striving self relaxed and placid as an ordinary priest, but miserably vexed on all sides as a dean. *Horace, Lib. 2 Sat. 6. Part of it imitated* (1714) describes Swift at Oxford's reception, where some condemn his pride while others complain of the violence with which he elbows aside the crowd (like the fat man early in the *Tale of a Tub*). In *The Author upon Himself* (1714), he has been singled out for suffering, Juvenal's good man among beasts and devils, the victim of venomous and stupid routineers of his own profession and of "an old redhair'd, murd'ring Hag. . . ,/ A Crazy Prelate, and a Royal Prude." His sense of being at the focus of attack did not decline with age and exile, nor did his skin grow thicker.

Swift's temperamental mistrust of fortune often expressed itself in a fear of just missing his goals, which became involved in his feelings about guilt and death, the inevitable confutation of all human schemes. All such disappointments, from the time he was kidnapped by his nurse and not restored for three years—the surprising failure of Temple or his friends to provide adequately for him, the unwillingness of the Irish prelates to give him credit for gaining the "first fruits," the always-elusive bishopric, Queen Anne's cataclysmic death—are caught and symbolized, as he intended them to be, in a letter to Bolingbroke and Pope of April 5, 1729: "I remember when I was a little boy, I felt a great fish at the end of my line which I drew up almost on the ground, but it dropt in, and the disappointment vexeth me to this very day, and I believe it was the type of all my future disappointments" (*Correspondence*, III, 329). But if this myth of recurrent victimization is a true picture of his life, it is not the only one, and he is at all points aware of the absurdity of thinking it so.

Like Johnson's wooing widower, Swift persisted in hoping despite his experience. He had an acutely expectant as well as an acutely suspicious temperament; like his personae, he was both projector and renouncer. In a typical letter from his Irish exile, to Bolingbroke on October 31, 1729, Swift could imply that ambition for lasting fame is childish: "The desire of enjoying it in after times is owing to the Spirit and folly of Youth: but with age we learn to know the house is so full that there is no room for above one or two at most, in an age through the whole World" (*Correspondence*, III, 355). But as his last will showed, he could no more learn such a lesson from life than Browning's Bishop of St. Praxed's could assimilate it from Ecclesiastes. Although his letters and such attempts to evaluate his life objectively as the *Family of Swift* or the histories present a course of disappointment after disappointment, until his final helplessness he kept making plans and throwing himself into battles for his own dignity, for his friends, church, parishioners, and nation, and for civilization. While his reflecting self knew that almost no one is remembered, his other self—to the world's great advantage—caught hope from the vision of the extraordinary one or two.

Fascinated by his own singularity, Swift also repeatedly noticed that he aroused stereotyped responses as Irishman, priest, author, and political figure, and even as a man of a certain size and shape. Each category had its general associations which could be caught in a "character" of the sort popular since the seventeenth century: the Hack, the Tory, the Country Vicar, the Irish Teague, the Projector, the Bluff Briton (Arbuthnot's John Bull). Because these character groupings were solely external and partial, they were necessarily false views of himself or of any man. It is the partial nature of this self— the insensitive practitioner of group thought that was to become the typical persona-butt—that Swift insists on; in the process of acknowledging its existence, he affirms the value of the total observing self.

To judge by Swift's repeated complaints, the most immediately distorting qualities which an Englishman would assign him derived from his Irish nationality, and like the Englishman he found these qualities absurd. Rarely bothering to distinguish between the Catholic mass of the peasantry and the mock-English, mock-rational, mock-civilized, mock-universal Anglo-Irish establishment, after his return to Ireland in 1714 he wrote often of the ignorance and poverty, of the contentiousness, triviality, and slavish temper with which he feared his compatriots' habits would tarnish his impression on others.[9] At times, however, he could make the allowances in his letters that he was implicitly making in his life and political pamphlets. Writing on August 2, 1732, for example, he insisted that the main character defects in the native Irish were occasioned by English tyranny (*Correspondence*, IV, 51). Similarly, his various subversive pamphlets, such as the *Proposal to the ladies of Ireland* to wear Irish cloth and *A Modest Proposal*, steadily attacked the wealthy Anglo-Irish for their absence and for their exploitative, frivolous, and selfish attitudes which maintained, if they had not caused, the barbarism of the native population.

Inevitably, and despite his birth, long residence, and patriotic achievements in Ireland, Swift tended to see himself as an oddity among the Anglo-Irish. A poor relation of a colonial establishment (like the ambiguous figures in Kipling, Forster, and Graham Greene), he is finally saved from desperation by observing his own absurdity in the world of mock-England. In a letter to Lord Castle-Durrow of December 24, 1736, he writes: "I often reflect on my present life as the exact Burlesque of my middle age, which passed among Ministers, in those days that you and your Party since call the *worst of Times*. I am now acting the same things in Miniature, but in a higher Station, as a first Minister, nay sometimes as a Prince; in which last quality My Housekeeper, a grave elderly woman, is called at home and in the Neighbourhood Sr. Robert. My Butler is Secretary, and has no other defect for that office but that he can not write yet that is not singular; for I have known three Secretaryes of State upon the same level, and who were too old to mend, which mine is not. My

Realm extends to 120 Houses, whose Inhabitants constitute the Bulk of my Subjects; my Grand Jury is my House of Commons, and my Chapter the House of Lords; I must proceed no further because my Arts of Governing are Secrets of State" (*Correspondence*, IV, 555). Not the indignant, drubbed participant but the spokesman for universal man can accept such a consummation of high ambition. Out of mankind's whole experience, he can know that even the real thing—English power and grandeur—is itself merely a prouder joke which man plays on himself.

Not only was Swift clearly an Irishman but throughout his active adult life he was immediately identifiable as an Anglican priest. He entered English political life through Irish church business, and after becoming involved in larger affairs he continued to insist on being known as a priest.[10] His pictures of the clergy, especially in his verse, tend therefore to show how he thought he looked to others in this role. As always when directly showing himself, he is ironic; and to the extent that he examines people limited by narrow mutual concerns, he is contemptuous as well. In the clannish, censorious, and sycophantic attitudes which nourish the self-interest of clergymen, he finds materials to fit out one recurrent villain in his works, the complacent conformist.

In the poems dealing with clergymen, Swift is likely to stress their low status, the contradictions and ambiguities of their social conditions, or their self-aggrandizing tendencies; and as against the universal, aristocratic implied observer, they seem often less than manly. In *The Humble Petition of Frances Harris*, for example, the maid's expectation that Swift might marry her suggests his low standing as chaplain, while his muttering and gestures mock his grander pretensions. Much of the fun of the more urbane *Baucis and Philemon* lies in the transformation of Philemon into a caricature of the country vicar sunk in laziness, stupidity, servility, ignorance, secularism, cupidity, and pride—all the qualities which justify his plea,

> I'm good for little at my days;
> Make me the Parson if you please.

In *Apollo Outwitted*, the god condemns Anne Finch to various punishments for rejecting him, of which the culmination implies sexual frustration with a clerical husband:

And last, my Vengeance to Compleat,
May you Descend to take Renown,
Prevail'd on by the Thing you hate,
A ——, and one that wears a Gown.

The Progress of Marriage (1722) despises a "rich Divine" of about Swift's own age who wooed and married a belle but could not satisfactorily bed her. Sexually, as in other worldly activities, Swift's clergymen combine vain aspiration with a tendency. toward sluggish dullness, one kind of delusive lifelessness to which man is tempted.

Preferring the attitudes of the humane world at large to the partial or factional interests of a narrow group, Swift in his autobiographical sketches tried to distinguish himself from other clerics. In his version of Horace, I, vii, he describes himself as

A Clergyman of special Note,
For shunning those of his own Coat;
Which made his Brethren of the Gown.
Take care betimes to run him down.

In *The Author upon Himself* (1714), a fairly extensive examination of his impact on the world, he complains of being mistreated by his mindless colleagues for participating in the larger life of England. As opposed to them, he considers himself graceful in manner and frank in expression:

He reconcil'd Divinity and Wit. . . .
At *Child's* or *Truby's* never once had been;
Where Town and Country Vicars flock in Tribes,
Secur'd by Numbers from the Lay-men's Gibes;
And deal in Vices of the graver Sort,
Tobacco, Censure, Coffee, Pride, and Port.

As Gulliver sought affiliation with another species when he noticed his resemblance to the Yahoo, faced by the petty selfishness of herding clergymen Swift asserts his real identification with the civilized norm—the aristocratic universal self.

Where Swift the priest registered his fellows as conformist blockheads who lacked and feared virility, Swift the author associated himself with sensitive, energetic actors before the public enjoying rare opportunities for original, substantial, and memorable achievement:

as he wrote to Gay on November 20, 1729, "The world is wider
to a Poet than to any other Man. . . . For as Poets in their Greek
Name are called Creators, so in one circumstance they resemble the
great Creator by having an infinity of Space to work in" (*Correspondence*, III, 360). Aspiring as individuals where the clergy are
normally content to flock, priestly authors like Swift in *The Author
upon Himself* run special risks of being resented

> By dull Divines, who look with envious Eyes,
> On ev'ry Genius that attempts to rise;
> And pausing o'er a Pipe, with doubtful Nod,
> Give Hints, that Poets ne'er believe in God.

Nevertheless, even the clergy have a point: authors use metaphors
and are therefore liars who say the thing which is not; and as servants
of the imagination, they are peculiarly subject to madness.[11] When
Swift as harmonious observer sees his idiosyncratic self in the limiting role of author, he ironically suggests dignities and responsibilities
which tremble on the edge of pretentiousness. After a quarter century of thinking of himself as a poet, the mature Swift of *The
Progress of Poetry* (1720) anatomized the poetic nature as deluder
and deluded. When his poet-goose succeeds with the public, he is
dragged to earth by his fat, turned into a dull and complacent equivalent of the conventional priest; but when he fails,

> Now his exalted Spirit loaths
> Incumbrances of Food and Cloaths;
> And up he rises like a Vapour,
> Supported high on Wings of Paper;
> He singing flies, and flying sings
> While from below all *Grub-street* rings.

Elsewhere, and similarly, Swift often sees the author-self as a performer, a Presto who even to his most intimate friend hints and winks
about his works, a battler before the public who shares the stage
itinerant with the priest, one who seeks to vex, mend, and anger
mankind.[12]

Steadily, through these major personae which he built out of his
vision of himself acting before his fellows, Swift delights in complexity, in apparent obscurantism and obliquity. Absolutely central
is his uniting of priestly gravity and poetic absurdity to expose soci-

ety's chief vice, the corruption of right discrimination through the self-serving clichés which turn groups into conspiracies. As in all of Swift's visions of himself, of his surrogates in the world, and ultimately of representative man, the struggling mind is constantly in danger either of sinking into mindless convention or of evaporating as a vain absurdity.[13] Although man's highest qualities should be concentrated in the vocations of priest and poet, when their practitioners succumbed to the opposing but easily coalescing temptations of laziness and pride they symbolized the greatest betrayal, the abandonment of their special obligations to find the way and show it to others. In his visions of man's fundamental failure, the priest's mask of sober conformity covers the wild, prideful mind of the poet in a parody of the harmonious union of universal and idiosyncratic selves.

Two of Swift's most effective works, *A Tale of a Tub* early in his career and the *Verses on the Death of Dr. Swift* toward its end, directly reflect such visions of himself in the world. *A Tale of a Tub*, which alternates the self-expression of a mad rhapsodic poet and his narrative of three brother priests, thrusts before us the irresponsibly prankish, wildly prideful, delusive, and narcissistic self in an unaccommodating world, while the implied normative self observes the antics with amused contempt.[14] The Grubaean Hack characterizes bad times, bad authors, bad scholars, critics, and theologians—bad and mad men generally; but he also seems in many ways a deliberate reflection of his creator. He is competitive like Swift and urgently ambitious, intending his book for "the Universal Improvement of Mankind" in a burlesque of Swift's youthful hopes for his odes. Again like Swift, the Hack is fascinated by the involutions of learning and the possibilities of language. But his identity lies less in specific interests than in a quality of mind, an abandonment to the possibilities of fantasy, an adolescent Faustian striving of which Swift had been proud a few years earlier. In a letter to John Kendall of February 11, 1691–92, Swift had written: "There is something in me which must be employ'd, & when I am alone, turns all, for want of practice, into speculation, & thought; insomuch that in these seven weeks I have been here, I have writt, & burnt and writt again, upon almost all manner of subjects, more perhaps than any man in England. And this is it, wch a person of great Honour in Ireland (who was pleas'd to stoop so low as to look into my mind) & us'd to tell me, that my mind was like a conjur'd spirit, that would do mischief if I would not give it employment" (*Correspondence*, I, 3–4). Examining the implications of this last image, Swift seems to have recognized in himself the contemporary temper, an aggressive mental character shaped to defy the universe and cower before it, a Yahoo self fundamentally dangerous to civilization and humanity.

Assuming throughout his career the position of the satiric butt in a world full of absurdities, Swift discovers for us the immense differences in modulation with which time can tempt man, the absurdities especially congenial to one's years as well as to one's period. In his first, difficult major work, the implied observer joins with the reader to judge and deride man's irrationally aspiring other self—in Swift's day and person, the Hack. When Swift was young, he saw the horror in this mad spirit of youth mixing the world's chaos with its own. In his maturity, he centered the madness in middle-aged orthodoxy, mindless complicity in the lie of one's group, which destroys the possibility for harmonious man to flourish in a harmonious world. At that stage, comfort exalts the self-interested faction— whether a cabinet ministry, the clerical profession, or even the genteel establishment of England—above the legitimate claims of the individual imagination and of general humanity.

As an aging man, in the *Verses on the Death of Dr. Swift* he affirms the embattled self's hope to speak for the eternal virtues in the face of selfishness, boredom, faction, and time. The poem leads us first to the self in life, then to the day of death, and then—in the longest part—to the judgment by universal mankind. Living and dying, he is no longer an agent, but rather the cause of response in others. After his death, when men's self-interest can partially relax its force, when their striving selves can desire no more from him than corroboration for their attachments, their more nearly normative selves can deliver judgment. The presumption of self-interest on all sides provides the element of irony inseparable from Swift's examination of himself, as does the attempt, inevitably doomed, to delineate one life within the chaos of superficial social and psychological forces.[15] After suitable deductions, the judgment seems to be what Swift wants us to hold: that he was a good man fighting hard to be virtuous, but always in danger of subversion from within. While his struggling self sought distinction from childhood to maturity, his observing representative of mankind was always present to apply or at least imply the rules: fairness, unselfishness, leadership for the benefit of others above the self, and even some understanding that aberration was inevitable. His writing became a dialogue between his selves, the projected roles always providing the greatest possibilities of fruitful achievement or dreadful moral betrayal. Perhaps that is why he, above all his contemporaries, is a favorite in our time.

2. Personae: The Projected Selves

Responding to the contemporary popularity of the character—a sketch of a social or psychological type—as a genre and trained in the homiletic stances and technique, Swift found the dynamic emblem more congenial than a narrative fable of man's movement through life. He shaped the projected fragments of himself into dramatic visions of man, in a psychological range from the genteel sanity of his spokesmen to the varied representative lunacies of the Hack, the Modest Proposer, Simon Wagstaff, and the author of *Directions to Servants*. Into the figures at the center of his ironic vision, he poured his resentments about his Irish nationality, his uncertain class, and the inferior positions that he believed awaited him, as well as elements of the perverseness that he admitted. Of his Irish roots and partly voluntary Irish exile, for example, he made an excuse, but also much more: Ireland became for him a retreat, a madhouse, a salve to his wounds, a weak protégé, an arena and stage itinerant, a pulpit and a bench and a flying island from which to attack England, a surrogate self full of his own oddities and distortions to warn of the consequences of ill discipline. His showman for this monkey, his implied or present norm, is the well-bred, pious, harmonious observer, heir of the most sober classical tradition, who yet is certain enough about the Fall to beware himself.

Reflecting his view of the self in the world, Swift's personae consist of two main kinds, the mad conformist-individualist or priest-poet and the civilized, humane figure who speaks for the universal values that make society tolerable. The modest persona is a more gentle and polished Juvenal, a plain man, a man aware that compromise can usually be achieved without abandoning virtue. An even-tempered, public-spirited citizen, a well-bred, honorable, reasonable spokesman for western and Christian civilization, he is basically the gentleman of the renaissance conduct books and aristocratic theory;

in accordance with that theory he can also be a gentle priest or even a merchant.[16]

Although such a persona exhibits local details suitable to his position—his attributes as political journalist or drapier—and emblematically fills the stage before us like the madmen, he shares the temperament and attitudes of the observing self. Even if the corrective of history tells us that "moderate" to the Examiner means "quite Tory,"[17] and if the *Journal to Stella* shows us Swift coolly dressing party sentiments in the trappings of impartiality, this persona still provides few indications of authorial obliquity. If he pursues no private ends and exhibits no mental distortions, we have no reason to doubt that he speaks for Swift. The author of *The Sentiments of a Church-of-England Man, with Respect to Religion and Government* (1708), for example, advises moderation and can say with every appearance of justice that "I have gone as far as I am able in qualifying my self to be such a Moderator: I believe, I am no *Bigot* in Religion; and I am sure, I am none in Government" (*Prose Works*, II, 2). A similar "Person of Quality" argues in *A Letter to a Young Gentleman, Lately Entered into Holy Orders* (January 9, 1720), for simplicity, moderation, liberal education, all the absolutes associated with the classical-Christian tradition in the eternal battle with divisive self-interest, pride, and faction.[18] In the *Letter to a Young Lady, on her Marriage* (1723), a similar persona applies the classical-Christian tradition to wifely duties, urging the bride to cultivate her mind so that she can properly interest her husband as a "reasonable Companion, and a true Friend through every Stage of his Life."[19] Such a view, no doubt encouraged by Swift's early intimacy with the Temples and applied in his relations with Esther Johnson, makes him more consistently and humanely modern than many of his gentler contemporaries (for example, Fielding). The voice of universal humanity, for Swift, transcended sexual difference as it transcended all the other accidents of life.

Where in those pamphlets on private life Swift's observer advises aspiring young people on how to achieve his civilized stance, Swift's well-bred political Examiner occasionally animates the proud absurdity of the opposition before our eyes. No. 19 of *The Examiner*, for example, castigates the follies and crimes of the Whig leaders, who become hints for satirized personae. In No. 22, the Examiner parodies his various answerers through a Whig persona who has some of the wild lunacy of the Grubaean Hack. In No. 28 he quotes—or writes—letters from crazy Whig and odd Tory personae attacking him, ostensibly proving his impartiality but actually moving the point of sane agreement a good way to the right of center.[20] In general, such pieces, as well as some other political pamphlets—*A Preface to the Right Reverend Dr. Burnet, Bishop of Sarum's Introduction* (1713), by "Gregory Misosarum"; *A Letter . . . Concerning the Sacramental Test* (1709), by a member of the Irish parliament; *The Story of the Injured Lady, Written by Herself* (1708)—depend for their effect on routine satirical devices rather than on the complex persona. In such specific and ephemeral practical pamphlets, Swift provides the traditional world of the sane satirist and his mad butts instead of a complete symbolic microcosm.

As the Examiner is Swift's most extensively presented gentleman, a well-educated, politically moderate, public-spirited observer of society, so the Drapier is his most thorough adaptation of this figure to the average decent English tradesman. The individuating touches are fairly slight, though enough to move from aristocratic distance to elicit from middle-class readers Swift's most striking political success. The first Drapier letter, "to the Tradesmen, Shop-Keepers, Farmers, and Country-People in General, of the Kingdom of Ireland," neatly presents both the argument and the eternally reasonable, practical, independent, public-spirited self in the guise of the small bourgeois, the figure that Benjamin Franklin was to cultivate a few decades later: "For my own Part, I am already resolved what to do; I have a pretty good Shop of *Irish Stuffs* and *Silks*, and instead of taking Mr. WOOD's bad Copper, I intend to Truck with my Neighbours the *Butchers*, and *Bakers*, and *Brewers*, and the rest, *Goods for Goods*, and the little *Gold* and *Silver* I have, I will keep by me like my *Heart's Blood* till better Times . . ." (*Prose Works*, X, 7). To reinforce the permanence of the moral and social values that concern Swift, the third letter addresses not the Drapier's equals but "the Nobility and Gentry of the Kingdom of Ireland," with a homely apology for his undertaking the subject. In the Drapier, the individuation and its consequent obliquity are always subject to variation for the sake of the immediate political end; in the great satires, particularly the one conceived at the same time as the Drapier but aimed at bourgeois sickness, not health, those characteristics take on a visionary autonomy.

Although such harmonious versions of the universal self may vigorously fill our vision, the memorably "Swiftian" personae are the mad, fragmented figures like the Grubaean Hack and the Staffs, the gallery of servants, projectors, politicians, poets, prophets, voyagers, and other assorted knaves and fools. Enacted or implied, the drama of

Swift's work opposes their distorted, chaotic bits of reality to the orderly world of norms, which, since it is whole, includes but transcends them. To begin with, these oddities are burlesques of the moderate man; they try to cover the frenzy of the hack poet with philanthropic prudence but manage only a selfish, tattered film of caution. At once cynical and naive, they offer to connive with the reader to diddle their fellows, just as the moderate personae wish to join with the reader for mutual improvement. As the humane personae speak to equals, the personae-butts assume their audience to be self-interested fools and knaves. Sealed off by a Cartesian-Lockean inability to recognize otherness,[21] their world is a Hobbesian fragment, the jungle of Defoe's people run by what has jestingly been called natural law.

Awkwardly grasping at eminence, the mad personae beckon us to join them in mocking all the values of the harmonious personae, and thus in affirming the sole reality of hell. They extol reason and public service, but confide that reason means self-interest and the public is an ass. In Swift's bagatelles, figures like Simon Wagstaff or Bickerstaff are trivial versions of the gaseous poet, logicians and connoisseurs of the worthless incapable of touching real human issues. But when such a persona is self-conscious, like the Hack of the *Tale*, the projector of *Abolishing Christianity*, or the Gulliver of Book II attempting to fool the Brobdingnagian king, he becomes the mocking devil of tradition, the old Vice or Goethe's imminent Mephistopheles: the low, knowing self always alert to strike with doubt the self which struggles toward wholeness. Confined to the surface of things and motives, this self cheerfully assumes that any claim or ideal of unity is a jest. But if like Gulliver it hears the sound of human voices, it can drown.

As Swift's own perpetual thinking and writing to instruct his countrymen takes ironic shape in the figure of the projector—a combination of imaginative poet and philanthropic priest—so Swift's drive to expose false appearances becomes a staple rhetorical device for his prideful personae, beginning with the brilliant variations on this theme in the prefatory matter of *A Tale of a Tub*. Most of these idosyncratic personae are even more ambiguous than the Hack, for where the Hack pays no attention to our veneer of conventional decency, they seem at first to share it. The author of the *Argument [against] Abolishing Christianity* (1708), for example, seems on the surface to combine principle and practical reasoning like the humane Church of England Man, but practicality to him (as to the Hack) means the Hobbesian opportunism which denies principle.[22] In combining an uncontrolled fancy, as in his list of the ways in which people behave on Sundays, with assumptions of universal indifference, such a persona embraces the poles of madness represented by the quicksilver Hack and the priest deadened by port. As a self-conscious performer, he follows the Hack, and in supporting conventional piety and fearing primitive Christianity, he joins the great mass of accomplices in evil. Where the humane persona, the good man, seeks to inspire men to exert themselves for others, the selfish butt exhorts his fellows to rationalize as prudent and moral the corruption in which he flourishes.

Blinded to the concerns of mankind at large, such personae-butts sometimes betray each other, as in Bickerstaff's quarrel with the writer of the Letter on the death of Partridge. Although the figures appearing before us in this series of spoofs on popular fortune-telling are not, like the Hack, assertive in their madness, they are built on a core of blind, pedantic, and pompous materialism, which unites the credulity and willfulness that in other situations could destroy civilization. Such a figure does not urge atheism or political faction, but by championing the insignificant as the center of life he breaks down the distinctions fundamental to order and harmony.

In their contentions, these puppets on the stage itinerant expose themselves as well as their opponents. "The Translator to the Reader" of *A New Journey to Paris . . . By the Sieur de Baudrier* (1711) explains out of self-defeating malice that the persona is a "mean Man" who represents the vanity of the French by claiming aristocracy when he is no more than a menial (*Prose Works*, III, 208). In *Mr. C[olli]ns's Discourse of Free-Thinking* (1713), the Whig describing his "wise leaders" obtusely reveals that they are subverting religion for political ends. *Lord Wharton's Letter to the Bishop of St. Asaph* (1712) neatly associates the Church Fathers, the Bishop, and God with Wharton's own blasphemous arguments that the people owe the king no obedience: "This you say is the Opinion of CHRIST, St. *Peter*, and St. *Paul*: and 'faith I am glad to hear it; for I never thought the prigs had been Whigs before" (*Prose Works*, VI, 152). One isolated madman judges another, but in the jungle where these creatures move there is no norm. Only the world of the classical-Christian tradition, the world of the observing Swift and his reader, can provide the valid truth by which to judge the shared lower self.

Toward the end of Swift's career he concentrated folly and knavery, as distinctly as the connections that he sensed would allow, in two reflections of old age, Simon Wagstaff and the bitter footman of

Directions to Servants (1745). Wagstaff, the author of *A Compleat Collection of Genteel and Ingenious Conversation* (1738), parodies his creator's wish to serve the public through the grandiose avowal of selflessness by which Swift warns us of stupid cunning. A burlesque of contemporary scientists, he also apes a private practice of Swift's old age: he has been keeping notes for decades on his chosen subject, conversation among the upper classes.[23] Substituting fashionable chatter for the total of human culture, he is both the poet of a mad society and its worshipful priest, an early grand master of U and non-U, a projector neatly symbolizing for us the foppish intercourse he describes.

But as always for Swift, knavery—the agent of pride, of which folly is the victim—is more insidious than folly, with an assured grin addressing its fallen reflection in every bosom. Where the fool Wagstaff is a laughable symbol of what we may be, the knave claims to see us as we are. In contrast to Wagstaff's elderly dedication to comfort, the old rogue of *Directions to Servants* has spent his life intriguing and struggling for small prizes, and he sees only Hobbesian chaos in the social world. Since he has known only a permanent class war, he prescribes ceaseless guerilla tactics: "I do most earnestly exhort you all to Unanimity and Concord. But mistake me not: You may quarrel with each other as much as you please, only bear in Mind that you have a common Enemy, which is your Master and Lady, and you have a common Cause to defend. Believe an old Practitioner: whoever out of Malice to a Fellow-servant, carries a Tale to his Master, shall be ruined by a general Confederacy against him" (*Prose Works*, XIII, 11). Like the author of *Abolishing Christianity* or Lord Wharton, this retired footman is well adjusted to his jungle, not patently mad like the Hack or Simon Wagstaff: but this may mean only that his world is close enough to our dismal experience to seem real, that we can almost be fooled into thinking it complete. Because of the limitations imposed by class, however, his mind is repellent but not dangerous to the judging self—like Fielding's Jonathan Wild, too narrow to persuade us that he is symbolic man. As he stands, his cynicism is only a symptom of the general corruption of society, in which the Hack, the Modest Proposer, Simon Wagstaff, and preeminently Gulliver are at the center.

And Gulliver is, of course, the final triumph of Swift's art, more substantial than the Hack or the Modest Proposer, more imaginative than the Drapier, more painfully ourselves than any other creation of his century. Past its levels of brilliant narrative, literary and social burlesque, and political satire, *Gulliver's Travels* is Swift's fullest vision of man acting in the whole world, a clinical examination of human nature that ends as it must in the exemplary mind of the hero.[24] By the imaginative projection of the elements of his self-vision in Gulliver and the figures around him, as by casting light through a prism onto a screen, Swift creates and observes his own and humanity's looming, foolish, sinful transformation of real unity into a fragmented, enclosed world.

In its first three parts, Swift's only extended narrative follows the symbolic pattern of his satiric visions: exposure to the judging self of the assumptions on which the ordinary striving self acts. The Gulliver of Part I is conventional and orthodox: a bluff, decent Englishman following close on the Drapier but faced with much wider problems. Although he is chained in a temple-doghouse and occasionally tainted by perverse urges, although like the deranged butts he has written an ambitious history (of Lilliput) and is gulled into gravity by the grotesque rumor of his affair with Flimnap's wife, nevertheless he appears to represent us and the normative self; since the Lilliputians exhibit many of the worst qualities of the prideful, striving self, we are led to minimize his mental and moral deficiencies and to make much of his ordinary virtues. In Part II, however, where Gulliver confronts one embodiment of the humane and noble tradition, he eagerly identifies himself with a Europe which has institutionalized corruption. Partly through the tricks Swift can play with our vision of the tiny Gulliver puppet (which appears as a freak, a doll, a toy, a baby monkey) but also by its attempts to discourse, we learn of representative eccentric or demeaning elements in the conventional Englishman (no longer an analogue of a specific political figure like Bolingbroke or Temple) of which the puppet and the Englishman are ignorant: notably, vanity and a complacent willingness to tolerate profitable evil. Unable to distinguish between what is and what ought to be, Gulliver even asks us to join him—like all of Swift's opportunistic butts beginning with the Hack—in scorning and misleading the honest self. By contrast, and particularly in the famous conclusion to Chapter VI, the king of Brobdingnag speaks magisterially for universal humanity judging the bustle and pride of striving, time-bound man.

The king, however, is not an allegorical figure or an oracular spokesman for all classical-Christian tradition. Limited by the isolation of his culture and by the cares of family life and office, he has little of the Examiner's urbanity or the Drapier's easy good nature. He is a specific example of Man as Humane Ruler (or Bolingbroke's

Patriot King); for the book's vision of the whole normative self, one would need to add the kindness of the various captains culminating in Pedro de Mendez, the courageous decency of Reldresal, the warmth of the Brobdingnagian Queen and Glumdalclitch and Gulliver's own wife, the framers of the ancient laws of all the utopias, the public spirit of Munodi, the courteous intelligence of the Houyhnhnms, and the implied sanity opposing the idiosyncrasies of Part III. Even if any of these figures, Don Pedro for example, could sum up the harmony at the core of a world of varied appearances, the role of such a character is necessarily limited and distorted by the hero's needs and self-pleasing conceptions.

As the central representative of mankind makes his way through the world like Christian and Don Quixote in two of Swift's favorite books, we observe his peculiarities afresh in each encounter. Unlike Bunyan's Pilgrim, Gulliver lacks both guide and certain goal. When the smooth curtain of delusion slips, his lifelong failure to seek and absorb the universal humane tradition leaves him defenseless against chaos. In Chapter X of Part III, for example, to his normal, unthinking delight at the idea of immortality, Swift counterpoints the struld-bruggs, a vision of the inevitable doom to which a fleshly creature is subject. The absolutely archetypal, absolutely universal fantasy, the greatest of all delusions, the unformulated, prideful assumption of immortality suffers the greatest of all exposures; Swift's only alternative to death, progressive decay, is simply an adumbration and reminder of death. But powerfully as readers have been struck by the shock of animal mortality, which in other forms taught Every-man and Christian to choose the true path, Gulliver as a healthy man remains an untouched fragment of the self and not a whole, merely a traveler with an oddity to report. He has now, however, seen all the necessary elements of life; the struldbruggs help Swift to move past exposure and on to recognition and its consequences.[25]

Where in Part II Gulliver had unconsciously scorned the humanity of others and glossed over such horrors as naval warfare, legal corruption, or political depravity on the implied ground that other people do not exist, in Part IV he awakens to a vision of union with his kind and goes mad. Faced with the Yahoo, a reductive symbol of all that is basest in man, he identifies with it, distorting himself, the horses, and all existence. Realizing that his arguments before the Brobdingnagian king have their roots in sensuality and self-interest, he cannot imagine human society based on larger principles. He has recognized his own evil, like Fielding's Old Man of the Hill or Young

Goodman Brown of Hawthorne's story, and has believed it to be the sole truth about himself and the world. Since he sees only a fragment of the truth, he accepts only fragmentation as true. He conceives the world only in the extremes of mindless violence or passionless calm, overlooking the existence of charity in many people whom he has known and in the Portuguese sailors and captain whom Swift thrusts upon him. He has despaired because he has no equipment in the humane tradition to bid him hope.

But where the unchanging earlier Hack and later Footman, like the devil, delight in the vision of universal depravity, Gulliver deserves and receives some sympathy, because he affirms a world where goodness can exist somewhere, even if its home is an impenetrable utopia of courtly horses. Unlike Christian—but like Swift—Gulliver has had to strive in a morally ambiguous world, has had to fight his way through the mists of his own desires and the confusion provided by others, has had to affect the lives of others as well as nurse his own salvation. He has been defeated, as is inevitable for any man dreaming fiercely of permanence, and like his creator describing "the Dean of St. Patrick's sitting like a toad in a corner of his great house" (*Correspondence*, III, 114), he has retired to rail at the world of flux. Among Swift's personae, he is unique in having changed, in having wrenched one sort of truth from the battle: he refuses to return to easy glosses and conventional self-interest. In his stable with his respected horses, alone at his dinner table, or writing a letter to his Cousin Sympson, he repudiates his heightened impression of our routine world of surfaces. Between this world—the Footman's hell which he observes from isolation—and the Drapier's sane and harmonious vision which also belongs to Swift, the degree of obliquity is great.

Swift's personae play imposing parts in his visions, reflecting elements within himself that he controlled and artfully shaped for public communication: the time-bound, ambitious, consciously proud and individualistic self—either nakedly grasping or disguised with the complacent acceptance that Swift understood more as his advancing age demanded more comfort—performs variously before the self which has been forged by the humane consciousness of the apparently timeless, aristocratic, classical-Christian tradition. In his satires, dualities fly off in extremes, which are embraced by madmen like the Hack but must be judged by the observing self: not to establish a compromise, but to see what virtue has been distorted. Originality and order, both virtues, become fragmented wildness and rigidity in Irishman and Englishman, poet and priest, Footman and Wagstaff—all partial reflections that Swift saw in the mirror of his mind. The foolish and mad aspects of the self provide distorted pictures of a chaotic world with which they wish to collaborate; the relatively sane, harmonious self, an echo of the divine but yet modified by an understanding of the idiosyncrasy inescapable in the real world, conceives of a harmony which includes the fragmented chaos but far transcends it.

Using the idiosyncratic persona, Swift creates eccentric visions different from the traditional satiric world of *The Dunciad*, in which the unambiguous author-satirist attacks or is attacked by the forces of evil. Far more aware of an attraction to the devil's side than Pope was, Swift joins with that side rhetorically and causes us also to divide ourselves, to identify with the deluded sinner and to be our own final judges. If this is satire, it tips suspiciously toward tragedy.[26] Not only the classical attitudes of Homer and Virgil guide our contemptuous gaze to the mess which our contemporaries have made of the world: all of mankind's cherished values, the distillate of its hopes for this world and the next, provide hapless laughter at what has become of us as we fondle our stone horses, ward off our wives and children, and threaten our tormentors, versions of ourselves, with legions of avenging Houyhnhnms. By projecting his sense of his own individual obsessions into symbolic visions of man, Swift ties himself to us through poet and clergyman, projector and rogue, and most powerfully through the well-disposed citizen, the mock observer who in conniving at the world seems to confer on it the approval of general mankind. By drawing on the ideal vision of man that he shares with his time, Swift provides the composite and implied observer—general man at his best—who can correct our eyesight and guide our realistic judgment.

3. Man in the World

Imagining man in the world, Swift saw at the center a creature in desperate need of guidance, beset by the immense pressures of a seductively congenial chaos. Such a vision constantly raises painful moral questions even during the routine of life and forces serious concern with matters which sometimes seem ludicrous. How is a man to live sanely if he must always stumble amidst chaos even in his diet or among his servants? if in seeking the truth, which must in essence be simple, he finds only permanent grotesqueries—in religious observances, in the social behavior and diction of sober adults, in a nation's coinage, in its political and financial customs? if he can know as certain only what he perceives for himself and yet must rely on the wisdom of the species, the common perception of millennia and millions? Through traditional satiric metaphors which intimately mingled with and helped form his complex vision of himself, Swift was able to shape the paradoxes of man's condition in the world; they provided a context and a vehicle for the wild and deluded acting self, the chaos which it finds and creates, and the observing self which has been built out of divine concern and urbane tradition.

To seize the perverse human condition, Swift's imagination characteristically employs such fantasy-based symbolic situations or patterns of action as wrangling political factions or their psychological equivalent—madness—which when contrasted with national unity and sanity concentrate his vision of man in harmony or conflict with the world; the coming of catastrophe, of which the priest must warn; the use of magic, which is a combination of the pretentiously absurd and the dangerously mad, though it is also the province of the literary performer. Man's fears of madness, division, misunderstanding, and disaster, are versions of Swift's; man's better prospects, his admiration for deserved eminence, coherence, and sane command of order, and, above all, his hope to transcend by public performance the defeats dealt by accident and conspiracy, characteristically echo Swift's reveries. From the chaotic factional wrangling to the magical weaving of cloth, man's condition, like Swift's, is always precarious but not hopeless if he maintains faith in a harmonious world.

In one myth so recurrent that it seems to be an element in his imagination, Swift affirms the existence of an animal nature in man and even sees it in himself; as an artist, he finds the moral neutrality of animals a fine device by which to aggrandize or diminish mankind. Since an animal is less than a man, Swift can conceive the butt's despair of attaining a harmonious life as a yielding to the enticements of this limited self. Poems like the *Ode to the Honourable Sir William Temple* (about 1692), *Vanbrug's House* (1703), *The Description of a Salamander* (1705), *Phillis, or, the Progress of Love* (1719), and *The Progress of Marriage* (1722) envision petty kings as mice shaking mountains, architects and playwrights as insects, a general as a salamander out of Pliny, two socially mixed but constitutionally similar lovers as "Cat and Dog, and Rogue and Whore," and an elderly husband watching his wife and her friends at Bath as a hen at the periphery of a mud puddle, clucking while the young ducks swim. By acting like an animal, man has lapsed to the condition of an animal: if morally neutral in itself, yet loathesome for a being created *rationis capax*. However, though Swift uses the animal image for intense contempt in these poems and in party pamphlets like *The Public Spirit of the Whigs*, he sometimes argues that man does properly share limited worlds with the lower creatures. Since he was a complex person with varying ways of conceiving the world of phenomena and not a butt committed to one lifelong allegory, we cannot weigh his references to horses and find an average connotation (consider, for example, his letter comparing a talented statesman to a "mettlesome horse" [*Correspondence*, II, 333] and his description of Steele as a "hireling Jade" [*Prose Works*, VIII, 43]) in order to understand the Houyhnhnms, as we cannot argue from the trifling women who chatter like monkeys in the *Letter to a Young Lady, on her Marriage* (1723, when Swift was brooding over *Gulliver's Travels*) that Gulliver's stupendous abductor in Part II, Chapter V, is a charming fool. Swift's spiders are ugly, but they do spin beautifully. Bees, models for classical authors, bring sweetness and light. Horses may be spirited, vicious, lazy, enduring, or stupid, as the currently imagined world requires.[27]

A major cluster of images and patterns thematically connected to the faction-madness-animalism threat conveys Swift's strongly projected sense of impending catastrophe. In the London period of political involvement, when he felt particularly vulnerable to chance and whim, Swift saw a world of figures drowning, clutching at straws, or tossing out tubs for whales.[28] Even when his friends were in power and he nursed hopes for an imminent humane order, he tended to conceive not the millennium but the apocalypse, this present world of chaos in the throes of its necessary destruction: in the famous *Description of a City Shower*, for example, the filth and detritus of London collect in a flood of sewage, as in *The Fable of Midas* a torrent washes away the dirty spoils of politics. Swift's sanest persona before the Drapier, the Church of England Man, fears the kind of chaos which had overwhelmed Ireland in Swift's youth and seemed always potential in the world of the surface.[29] He would defend episcopacy "by Arms against all the Powers on Earth, except our own Legislature; in which Case, he would submit as to a general

Calamity, a Dearth, or a Pestilence" (*Prose Works*, II, 5). One of the maddest of the personae of the same time, the author of the *Argument [against] Abolishing Christianity*, also opposes drastic change in the Church, on wildly selfish grounds and in fear of a materialistic day of doom. Burlesquing the apocalytic fears of Swift's letters, this anti-projector luxuriates in dreadful visions of the restoration of primitive, genuine Christianity, which "would be to dig up Foundations; to destroy at one Blow *all* the Wit, and *half* the Learning of the Kingdom; to break the entire Frame and Constitution of Things; to ruin Trade, extinguish Arts and Sciences with the Professors of them; in short to turn our Courts, Exchanges, and Shops into Desarts" (*Prose Works*, II, 27). For the selfish man of the world, as for the earlier Hack, a smooth skin is absolutely essential to hide the flayed horror which he imagines underneath. Out of the chaotic, partial outside, this disorderly imagination weaves a delusive cloth to parody the divine coherence which for Swift's universal self underlies all. The antithetical personae are aspects of the opposing visions which Swift had indicated earlier in his play with clothing images: the Hack perceived the external garment as governing shape and meaning; the implied observer was aware of the animating spirit.

Since man must imitate the divine as best he can, this related cluster of movements and images for catching the world—the operations of magic and cloth-making—suggests the creative no less than the obstructive possibilities of the idiosyncratic self.[30] Swift was, after all, Presto to his dearest friend. Against the use of clothes in the *Tale of a Tub*, where the predominant connotation is of false surfaces, in Swift's allegorical defense of himself in the Drapier's Letter V, clothing becomes symbolic of fundamental civilization and its creator shines as a true pastor: "Some Months ago, considering with my self, that the *lower and poorer Sort of People* wanted a *plain, strong, coarse Stuff, to defend them against cold* Easterly *Winds; which then blew very fierce and blasting for a long Time together;* I contrived one on purpose, which sold very well all over the Kingdom, and preserved many Thousands from *Agues.* I then made a *second* and a *third* Kind of *Stuffs* for the *Gentry*, with the same Success; insomuch, that an *Ague* hath hardly been heard of for some Time" (*Prose Works*, X, 82–83). In his least ironic self-projection, Swift chooses to be seen as an imaginative protector: the priest-poet, the good magician who weaves pamphlets to ward off evil.

The active profession of magic, as might be expected of a satirist consciously following Cervantes and Butler, implies for Swift a proud, idiosyncratic diversion from right reason, often a combination of delusion and swindle. *Vanbrug's House*, for example, attacks the building as a conscious trick by the faddish, mad architect to fool the idiots who admire modern art; in *The Virtues of Sid Hamet the Magician's Rod* (1710) Godolphin deceives the citizens (and, like Thomson's later Indolence, hints at the connection in fantasy between trickery and sexual exploitation); the Partridge tomfoolery plays with the magical game of astrology and the folly of personae who quarrel over their skill in its practice. Steele in the imitation of Horace (1713); financiers in *The Run upon Bankers* (1720); the rascally Bishop Hort in *The Storm: Minerva's Petition* (1722); Wood, in *A Simile on our Want of Silver* (1725)—all are nasty, incompetent magicians attempting to substitute one fragmented vision of the surface for another. Whether villains or dupes, they are blind to underlying essence. They are the acting self cut loose without guidance or judgment.

But if Swift attacks magic as delusion or obscurantism, he himself wishes to work opposing wonders, to shock the mind to awareness of what it has hidden from itself. His spells are intended not only to destroy the illusion but also to heal the mode and organ of perception: the reader should see differently, more truly. In negating appearances, the detailed metamorphoses of *Baucis and Philemon* affirm the underlying essences.[31] Even more clearly, Presto waves away the deceiving surfaces of convention in the poems exposing the clichés of poetic mood, such as *A Description of the Morning* and *A Description of a City Shower*; in the surgical anatomies of a prostitute or of the mind of the lover who discovers that his beloved excretes; and in the progress poems, where shallow or vicious people shine out like rotten wood (to borrow an image from *A Tale of a Tub*). In *Phillis, or the Progress of Love*, Swift reveals at the end not what Phillis and her lover have suddenly became, but rather what they always were. In *The Progress of Beauty*, Celia moves from the hinted cant world of pastoral poetry ("When first Diana leaves her Bed"), a world of apparent serenity, to disintegration beyond the possibility of illusion. *The Progress of Marriage* opens with a situation which should be inconceivable but in a mad society is even customary:

> Aetatis suae fifty two
> A rich Divine began to woo
> A handsome young imperious *Girl*
> Nearly related to an Earl.

At the husband's premature death, the narrator destines the wife for a broken ensign who will

> turn her Naked out of Doors,
> And spend her Joynture on his Whores;
> But for a parting Present leave her
> A rooted Pox to last for ever.

Like the priest whose core of lecherous folly has waited fifty-two years before being fully revealed, she must follow her own nature, progressing from pampered aristocrat (her accidental, local quality) to rotting whore (her essence). In such poems, as in Swift's greatest prose, he has torn the delusive surface off to show the reader its corrupt foundation. He has also implied a standard of judgment which places the corruption within a moral order and therefore transcends it.

A world consisting only of surfaces breeds delusions, and all of Swift's personae-butts are mad. Locked in their minds, they inhabit partial and distorted layers of the world, from the absurdly thin slivers of the Staffs through the deeper societies of the Hack and the Modest Proposer, to the Europe of Gulliver—of such depth that it accommodates most of our own consciousness. When the butt has power, he erects a flimsy madhouse, a distorted, fragmentary imitation of the harmonious world; whatever he says or thinks, its principle of deformity is always selfish opportunism. A vision formed by Swift's own fears of drowning in chaos, the madhouse caters to those who hate and fear the world, men like the Hack who are too vainly aggressive to be tolerated by their peaceful fellows. Since this dangerous and absurd construction may fool an ordinary man—who after all acts much of his time in the world of surfaces—his observing self must destroy the hallucinatory enclosure with the classical-Christian vision of the limitless world.

A natural extension of private madness is the fragmented, embattled, mindlessly selfish world of faction, to which individuals—from modern writers in the *Tale of a Tub* to the presumed audience of *Directions to Servants*—abandon their powers of vision and judgment. In politics, religion, and literature, the weak and fearful, rendered anxious and despairing by their inability to fight off chaos, rush to accept the mental habits of a group. Inevitably, they find a fragmented view masquerading as integrity. Reflecting its source in the distortions of self-interest, factional thought cannot be the truth which its ambiguous clichés pretend to summarize. In contrast, the harmonious order which simply and clearly distills man's universal experience supports the whole of society against the professions, the established religion against the sects, the nation against the political parties. The difference between sanity and madness is the distinction between the universal, eternal truths provided by God's word fortified by human history and the mechanical rubrics set up by a party, profession, social class, province, dissenting sect, or, in short, any group with dominant special aims.

The difference is therefore both moral and simple, obvious to any man willing to abjure selfishness. But in the face of such serene assurance, Swift's irreverent mocker often rises to ask if a view held by whatever majority of the elite currently constitutes the nation is necessarily an eternal truth; how one can distinguish arrogant from perceptive independence in the individual who differs from the larger group; how, indeed, one can decide between the vitally harmonious and the most recent copy of established patterns. If "systems"—reductive generalizations—are probably mindless clichés while nonconformity is often a mere symptom of madness, where is man to find clear sanity?

Swift has no certain answer, except that one must live one's life seeking the union of order and vigor, which is truth, and doubting its easy imitation. The self is everywhere beset by temptations to yield its moral choice, and it simply must resist them; the extremes of individualism and conformity are aspects of each other, the Hack making common cause with all the moderns. Nevertheless, at any one time the extremes reflect the opposing temptations of Swift's gregarious, routine-bound Priest and his soaring, gaseous Poet. He repudiates both as dangerous lunatics; but forced to choose, he cannot help leaning toward the irreverent and idiosyncratic, who is at least certifiably alive. Throughout his career, Swift was suspicious of apparent calm of mind, which seemed to him either vacancy or submission to the dominance of the group.[32] In the *Journal to Stella* of March 5, 1711–12, for example, he attacks the clichés of religious observance in a manner unusual for an orthodox clergyman: "I wish you a merry Lent; I hate Lent. I hate different diets, and Furmity & Butter, & herb Porrige, and sour devout Faces of People who only put on Religion for 7 Weeks" (II, 504). Through the Church of England Man of 1708 he had said of party regularity what could apply to Lent: the reasonable man may compromise on minor practices, but in no case where moral issues are involved should he yield to the opinions of a group. Examining another sort of mass cliché which attempts to overrule individual intelligence in the late *Hints Towards an Essay on Conversation* and its elaboration by the snobbish dandy Wagstaff, Swift implies that a group of free human beings gathered for social pleasure can only suffer from the application of orthodoxies.[33]

Swift's leaning toward the idiosyncratic, however, is more a matter of his temperament than a formal element of his thought. Although he acknowledges the subversive lure of the obscure, the illusory, the trivial, the haphazardly concrete, and the grotesquely cumbersome, Swift affirms the orderly. All things considered, he concludes that man's most necessary and most difficult goal is to act independently and yet coherently. A man's selves must cooperate, so that he sees the valid distinctions invisible to the mindless herd, and acts not on the spur of pride or animal appetite but in the light of his humane vision. Therefore Swift refuses to be limited to two alternatives, since they may both be wholly or partially wrong, as rule by either passion or routine is wrong. Repudiating the paths provided by the isolated self of the Poet or the corporate self of the Priest, his sober letters, moderate personae, and implied guides recommend that living tradition be applied to the living moment.

Although as an imaginative and sensitive man the writer is beset by an immense number and variety of images, odd ideas, and analogies—by the obliquity of Grubaean and Gulliverian human nature—Swift says that great literature must hew to the divinely right, the general, the classical ideal of significance, simplicity, precision, decorum. Fortunately for us, however, the satisfying generalizations eluded him, as he admitted to Gay and the Duchess of Queensberry in describing his attempt to write a fable: "I remember, I acted as you seem to hint, I found a moral first, & then studyed for a Fable, but cou'd do nothing that pleased me, & so left off that scheme for ever" (*Correspondence*, IV, 38–39). For his own peculiar genius the concrete took precedence; while he reproves the chaos that presses on him from all sides, his mad poetic self leaps out with joyous appetite. Swift's special power lies in moral vision rather than moral statement—in the faltering, noble, painfully deluded, or grotesque figure, not the epigram. Although we are still divided on Swift's specific intentions in Part IV of the *Travels*, our memories are stamped with the sight of Gulliver tied by the Lilliputians, exhibited by the Brobdingnagian farmer, watching the execution of giants, fighting off a lusting Yahoo female, or discoursing with his Houyhnhnm master, and we are overwhelmed by the almost palpable presence of the lunatic Hack or the complacent horrors in the mind of the Modest Proposer.

Aside from professional observations on satire, wit, and humor in *Thoughts on Various Subjects to Mr. Delany* and in *The Intelligencer* No. 3, Swift as literary observer is most fascinated by language, which like clothing is both a separate fabric and a surface over something much more important. Like Pope, Swift sees language as an index of a writer's thought and manner, and beyond that of a writer's or a whole society's moral condition.[34] In his only acknowledged appearance as a projector, the *Proposals for Correcting, Improving, and Ascertaining the English Tongue* (1712), he applies this classical theory to English and advocates the establishment of an academy. If the English language can be preserved harmonious and clear above present corruption, it will serve as a fit instrument for great writers to communicate with a great reformed society of the future. Yet a part of him, available for the Hack's verbal contortions and Wagstaff's fussiness, constantly mocks the purist. In the contemporaneous *Journal to Stella*, as to the end of his life, Swift delighted in word play: his letters and notes abound in puns in several languages, doggerel, slang, dialects—in short, whatever grotesqueries languages could provide.[35]

Much as Swift enjoyed dabbling idiosyncratically with language—the chaotic surface of art—his fundamental concern is with moral vision, classically the essence of art. In drawing people, for instance, he is at pains to exhibit the specimen not changing or moving but fulfilling its nature in plain view. Thus in his *History of the Four Last Years of the Queen*, his portraits of the Whig leaders are "characters" built around single elements like Marlborough's avarice or Nottingham's constitutional treachery (*Prose Works*, VIII); Nos. 5 and 7 of *The Intelligencer*, attacking "Discretion: a species of lower prudence," contrast two such characters, Corusades—the prudent, hypocritical, successful mediocrity—and Eugenio, the lively, original, imprudent failure (*Prose Works*, XII, 38–45). When Swift does move the satiric object through a progress, he aims to classify it scientifically within a limited range of aberrations: an unnatural marriage, delusive beauty, sexual corruption. Only Gulliver passes through time and change, and his change is rooted in Everyman's or Quixote's, not in the special circumstance of meeting pygmies, giants, bestial men, and humane animals. From the Hack to the Footman, the personae are permanent elements in the nature of man—as they are in Swift—temporarily enlarged for our inspection and edification. Although a characteristic may seem to rise directly from Swift's own circumstances, as with Simon Wagstaff's memoranda on language or the Modest Proposer's advanced age, it is carefully fitted to the mental appearance of the character. Swift's self-vision in his successful work supports, and does not subvert, his public purpose.

Swift's verse is often even more overtly emblematic than his prose; it uses related images to make up for the support provided by the persona's unifying moral position in the prose. At times, as in *Vanbrug's House*, Swift begins the attack with a parallel denigrating fable or image which explicitly glosses what is to follow:

> Premising thus in Modern way
> The greater half I had to say,
> Sing Muse the House of Poet Van
> In higher Strain than we began.

Again, *The Description of a Salamander* opens with a series of analogies between animals and people, and then shows how the satiric victim, General Cutts, is psychologically equivalent to Pliny's salamander. After a picture of a father and his sons in *The Faggot*, "Here ends the Fable and the Moral." Announcing at once that the poet is like a goose, *The Progress of Poetry* presents first the goose's qualities and then their application to the poet. Such a device can work to reconcile Swift's aim for the general and his delight in the special, outrageously making the acting self an illustration of the owlish wisdom of the observer.

The elaborate parallel may be so deliberately incongruous as to subvert the sober statement, shed irony on the moralizing author, and turn him into a mild butt. The poet who compares a poet to a goose is himself exposed as unbalanced. By its violence or triviality the metaphor becomes a symbol of fundamental corruption, a crack in the delusive harmony of the surface which gives away the chaotic mind and passions beneath, as Gulliver's detailed admissions to the Brobdingnagian king, or the Anti-Abolisher's description of English life on Sundays, destroys the apparent order on which the speaker insists. When such juxtapositions are carefully controlled in Swift's prose, they support a double vision of life, where the wild, grotesque clutter is played against a possibility of harmony. But in the poetry, where intellectual argument is even by classical theory subordinated to emotional effect, Swift tended to indulge the concrete and chaotic visions. Just as the Poet concentrates Swift's idiosyncratic self—the rhapsodist of the early Pindarics, whom Swift even in the 1690s thought a conjured spirit—the poem can form the bursting channel for torrents of specific perceptions.[36]

As a gathering for such perceptions, Swift's pattern poem can be *The Bubble* (1720), a profuse and bizarre vision of overlapping partial worlds which smother the singleness of truth. After attacking as mountebanks the managers of the scheme of financial speculation (always nicely emblematic of chimerical hopes and destructive folly), Swift as traditional satirist and preacher shows us the investor, a "deluded Bankrupt" who stakes everything and

> The plunges in the *Southern* Waves,
> Dipt over head and Ears—in Debt.

Inhabiting a mental landscape of pastoral clichés, the feverish mariner

> with Rapture sees
> On the smooth Ocean's azure Bed
> Enamell'd Fields, and verdant Trees.

After an ironically trite parallel from the classical world, the myth of Icarus and Daedalus ("Rais'd up on Hope's aspiring Plumes"), Swift descends to the barnyard society of geese to show how one sharp speculator overcomes the many fools. Out of inexhaustible stores, he invents an apposite vision, a fable about an ass; another about fishes; an episode grotesquely conjoining social satire and remote folklore, about women gamblers who

> Ride o'er the Waves in spacious Hoops,
> Like *Lapland* Witches in a Sieve;

then more mythology, this time Venus descending to the sea to tie the visions of poetry to the squalor of finance:

> the Queen of Love intends
> To search the Deep for Pearl and Coral.

For the claim by the portentous and dishonest directors that the sea is covered with gold, the myth of Midas is a suitable gloss. Yet reality does exist, Swift tells us editorially, beneath the lying magic surface:

[63]

> So cast it in the *Southern* Seas,
> And view it through a *Jobber's* Bill,
> Put on what Spectacles You please,
> Your Guinnea's but a Guinnea still.

Additional myths, fables, natural history, and pervasive Biblical allusion combine to develop the scheme's grotesque lunacy. In short,
while the point is clear and general, for maximum effect Swift is
drawn toward the satiric manner of Butler backward to Donne and
the medieval preachers rather than to the decorum popularly attrib-
uted to his contemporaries. As soon as he approaches the bubble, the
whole world of man's delusion through time, multifariously detailed
and deliberately incoherent, assails him; and in his less guarded medium
of verse, he welcomes the chaos. Temperamentally and therefore
imaginatively, Swift is a long way from Gay as fabulist.

In his other emblematic writings, Swift further examines the distinctions between the singularity of metaphors and the complexity of
phenomena; between systematic, confined logic and the real world of
matter and people; between mythical or archetypal ways of expressing permanent truths and the inevitable petrifaction of these perceptions of reality. He wants to guide us along a path to the truth within
chaos, and will use every available device of language or thought,
but he knows that he must keep testing to see that he has not strayed.
While the truth remains the truth, chaos has a habit of shifting around
it and distorting it, even as his main characters undergo surface
changes (the Hack is sometimes critic, sometimes philosopher, sometimes poet; Gulliver is a surgeon, but also a ship's captain and a his-
toriographer), and as he himself played a variety of roles before his
own consciousness. The living whole and the enduring truth must,
therefore, be continuously approached afresh, and with the awareness (not granted to system makers) that the way is only certain
when it is illuminated by revelation.

The submission to chaos can take all sorts of social and political
forms. It can pose as the rise of a moneyed interest that wants to
rule the country (letter to Pope, January 10, 1721; *Examiner* No. 37);
as the substitution of powerful central control for the admirable
"*Gothic* system of limited monarchy" (*Correspondence*, IV, 303);
as the spread of religious dissent, from *A Tale of a Tub* to the end
of Swift's life the certain bane of the commonwealth. In every sphere,
falsehood is the unregulated, though sometimes poetic, chaos of
variety, the product and sign of willful pride. All his butts, from the

Grubaean Hack through the various Whig and deist figures of the 1710s to Gulliver, the Modest Proposer, Simon Wagstaff, and the grim Footman, form mutually exclusive closed systems that explain the universe according to partial and therefore delusive keys. Truth, by contrast, is single—in a prose made up of proper words in proper places; in episcopacy for religious order and purity; in the capacity of educated gentlemen to fill any public office; in the ability of man, instructed by revelation and the wisdom of the species, to act well in the world.

Like all memorable writers and thinkers, Swift envisioned a world of individual integrity and social harmony, for which he sketched suitable educational, legal, economic, religious, even linguistic programs. On the great issues more specific to his time, he agreed with his contemporaries and their models in preferring the eternal to the temporary, the substance to the surface, reality to illusion and delusion. He was more in sympathy with the cyclical view of history than some others like Pope or Johnson, and he saw his own time as a low point; he was more conservative than most others whom we remember, less willing to tolerate variety, which seemed to him error. But while Swift's ideas where important to him, they are not special to him or central in his literary achievement.[37]

The vision of man gyrating in a fragmented, distorted, and ludicrous world of immediate satisfactions, under the eye of an observer who knows both the harmonious ideal and his own distance from it, is surely more what Swift stands for than any group of ideas that we can call cyclical, conservative, classical, Tory, or even Anglican. Much more Swiftian than any "system"—to borrow his own scornful term—of ideas, personality, style, or genre, his oblique affirmation of harmony and overt delight in the irreverent, the disturbed, and the perverse create an observing self even larger than his contemporaries' favorite norm, the spokesman for the classical tradition. Because his idiosyncratic, striving self is not totally denied but placed in perspective by the evaluative, universal self, Swift like Rabelais can condemn its cynical pride and folly and yet bring into the larger human world its living elements: its delight in trivia and puns, its rhapsodic ingenuity, its sportive self-consciousness.[38] Through the self-mockery characteristic of his time and congenial to his temper, he can erect before us the comic as well as the noble, the herding priest and flying poet as well as the harmonious gentleman.

Where Pope projects the small and delicate and light as various ironic forms of the self, and Thomson the dreaming and sensual

escapist, Swift's imagination plays with the violent, mocking, burlesque Projector-Irishman-Whig-Poet and the orthodox Priest-
Teacher-Englishman-Tory. For each, the rejected antiself is recognizably a vision of what he saw in a mental mirror. All three writers,
more or less contemporaries and more or less satirists, scorn those
self-indulgent elements in the projected vision which yield to routine,
to destruction, and to suicide; but in the constitution of these elements
and in the shadings of response to them, each is clearly distinguishable
from the others. Perhaps because his sympathies were so antithetical,
and his resolution of them in the gentleman so precarious and ironic,
Swift's is the most vivid vision, his the most powerful and varied contribution to the amalgam of human nature fashioned in his century.

IV

JOHNSON

1. The Author as the Pattern Self

JOHNSON SAW AROUND him a psychological arena in which men tested themselves in conflicts with Johnson's own uncertainties and temptations. Only through continuous grappling with the chaos of experience could man hope to seize momentary harmony, which his imagination—not his reason—could temporally extend as "happiness." Man's fondest illusion equates happiness with rest, and his most profound shock rises from discovering that rest can mean the loss of energy to struggle. Since virtue's source is psychological—only a healthily active mind can rebuff despair—Johnson approaches morality with a descriptive, empirical, not (at least in the first instance) judgmental examination of mental processes. Where Swift as a fundamentalist in morality looks within for elements to condemn in contemporary man or all mankind, Johnson begins by trying to study psychology objectively. Searching his own nature for the laws of human behavior, he found the ironies and confusion and extremes which he projected through his figures.

Appraising himself as sufferer and as heightened representative man, Johnson saw both the equipment to overcome the hardest tasks and a tendency to yield before the unending strain of life. Although he could at times make allowances for his social and physical obstacles and for the magnitude of his goals, he was nagged by the consciousness of great abilities not sufficiently realized. As his personal papers show, he agonized over both specific deficiencies such as disobeying his father, sleeping late, or not providing comfortably for his wife, and a general failure to use productively the talents which God had given him. In his diaries, prayers, and meditations, he calls himself to isolated judgment even more sharply than in his letters, in which ameliorating comparison with others is inevitable. On his twenty-ninth birthday, for example, he writes of wasting time "in Sloth, Vanity, and wickedness," and in later entries, particularly after Tetty's death, he bows even lower with guilt.[1] He accuses himself of indolence and fears despair, sins as dangerous to the dissenting or bourgeois conscience as pride is to the aristocratic Swift or Pope or Fielding. Johnson acknowledges a temperamental violence, sometimes verging on madness. He condemns his own rebelliousness, calling himself willfully delusive, oppressive to himself, peevish, and obstinate.

But if Johnson's aspiring, ideal self held up a standard too high for serene accomplishment or indeed for any possible fulfillment, he could always oppose it with what he imported from general human experience. As Boswell makes clear, Johnson knew his feelings of guilt were morbid, had always been determined to resist them, and could bring to an examination of his struggles the saving judgment of larger humanity: "He mentioned to me now, for the first time, that he had been distrest by melancholy, and for that reason had been obliged to fly from study and meditation, to the dissipating variety of life. Against melancholy he recommended constant occupation of mind, a great deal of exercise, moderation in eating and drinking, and especially to shun drinking at night."[2] Where Swift's reflecting self assures its fellows that the will can vanquish its mad tendencies by following the classical-Christian path, Johnson's allows common survival to be at least a minimal virtue. Softened by distance, charity, and an awareness of the slighter abilities of others, such self-analyses help produce an important part of his observing self: an extraordinary sensitivity to the complexities of the general human mind, particularly to its fluidity and to the dangers of guilt.[3]

Since Johnson cultivated the habit of comparing himself with others—partly to oppose his driving self, perhaps, and partly to placate it—he knew his virtues: his vigorous response to all challenges, his willingness to keep fighting indolence and grinding chaos into order, pleased him as they do us. Although sometimes he seemed to himself a recluse, an uncourtly outsider painfully and even grotesquely abnormal in his society, like Pope he enjoyed attacks as clear proof that he had risen beyond anonymity and forced the world to acknowledge him.[4] Writing to Chesterfield on February 7, 1755, Johnson complains of his difficulties and loneliness, but the fame of the letter derives from his just pride in independent accomplishment. Ironically aware of the fruits of shining before others, he accepted his competitiveness because it allowed the life-giving use of his intellectual talents; and he was joyful when he could free his great powers of concentration and composition from prolonged passivity.[5] If Johnson was overly disgusted and pained by his excesses in drinking wine or sleeping late, he made proportionally grand attempts to overcome them, setting himself early schedules, fasts, abstentions, the translation of Greek testaments, and massive public undertakings like the *Rambler* and *Idler*, the *Dictionary*, the Shakespeare edition, the *Lives of the Poets*. Although he put his ultimate faith in God (the center as well of his greatest fears, the Being with whom he could not confidently compare his powers), in the sublunary grappling with life he knew that he would show up well.[6]

But such comparative achievements could not provide the sole necessary reassurance, the mental ease of satisfying the appetitive idiosyncratic self. On the contrary, in his gloomier moods he feels that they swell his representative deficiencies: his disappointments and anxieties, his unhappier aspects, rise not from specific failures but from a sense of heightened accessibility to general human weakness, a heightened susceptibility to the general doom of man. Fears of various sorts predominate in this negative condition—fear of his combativeness, of isolation, of wild fantasies, of melancholy, of insensitivity to stimuli, of madness, of death, of a waste of life, of boredom, of everything subsiding into falsely smooth surfaces. Palpable dangers like brawling mastiffs, a gang of angry Macphersons, or a fearful storm on a highland lake he could face easily; but vague fears and uncertainties lurked recurrent and unconquerable. As he wrote to Taylor on August 31, 1772, with increasing age his fantasies were sometimes barely tolerable: "I had formerly great command of my attention, and what I did not like could forbear to think on. But of this power which is of the highest importance to the tranquillity of life, I have for some time past been so much exhausted, that I do not go into a company towards night in which I foresee anything disagreeable, nor enquire after any thing to which I am not indifferent, lest something, which I know to be nothing, should fasten upon my imagination, and hinder me from sleep" (*Letters*, I, 281).[7] He feared the effects on him of his poverty (*Diaries*, June 15, 1732, p. 29), of his guilt about Tetty, of his intellectual examination of religion. Nevertheless, even to these fears he could oppose the moral courage which for specific obstacles directed him out into experience, perhaps an aspect of the same driving appetite which fed him impossible ambitions. Despite his shame at failing to fulfill resolutions, he says determinedly, "I will yet try."[8] The persistence showed itself in his famous unwillingness to transfer his worries to a convenient agency: although he feared above all death and the thought of what would follow, " 'an obstinate rationality prevents me' " from escaping the fear through conversion to Catholicism (*Life*, IV, 289). In his own view as in Boswell's, this resistance to a solace that he badly wanted shores up Johnson's independent stance in the face of chaos.

Although Johnson always knew that he had to battle a massive task, or chaos, or the fear of death, by himself, after Tetty died he often saw himself as even more alone, as emblematically isolated; and indeed Johnson as widower, with no formal profession or intimate dependents, approximates the archetypal wanderer in an alien world more closely than most writers of his or any time. As with other aspects of his psychological self-medication, his response was a steady and varied series of efforts to move outward, to fashion close ties with others.[9] He wrote to Thomas Warton on December 21, 1754: "I have ever since seemed to myself broken off from mankind a kind of solitary wanderer in the wild of life, with out any certain direction, or fixed point of view. A gloomy gazer on a World to which I have little relation. Yet I would endeavour by the help of you and your brother to supply the want of closer union by friendship."[10] However, even if he was "a kind of ship with a wide sail, and without an anchor" (*Letters*, II, 90), he had the resource of the internalized observing self, which could put his pain into a comic perspective. In a letter to Mrs. Thrale of September 30, 1773, he placed himself vividly on the stage before mankind: "You remember the Doge of Genoa who being asked what struck him most at the French Court, answered, 'Myself.' I cannot think many things here more likely to affect the fancy, than to see Johnson ending his sixty fourth year in the wilderness of the Hebrides."[11] His loneliness was every man's individual lot; but awareness of absurdity accompanies the pathos of the figure he cut before society.

Johnson's lack of family ties after the death of Tetty was more pronounced than his separateness from others, but he had learned to cope with painful distinction by then. Physically peculiar from childhood, he had always worked hard to make up for his deficiencies. Even in ordinary social intercourse, he needed and developed equipment by which his mind and will could make up for his deficiencies of class, physique, or appearance; in short, he developed the arts of the writer. Although he might be disconcerting in appearance, he had learned by persistent effort, by focusing the immense energies of his striving self, to break through his weakness of ear and eye and approach the kind of compensation which first Mrs. Porter and then the reading world could appreciate. Through the determined intensity of his response to life, he had succeeded: "He had early laid it down as a fixed rule to do his best on every occasion, and in every company; to impart whatever he knew in the most forcible language he could put it in; and . . . by constant practice, and never suffering any careless expressions to escape him, or attempting to deliver his thoughts without arranging them in the clearest manner, it became habitual with him" (*Life*, I, 204).

Evidently, Johnson had trained himself to literary performance, to the continuous organization of matter for an observing audience, in fact to the professions of teacher and author. Where Swift was definable at a distance in at least the varied guises of priest, politician, and author, Johnson assumed one role, although within it he might show the characteristics of scholar, journeyman, lexicographer, editor, dramatist, biographer, or poet. All of these he saw as serving a teaching function, a process of communicating to others the application of the millennia of humane thought to the world of contemporary chaos. The authorial voice becomes for him, therefore, not an oblique hint toward the exposure of character, but a universal self modified enough to speak familiarly to readers who were themselves receptively urbane. Except when he is deliberately using a persona, as in some of the letters in his periodicals or in passages of heavy irony in his own letters, the essential author, the author as centrally conceived in the scheme of a harmonious world, is for him close to the universal, observing self.

Authors are, however, also a particular category of actors in the chaotic world of experience, facing in a heightened way the same idiosyncratic appetites and confusions as other men, indeed projecting Johnson's own problems at large. He was therefore alert to the status of literary men, to their oddity before society, to their general neglect as well as paradoxical prestige. He championed their independence, for like his own it had to compensate for the isolation and justify the sense of superiority behind the oddity. However perverse or ironic his " 'No man but a blockhead ever wrote, except for money' " (*Life*, III, 19), it affirms that writing has economic value in society, a bourgeois view that is much more modern than Swift's and more straightforward than Pope's.

Sympathetically, he projects a self tossed with the crowd in Grub-street; like himself, his authors tend to be awkward, eccentric, aloof, ambitious, yearning for moral eminence, faintly absurd in the contrast of their aspirations and achievements. Accepting specialization of skills as legitimate on the surface level of human activities (unlike the traditional Swift), he shows apparent authorial idiosyncrasies as versions of central human ambiguities rather than distortions of harmonious clarity. In *Adventurer* 131, for example, elaborating the dangers of "singularity" in scholars, the eccentricity caused by their insufficient social experience, he generalizes a condition which he had seen in himself and described in *Ramblers* 177, 179, and 180. Social ease is not his *summum bonum*; but the oddity is symptomatic, like any other marked quality, and it reflects his fundamental fear of isolating oneself. In *Ramblers* 21 and 46 (and thirty years later in a discussion of Prior's *Solomon*[12]), Johnson also sees the writer as sharing in heightened form ordinary man's delusions about his achievements. On the whole, in making little difference to society despite their reveries, authors reflected not only Johnson's harmlessness as a grub, a lexicographer, and an editor, but any single ambitious man's inability to change the lives of his fellows.

Although in his late and sober *Lives of the Poets* Johnson was to hold a consistently high view of the poet, the works of his struggling middle age project the author through a wide tonal range in which ironic laughter at himself, as in *Ramblers* 16 or 161, is much more characteristic than the dignified unmasking of the last *Rambler*. No. 161, which surveys the successive residents of a cheap apartment, ends with a Grub-street poeta who even burlesques Johnson's physical mannerisms: he "lived very inoffensively, except that he frequently disturbed the inhabitants of the next floor by unseasonable noises. He was generally in bed at noon, but from evening to midnight he sometimes talked aloud with great vehemence, sometimes stamped as in rage, sometimes threw down his poker, then clattered his chairs, then sat down in deep thought, and again burst out into loud vociferations; sometimes he would sigh as oppressed with misery, and sometimes shake with convulsive laughter."[13]

As in the *Rambler* pieces, Imlac's claims of the poet's superlative knowledge, mental grandeur, talent, industry, and experience strike Johnson as comic exaggerations of the marginal difference between the very greatest men and anyone else.[14] Although he will not depreciate an authorial stance like Pope's in the *Epistle to Arbuthnot*, he knows himself to be a harmless drudge scrambling for subsistence. At the same time he respects his own efforts and achievements, and he respects his competitors so far as they are individually deserving. It is impossible to imagine Johnson writing a *Dunciad* or *A Tale of a Tub*. Where Swift derives imperfect writing from a corrupt soul, Johnson answers that in fact many bad writers are good men in pain or in harmless delusion. Since neither he nor they can be sure of a clear path in this world, his concern is to cure their mental wandering, not to damn them for it. Just as Johnson tends to see psychological revelation as the chief virtue to be attained by a writer, so he stands more as sympathetic psychological observer of his colleagues than as recording angel.

Everywhere Johnson sought to turn phenomena into general patterns—to create consciously the emblematic of which Swift seems to have had an intuitive perception—and the writer, like himself, became man writ large, particularly in his grand and often delusive hopes. As in seeking fame writers are merely more intent than other men to overcome time and death, their very lack of success confirms their representative nature. Since they can nourish new and ambitious hopes with every project, they most aptly concentrate the expectant in every man. According to *Rambler* 2, the illusion that the future will repay attention better than the present is natural to man, who goes so far from hope to hope that he will even undertake a periodical series out of fantasies of progressively increasing fame. In the penultimate *Rambler* 207, the writer is even more clearly man in his fundamental psychological struggle: reveries are so pleasant that we may prefer to leave them unrealized; and if we do assume an extended task, such as a periodical series, our fancied ideal dissipates into drudgery and triviality.

In both the private fantasies and the public activities special to writers, Johnson sees exaggerated the normal human tendencies toward harmony and toward violent, ruinous self-assertion. More sensitive than other men, writers may find the struggle more painful and so deserve more pity mixed with the ironic mockery that their pride earns from the judging self. But Johnson's judging self approves the good will of average, time-bound human experience even while it affirms the eternal rightness of distilled traditional human experience. Therefore, it sympathizes with rather than scorns the struggles of the other self, Johnson's projection of the deluded representative of all suffering men, at once the boundlessly hopeful poet and the limed soul yearning for freedom from the weight of self-generated guilt and folly. Aware of idiosyncratic, acting man's unfixed mind, untrustworthy senses, and unreliable social context, the observing self cheers and pities him in his battle with life, which may delude and must defeat him, but can alone give him the pleasure of tentative achievement. Unlike Swift, Johnson hoped to mold and appease his appetitive self, not force it down; projected into his art, the observed and observing selves are more like colleagues than antagonists.

2. The World Within: Johnson as Psychologist

Johnson's view of his projected selves focuses everywhere on the predicament of the mind and its reactions, not on its symbolic depravity or virtue. Fascinated like his contemporaries with mental processes, Johnson more or less accepted Locke's epistemology, as well as the faculty psychology which he inherited from the ancients and which still survives. But his insistence that all judgments and generalizations about human nature must be anchored in the details of human experience—one side of his practice of checking all possible data to correct the deficiencies of his physical senses—leads him to a fresh understanding of the psychological stresses of ordinary life. As against Swift's, his acting selves cover a range from the monomaniac fragment to the psychologically complex whole man, vigorous as well as guilt-stricken, sober and affirmative as well as fearfully ridden by fantasies. The observing self, whether Johnson mocking Johnson in a letter or the surveyor of acting men from China to Peru and from Xerxes to Swift, yet sympathizes with every man's struggles with confusion, flux, isolation, and guilt, and mourns our inevitable defeat. The acting self is for Johnson often deluded by a league between its own desires and the chaos outside; the observing self, aware of the discrepancy between appearance and reality, also knows the power of appearance too well to condemn its victims. Like Johnson in his ideal vision of himself, it is a teacher, not an anointed judge.

The fundamental cognitive operations of the mind appeared to him pretty much as they had to Locke, as the complementary processes of perception and reflection (the respective provinces, more or less, of the acting and evaluating selves). In a letter of August 5, 1775, to Mrs. Thrale, Johnson says that after early adulthood most people learn little that is new, and some develop by reflective generalizing rather than acquisition: "Not only because as more is known there is less to learn, but because a mind stored with images and principles, turns inwards for its own entertainment, and is employed in sorting those ideas which run into confusion, and in recollecting those which are stealing away, practices by which wisdom may be kept but not gained."[15] In describing communication, Johnson also (again like his contemporaries) relies on Locke. *Rambler* 151, for example, unequivocally accepts Locke's epistemology, affirming that the man who can divest himself of accidental pecularities will identify sympathetically with the permanent and fundamental condition of others and thereby understand them. Despite the great variations in character produced by different environments—which provide the accidental peculiarities—man universally develops in the same way: "We all enter the world in equal ignorance" and see the same objects tending to our earliest "aversions and desires"; although we go different ways, all minds work through the body and are affected by it; and those who stray far from the norm "are recalled from excentricity by the laws of their existence." Furthermore, we understand each other by evoking identical responses, as Johnson implied to Bennet Langton in a letter of 1781: "We have been now long enough acquainted to have many images in common, and therefore to have a source of conversation which neither the learning nor the wit of a new companion can supply."[16]

In such a mechanism, acting and observing self need each other, as in Sterne's figure of Locke's wit and judgment as the complementary knobs of a chair. For Johnson, the perceiving, acting self provides the new experience, which interacts with universal experience; and the new generalization which explains the result is guided, not dictated, by the universal self. The psychological bridge between the two selves—sympathetic understanding, by which the mental state of one figure is communicated to another—is neatly appropriate in a time when even a damaged Tristram could act as mediating humanity for the eccentric Walter and Toby. The mid-century's Lockean emphasis on sympathy as the means to knowledge reinforces Johnson's awareness that without an ambition so extreme as to tie him to madmen he could not have fought his way out of his poverty and illnesses. Neither the time nor his own psychological orientation permits him Swift's superiority to the idiosyncratic self.

But Johnson is much more alert to the mind's deficiencies than Locke, much more concerned with it as an organ than a machine.

In his notion of the mind as the appetitive self, it is almost formless, uncertain of its own needs, indolently following impulse, and requiring external pressure to maintain its own resolutions. Writhing over a *Rambler* essay, Johnson exemplarily faces and resolves the general human problem of choice: his mind roves and trifles until the deadline and then, delighted to act, pounces on what happens to be filling it (*Rambler* 184). In crises one cannot be sure even of one's own motives, as he wrote to Mrs. Thrale on July 20, 1774: "I am glad you went to Brighthelmstone [where her dying child had been treated], for your journey is a standing proof to you of your affection and diligence. We can hardly be confident of the state of our own minds, but as it stands attested by some external action; we are seldom sure that we sincerely meant what we omitted to do" (*Letters*, II, 70). He does indeed affirm the possibility—the urgent need—for the mind to overcome its inertia and lack of order, but this is a long way from his century's supposed trust in reason and even from Swift's assumption that a healthy mind can open a clear path and can will to follow it. In Johnson's descriptions of the mind's determination, as in his own actions, convulsive and sudden motions predominate, not steady tugging at the oars.

Passing beyond Locke's epistemology, Johnson sees the mind as organic, responding to what it apprehends in maturity through idiosyncratic patterns developed earlier. In a brilliantly precise passage that I have already quoted (see Chapter I above), he told Mrs. Thrale that the fully developed mind can acquire additional information, "but its power of thinking remains nearly the same, and unless it attains new subjects of meditation, it commonly produces thoughts of the same force and the same extent, at very distant intervals of life, as the tree unless a foreign fruit be ingrafted gives year after year productions of the same form and the same flavour" (*Letters*, II, 79).[17] In the *Journal of a Tour to the Hebrides*, Boswell records a further element in such a view, that the organic mind may be early trained and modified toward the bearing of particular fruits: "—*Johnson*. 'No, sir; it is only, one man has more mind than another. He may direct it differently; he may, by accident, see the success of one kind of study, and take a desire to excel in it. I am persuaded that, had Sir Isaac Newton applied to poetry, he would have made a very fine epick poem. I could as easily apply to law as to tragick poetry'" (*Life*, V, 35). While the tablets of the mind might have been clean at birth, they varied enormously in size. This important idiosyncratic factor allowed, Johnson implied further that the number of possibilities for development would be limited if the mind applied itself seriously to any. As always, he sees the need to choose paths in life, to abandon some possibilities of achievement, as both necessary and regrettable, an emblem of man's painful condition.[18]

But if the mind can direct its cognitive, intellectual powers with effective concentration in response to an early dominant impulse or stimulus, where its observing and evaluating element is undeveloped it typically remains fluid and painfully free in its capacity as guide to practical and moral action. The worst decision, as Johnson says often in *The Rambler*, is the yielding of decision to the contents of the mind at the moment, the moral dominance of chance which was vicious folly in Swift's Hack and a looming danger for Locke—but for mid-century sentimentalism, the sign of sincerity. Human wishes are vain, Johnson shows, because they are formed without consideration of their consequences and manifested on impulse after vacillation, issuing from a frightened recklessness that can only send man to roll darkling down the torrent of his fate. In *Ramblers* 6, 29, 134, and 184, Johnson describes through a variety of tones how striving man, uncertain of the guidance of a universal self, forsakes reason, its tool, to seize on some element delusively thrust up from chaos. Man *must* choose right, Johnson the moralist insists; but as psychologist he sees most men, like Rasselas and his entourage, as so confused by the fluid uncertainty of all phenomena that they are fortunate to be able to act at all, let alone to act wisely. Before Johnson's gaze, man struggles as an almost impossibly fluid mind obliged to act firmly in a plastic universe. The vastness of the impediments leads both to Johnson's tolerance and to his high regard for moral achievement.

Although Johnson recommends some self-regulation to help fix the mind, as in his advice to Boswell to keep a diary, he suspects habits, as he does traditions, authorities, and philosophies, because they substitute arbitrary machinery for individual choices.[19] *Rambler* 73 is typical of a fairly large number of case histories among the essays in showing the destructive effect of narrow, rigid training: brought up to anticipate future riches, Cupidus in his old age cannot enjoy his wealth because he has "a mind, corrupted with an inveterate disease of wishing, and unable to think on any thing but wants, which reason tells me will never be supplied." Similarly, Johnson distrusts vows and resolutions as tricks upon ourselves, for they can lead us to squeeze specific complex situations within simple formulas or to suffer guilt when we fail to keep our promises.[20] Habits and vows, like all other means (except religious faith) for helping the evaluating self to guide the struggling self, limit the range and vitality of both selves. Only the vital ties of human or divine sympathy can strengthen the evaluating self from without in its prime function.

Particularly in intellectual operations, some fine minds can pounce directly on essentials, like Thomson's scientists: "To find the nearest way from truth to truth, or from purpose to effect, not to use more instruments where fewer will be sufficient, not to move by wheels and levers what will give way to the naked hand, is the great proof of a healthful and vigorous mind, neither feeble with helpless ignorance, nor overburdened with unwieldy knowledge" (*Idler* 36). But for moral and social problems such efficient application of digested experience to raw experience can be imagined only in fictional teachers, like the Rambler and Imlac, and even there must be weakened to be credible. More usually, the mind muddles, manufacturing vain wishes and unsatisfying pleasures out of the materials supplied by society and its own appetites. Wandering in a maze of chance and delusive impulse, man meets his only hope in an arbitrary, internal portion of "celestial wisdom," a capacity for serene cooperation between the striving and judging selves.

With or without such wisdom, the mind faces great difficulties in directing itself to action in a world of phenomena different from itself. Should man be lucky enough to receive the gifts of *The Vanity of Human Wishes*—a healthful mind, obedient passions, a resigned will, love, patience, and faith—and add to them Pope's health, peace, and competence, he can fashion a temporarily harmonious world, the nearest thing to happiness possible for a mortal who must eventually face a stern judge. Even then, however, he must still search for suitable goals: in *Idlers* 62 and 64, as in *Rasselas*, the problem is how to find happiness when one is provided with leisure and wealth, and yet has a mind too decent and literate for the fashionable delights of patronizing a fiddler, keeping an opera singer, or having one's portrait painted. If, on the other hand, the mind is narrow, weak, or unhealthy, it will seize on whatever promises immediate rewards—building a distorted world around an obsession, cherishing a pimple as its whole circle of life. Such a mind can shape all its energies to tyrannize over a family (*Rambler* 11, *Idler* 46), clutter a house with useless bargains, collect insects, or simulate gentility or critical sophistication; all the while, it is storing up retributive dissatisfaction and guilt. The universal self, acting through education in the classical-Christian tradition, can help to provide the mind with materials for a vision of the whole world; but if the mind is ill, it can only be brought to focus on reality by a strong stimulus, like the impact of Pekuah on the astronomer.

Since the waking, struggling self will be busy no matter what, to prevent its destructive turn inward the observing self should feed it with external matter that is innocent and, if possible, useful. Recording such sights as a regatta, a storm along a river, Carnarvon Castle, or the Little Trianon, Johnson was likely to value them by their success in filling the mind, often in terms which evoke the quantitative implications of Burke's psychology of the sublime. One of the assumptions of his *Journey to the Western Isles* he makes explicit toward its end, that significance lies in mental responses, not in physical stimuli: "We were now to leave the *Hebrides*, where we had spent some weeks with sufficient amusement, and where we had amplified our thoughts with new scenes of nature, and new modes of life. . . . Of these Islands it must be confessed, that they have not many allurements, but to the mere lover of naked nature. The inhabitants are thin, provisions are scarce, and desolation and penury give little pleasure."[21] Perhaps such superiority to Scottish scenery and rural life is to be expected of an elderly Londoner with weak eyes, but it is also a legitimate attitude for the moral psychologist who finds in physical nature substance insufficient to engage the only centrally human faculty.[22] Although the mind needs filling, stuffing it with the trivia of lakes and mountains—like drowning the vigorous powers with music, wine, or sleeping drugs, all of which Johnson repudiated in various situations—partakes of suicide.

In *Rasselas* the impossibility of keeping the mind's appetitive faculty legitimately employed decisively colors Johnson's vision of man stumbling through life. Summarizing a large segment of Johnson's theory of motivation, Imlac says that "some desire is necessary to keep life in motion, and he, whose real wants are supplied, must admit those of fancy."[23] One of the Prince's early stages of hope came when he discovered a goal, to leave the valley, and consequently had something constructive to think about (chap. iv). Imlac also knows the fundamental element in mental survival, the provision of food for the machine: in the Happy Valley, " 'I am less unhappy than the rest, because I have a mind replete with images, which I can vary and combine at pleasure,' " while the others " 'are either corroded by malignant passions, or sit stupid in the gloom of perpetual vacancy' " (chap. xii). But Imlac speaks only of greater or lesser unhappiness, and other experienced people have found that no amount of activity guarantees fruitful health. The hermit, for example, knows that with-drawal encourages the mind to waste itself on foolish reveries, but in society he merely finds more choices to confuse him. Society's toys and drugs to fill the vacant mind, such as the easy clichés of romantic love (chap. xxix), can be as delusive as the private fantasies that they codify.

In the chapters on the pyramids and on the old astronomer, Johnson provides his most concise summation and his most affecting exhibition of man's general psychological dilemma. The immense Great Pyramid, Imlac observes, has been built for no commensurately useful purpose: " 'It seems to have been erected only in compliance with that hunger of imagination which preys incessantly upon life, and must be always appeased by some employment. . . . I consider this mighty structure as a monument of the insufficiency of human enjoyments' " (chap. xxxii).[24] A modern parallel to the ancient phar-aoh, the astronomer has been driven mad by his mind's reaching within, in solitude, for material on which to feed. He has followed a horrifyingly normal, even archetypal progress from indulgence in self-pleasing reveries to obsession complicated by guilt to habitual delusion (chap. xliv). Where Swift would have seen in the astronomer an aberrant lunatic self, a version of the Grubaean Hack, to Johnson he is the ordinary self cut off from the evaluative balance, the external support, of other minds. His striving self did not reach madness through proud aggression, but rather yielded to incoherent fantasies when the judging self (as with the pharaoh) could provide no counter for them, no evidence of limitation by reality. He is victim of his misfortunes, not solely actor. But while his progress was an exaggera-tion of the normal, the chance that led to it was special to him, and to that extent he differs from Rasselas and his companions.

All the people whom the prince and his friends meet or discuss have chosen fragments of the human vision. The travelers themselves represent general man in his career of seeking, man still wishing and not yet ruined through the granting of his wish, rather than specific man who has shut off much of experience for the sake of the little he can master. Shocked by the astronomer's condition, they see that they must rule their fancies to maintain freedom to choose; aware at least for the moment of the clichés they nourish, they resolve to surrender them for outer reality. But as Johnson shows in his final chapter, they cannot help nurturing mental elaborations of the past and pleasing visions of the future. Since the mind's nature is to devour matter, it must be fed enough from without to absorb most of its energies in thought and creation. When the mind is unoccupied, it easily succumbs to its own imaginings—Johnson's tyrannical, sensuous, and sadistic reveries—which call forth the terrors of retributive guilt. For all living, fluid minds, an ideal balance is impossible, and therefore happiness is a chimera. Disappointment and the wish for change inevitably follow all accomplishment, since reality cannot fulfill what hope promises and any pause to contemplate happiness stimulates the hunger of the imagination.

Doomed to spend most of its time and energy in futile reverie, the acting self must yet wrest enough control over itself and its present environment to provide a measure of self-esteem and social affection. Not unusual folly but normality is its nature and fate, as like Johnson it pulls itself by hope from the temptations of despair. The observing self, offering advice and exhortation from its knowledge of universal human experience, can admire the vigorous fighter or deplore the coward that yields to dominance by immediate and therefore fragmentary experience. Johnson agrees with Swift on man's moral responsibility, but out of his own struggles with his fantasies he is far more aware of the difficulties of asserting the observing self against the chaotic hunger within, and hence far more fearful of the ultimate judgment. For both, irony helps to reveal the constant temptations that all of us have, but Johnson sees our difficulties as so great that he sometimes allows a sip of homeopathic delusion and reverie. He almost forgives us if, in our lifelong battle with madness, we lose a skirmish or two.

3. Moral Views: The World Outside

Man's foremost duty in Johnson's scheme is to acquire experience and act upon it, translating mental shapes and urges into intercourse with what is outside. Having looked both within and without at chaos, he insists that a healthy man must fill up the vast emptiness of life, creating order and meaning to replace or beguile his fears.[25] His occasional success in rising early, he wrote to Langton, was a great triumph because "it is no slight advancement to obtain for so many hours more, the consciousness of being" (*Life*, II, 17). Although happiness was a delusion or at best an occasional lucky moment, increased consciousness of being was the one substantial, precise psychological good available to everyone who sought it in almost any active way. Like Johnson, man finds his great temptation in sloth, a tendency to abandon oneself to reverie or to mindless drifting among phenomena. Johnson's prescription, psychological as well as moral, is alert seeking for external stimuli. As he wrote to Mrs. Thrale on June 21, 1775, she should not have any qualms about stooping culturally to attend a regatta, because "Company is in itself better than solitude and pleasure better than indolence. Ex nihilo nihil fit, says the moral as well as the natural philosopher. By doing nothing and by knowing nothing no power of doing good can be obtained, he must mingle with the world that desires to be useful. Every new scene impresses new ideas, enriches the imagination, and enlarges the power of reason, by new topicks of comparison" (*Letters*, II, 50–51). Needing to engage experience from outside as well as from within to stay healthy, the mind functions efficiently—in moral terms, virtuously—when it can turn experience and reflection into order. The attribute and reward of health, virtue must be continuously reaffirmed through combat with chaos.

Since experience is flux and truth may be mauled or blotted into error, to act well man must keep creating new guiding generalizations. Perhaps because of Johnson's sensory deficiencies, the observing self sees a surface of constantly changing patterns. Unlike Swift, Johnson comes close to suggesting that sublunary truths, the conclusions of fallible man, are relative. Swift's one right way becomes for Johnson a multitude of ways; every new datum of experience implies modification of previous hypotheses, a stimulus toward action, movement, moral sallying out into the world. For the healthy mind, the wider the experience, the more trustworthy its perceptions and the more substantial and valid the generalization. " 'Human experience,' " Johnson said in a concentrated expression of his thought, " 'which is constantly contradicting theory, is the great test of truth. A system, built upon the discoveries of a great many minds, is always of more strength, than what is produced by the mere workings of any one mind, which, of itself, can do little' " (*Life*, I, 454). But a man must resist familiar theories, because phenomena may well have altered after their original, legitimate formulation, and he should suspect large, simple theories—like the organization of the world by a great chain of being—as possible evasions of complex experience. Like Johnson himself, every man alone must painfully stumble among the false, the outworn, the partially true, and the true, if he is to make his path. For Johnson, therefore, salvation is far more an individual obligation than for Swift; where Swift sees the idiosyncratic self as needing to be mastered by the universal self which speaks for all mankind, for Johnson the current individual actor and the universal observer are equal and sovereign.

Animated by Johnson's own religious and psychological needs, his morality argues that since we must spend time whatever we do, we should use it profitably where we can. Although *The Vanity of Human Wishes* mocks fantasies of personal greatness, it admires the achievements, like Laud's scholarship, which may support them, and it ends by advocating not contemplation but quiet activity. *The Rambler*, which follows soon after, prescribes action as the key to decent living in, among others, Nos. 17, 19, 25, 63, and 86, and especially 134: "The certainty that life cannot be long, and the probability that it will be much shorter than nature allows, ought to awaken every man to the active prosecution of whatever he is desirous to perform. It is true that no diligence can ascertain success; death may intercept the swiftest career; but he who is cut off in the execution of an honest undertaking, has at least the honour of falling in his rank, and has fought the battle, though he missed the victory." As this passage exalts the moral value of engagement, *Adventurer* 111 (November, 1753) stresses its contribution to happiness: "Life affords no higher pleasure, than that of surmounting difficulties, passing from one step of success to another, forming new wishes and seeing them gratified," and "To strive with difficulties, and to conquer them, is the highest human felicity; the next, is to strive, and deserve to conquer. . . ." The themes are echoed throughout the *Idler*, where in keeping with the title they are often negatively illustrated by the deluded and unemployed. Johnson's personal advice usually tended toward this direction, particularly to his most famous external idiosyncratic self: "He bade me also go on with collections which I was making upon the antiquities of Scotland. 'Make a large book; a folio.' BOSWELL. 'But of what use will it be, Sir?' JOHNSON. 'Never mind the use; do it' " (*Life*, II, 92).

In *Rasselas*, Johnson demonstrates at length that only in struggling for virtuous action, the sole good under man's control, is there a chance for happiness. Since no mortal has the time or the mental range and power to formulate unexceptionable bases for acting (chap. xvi), Imlac has advised his companions to cut short doubt and act— even without certainty. Sallying out into life necessarily produces disillusionment, but it may lead to human contact, and it surely enlarges the store of food for the mind. By contrast, the acting self which has denied its nature by withdrawing from the struggle, whether the hermit, the astronomer, or a monk, is pitiable and unhappy, at best harmlessly sterile. Observing with mingled pity and laughter, the evaluating self can hope by sympathy to break through to the bravely alert, but not to the defensive, withdrawn, despairing.

Johnson's world is too rich a diet for the weak mind. Even the man eager to battle with chaos fears the great danger of madness, the defeat of the will to order; but he who selects a trifling slice of experience to organize has doomed himself to indolence or the miserable verge of madness. In *The Idler*, written when Johnson was most extensively evaluating himself and mankind, he provided a plentiful variety of such objectifications of his temptations to despair, defeated figures rolling down the torrent of chaos. Peter Plenty's wife in No. 35, for example, floods her household with disorderly matter, which she has gathered under the housewifely rubric of bargains: "The servants can scarcely creep to their beds thro' the chests and boxes that surround them," and "my house has the appearance of a ship stored for a voyage to the colonies." But usually the deficiency reflects a relaxed will, not the strenuous lunacy of Mrs. Plenty or her more pretentious equivalents, the collecting virtuosi of *Idler* 56. Philosophers and moral teachers, Johnson says in No. 27, have told man to examine himself, but man would rather philosophize and teach morality than face truth and act upon it. In No. 40 he complains that advertisers follow each other mindlessly, muddling distinctions in words and values to create chaos. No. 57 shows that cold prudence is lazy flight from life, and No. 92 stresses the impotence of cunning as the facile ape of wisdom: "The whole power of cunning is privative; to say nothing, and to do nothing, is the utmost of its reach." Although Johnson's satiric targets are traditional, their motivation is not so much Pride as a combination of Sloth and Despair, the giants that loomed in the revivalist religion of Law and the puritans and also rose from his fears for himself.

To act vigorously in the world—almost the whole duty of man— one desperately needs to see clearly, as Johnson insists following a moral tradition that stretches at least from the Prophets and Socrates. Despite the immense temptation of illusion, one must choose reality, keeping open and constant the traffic between the idiosyncratic self of individual, current, chaotic experience and the self which acts as reservoir and judge of accumulated experience. Much more even than Swift, for whom the spark of idiosyncrasy spontaneously explodes into cautionary madness, Johnson sees the average man as a pilgrim dazzled in a bazaar of facile systems which offer to solve all his problems, from choosing a London residence to settling on a religion. Inevitably, these systems conflict with experience, which is always in flux and therefore always needs to be organized anew. Even formulations that have served adequately for centuries, like the critical theories of the dramatic unities, may be shown up as delusion, not the true perception of universal humanity. Guiding ideas of more recent discovery are naturally more suspect as possible fads for the lazy.

The persistent danger to the decent mind is not glaring evil, which as Pope said had only to be seen to be hated, but the routine, the cliché, the pretended shortcut to the good life. *Idler* 10, for example, aims directly at the credulous and indolent who prefer systems of politics or philosophy to the complexities of reality, who "resign the use of their own eyes and ears, and resolve to believe nothing that does not favour those whom they profess to follow." Not evil but folly will seduce such a mind, but since the two are connected (as in the parable of the talents, which haunted Johnson), one must be constantly alert for its onset in all evasions of thought. Comfortable social theories, for example, may just be rationalizations: " 'Sir, all the arguments which are brought to represent poverty as no evil, shew it to be evidently a great evil. You never find people labouring to convince you that you may live very happily upon a plentiful fortune' " (*Life*, I, 441). Fashionable sentimentalism, like all cant, is facile and self-serving: "BOSWELL. 'I have often blamed myself, Sir, for not feeling for others as sensibly as many say they do.' JOHNSON. 'Sir, don't be duped by them any more. You will find these very feeling people are not very ready to do you good. They *pay* you by feeling' " (*Life*, II, 95). Most advice, according to *Rambler* 87, consists of general clichés; only people who blindly reject experience for systems can believe "that the lots of life are equal," in *Rambler* 128; and *Rambler* 202 deplores the nonsense with which poets and philosophers sing the joys of poverty when they mean merely the absence of wealth. In various conversations and writings, Johnson argued that fashionable philosophical speculations like Lord Monboddo's anthropology and Soame Jenyns' cosmological theories delude their readers, flitting lightly over gaps in evidence and thought for the sake of grand answers; that Mandeville's equally fashionable perversity plays with words, avoiding experience; that except for a few fine works like Law's *Serious Call*, religion tended to be disseminated in clichés. When Johnson met the old pious formulas on the most painful of all subjects for him, he insisted that they would not do, that he himself was right to fear death, and that no decent person could await the divine judgment complacently.[26]

In the periodical essays, Johnson as teacher liked to seize on the current easy cliché, often in an ironic tradition at least as old as Horace directing us to the delusions of the idiosyncratic self by slipping into its phrasing. The characters do not necessarily oppose what Johnson saw as the valid tentative orderings of the whole of experience; but their language betrays its function to protect the timid mind against the vastness of the world. *Rambler* 25, for example, exposes the rituals by which intellectuals frighten themselves into mental passivity: "One study is inconsistent with a lively imagination, another with a solid judgment; one is improper in the early part of life, another requires so much time, that it is not to be attempted at an advanced age; one is dry and contracts the sentiments, another is diffuse and overburdens the memory; one is insufferable to taste and delicacy, and another wears out life in the study of words, and is useless to a wise man, who desires only the knowledge of things." *Rambler* 23 provides the clichés of literary critics, which recur also in *Idler* 47 and bloom in Dick Minim of *Idlers* 60 and 61. *Rambler* 36 exploits the clichés of nature lovers, which also plague Euphilia of *Ramblers* 42 and 46 and Dick Shifter of *Idler* 71. Suspirius, who dominates *Rambler* 59, soberly burlesques Johnson's own estimate of human wishes, and Prospero of No. 200 hashes over Johnson's views on happiness inappropriately and in stale language. *Rambler* 50, on old age, rebuts the trite charges of impatience, irresponsibility, and ignorance with which the old habitually attack the young, while *Rambler* 186 patronizes the clichés which express the hopes of youth. Johnson tends to sympathize with manifestations of his own surging, idiosyncratic, youthful hope, but he does not judge a generalization by its effect on the spirits any more than by its popularity. Rather, his test is whether it grasps the largest relevant area of experience, whether it reflects a direct contact with chaos or merely echoes the struggling of others.

Again in the later *Idler*, no personal oddity is more frequent than delusion, the substitution of fantasies for much more troublesome actuality. Anticipating the doubt of prudent planning in *Rasselas* (which was probably maturing at this time, August, 1758), No. 19 exposes evasive indecision through Jack Whirler, "whose business keeps him in perpetual motion, and whose motion always eludes his business; who is always to do what he never does, who cannot stand still because he is wanted in another place, and who is wanted in many places because he stays in none." In No. 30, readers who seek easy answers and writers who cannot think corrupt each other, joining in responsibility for clichés like those that masquerade as war news. Tom Restless of No. 48 seeks a fashionable learned image without reading, because books "destroy that freedom of thought and easiness of manners indispensibly requisite to acceptance in the world." In *Idler* 49, Will Marvel magnifies himself by describing an ordinary trip in the mindless clichés of the sublime. Sophron, the unpleasant prudent man of *Idler* 57, avoids involvement with others through evasive clichés: when asked for advice, he "observes that a man may be as easily too hasty as too slow, and that as many fail by doing too much as too little; that 'a wise man has two ears and one tongue'; and 'that little said is soon amended'; that he could tell him this and that, but that after all every man is the best judge of his own affairs." In No. 83, Robin Spritely and his circles of fashionable vacationers speak according to their particular diverse branches of the trite, and No. 86 provides the pat phrases appropriate to apartment hunting in London. Among fragmented people unaccustomed to independence, identity crisis and adolescent rebellion are expressed in the crossing of stereotypes, so that Tom Wainscot's son in No. 95 nods sympathetically as befits a tradesman but borrows phrases from the young army bucks whom he admires. At times, Johnson allows for the element of universal truth in the clichés, but his point, as in Dick Minim's literary criticism, is that even a truism is fantasy if its speaker has not earned it. Like the exaggeration in Imlac's list of qualifications of a poet, clichés do not destroy the ideal, but rather emphasize its separation from actual human experience.

The opening of *Rasselas*, Johnson's most extended examination of our unwillingness to seek life instead of words and attitudes, addresses a representative acting self which reflects his own immoderate expectations. Like Johnson in his fantasies, we are all consumers of the consoling clichés "who listen with credulity to the whispers of fancy, and pursue with eagerness the phantoms of hope; who expect that age will perform the promises of youth, and that the deficiencies of the present day will be supplied by the morrow. . . ." To move the plot, Johnson regularly juxtaposes verbal and behavioral clichés with experience: Rasselas' affectation of *weltschmerz*, the sentimental pedantries of his old teacher, the inflated claims of his aeronaut, Imlac's discussion of his own profession of poet, and all the expectations not only of the protected young but also of the wise and elderly. Beginning with exposure to brutal shepherds and abject hedonists, the companions find not real choices of life but simple and therefore delusive schemes of happiness. Even considered and disinterested wisdom cannot guide the spontaneous responses of living people: Imlac thinks the learned astronomer will disdain teaching the rudiments of his science, but his generalization overlooks the attractions of the young Pekuah and the sage's pathetic boredom with his own company. Again and again, Johnson warns that only experience, that which is the peculiar goal of the struggling self, can provide matter for the observing self's wise generalization, which in turn may help in the continuing struggle. Such a view, as centered in flux as Sterne's,[27] can frame no plausible conclusion either in the novel—an abstract system—or in this life.

The world which Johnson sees about him differs from Swift's mainly in that its changing surface of experience, not only man's accumulated knowledge of the true, forms a base for generalization. To make order of this flux, Johnson argues that the self which considers man's distilled experience must encourage the acting self to grapple with life. A primitivist reliance on the instincts, popular in his day as in ours, he contemptuously rejects as cant that denies all the testimony of experience. Despite its deficiencies and weaknesses, which he registered as subtly as any contemporary, the human reason—the self as pure observer, not agent—seemed to him the only available guide through the chaos of external phenomena and internal fancies and appetites. God has provided revelation as a fountain of truth, and Providence oversees the larger operations of the world; but our understanding of both is uncertain, and therefore every man must rely for sanity and virtue on the application of human reason to his individual experience. Like his contemporaries, Johnson counsels uniformitarian introspection (as in *Idler* 28), the examination of the idiosyncratic self in search of general truth by the light of the eternal human experience.[28]

As might be expected, the same concern for applying the widest knowledge of mankind's life in the world to the struggles of the idiosyncratic self animates Johnson's social thought. Cant, no matter how conveniently conservative, could only subvert right action. While he advocated subordination because his reading of history had taught him the vast dangers of competition, he refused to justify with theories the stunting of actual human beings: the boy rowing on the Thames deserves the Greek for which he would give his all; a literate maid in *Idler* 26 is better than an illiterate one; his young Negro servant is worthy of a proper education (and Johnson provided it). Johnson's social world is even more dynamic than Pope's, for the seesaws of pressure and response, the interactions of mind and phenomena, shift their fulcrums. Changes in government, he argued, as in other areas of life, occur when the forms are no longer based on all the available experience;[29] people will not tolerate the intolerable (*Life*, II, 170), and martyrs may indeed bring new revelations. With a kind of vigorous sadness, Johnson presents a world where institutional change, though perhaps no more desirable than it had been for Swift and Pope, must reflect the eternal fluctuations of life.

Johnson's most complex vision of the course of human life, *Rasselas*, is a search for the universally true as a guide to experience. Pursuing direct answers to final questions, the Prince and his companions struggle to raise the idiosyncratic and flawed self to the level of the impersonal, almost divine consciousness of universal humanity. By refusing to stop short at the systems of life displayed to them, they earn whatever success is available to the human reason and spirit. They are no Fausts, but cultivating gardens will not satisfy their aspirations. Although nothing can give us certainty in this world, they find that action can prevent the stagnation and loss of the idiosyncratic self, and that learning of other times and other places can teach us something about man's possibilities, about the recurrent ways of dealing with a chaos coeval with earthly life. As their career suggests, all experience and all life must be brought directly to the service of our present and individual need in order to make meaning. In affirming his century's bourgeois pragmatism, its insistence on the primacy of emotional communication, its dissenting focus on the individual's moral decisions, and its Lockean sense that the mind cannot know phenomena with certainty, Johnson is attempting also to fuse the specific and the universal selves for the intense illumination of the moment before him.

4. Self in the World: Character and Narrative

As he forms his visions of man coping with the chaos around him, Johnson speaks through a version of his basic mask, the observer and guide, to describe a variety of projected characters. These characters, whether briefly sketched or developed into personae who write letters to Johnson's periodicals, are usually individualized actors struggling in the world, in one way or another projections of Johnson's vain wishes or aberrant tendencies. Even when such figures seem to vary in the sources and manifestations of their oddity, they are united in reflecting Johnson's sense of his own dangers as Swift's butts are united by his priestly-authorial view of himself. In contrast, when in the last *Rambler* he quotes Castiglione as saying that the mask " 'confers a right of acting and speaking with less restraint, even when the wearer happens to be known,' " he clearly means not an idiosyncratic self like Swift's Hack but a limited, conventional, borrowed face. Behind it is a universal and evaluative self.

Johnson's full-scale mask is always "a majestick teacher of moral and religious wisdom," as Boswell described *The Rambler*: schoolmaster to mankind, the role which Johnson played on the stage of his private life as well. In *The Vanity of Human Wishes* and *Rasselas* and to a lesser degree in the mildly familiar periodical essays the dominant voice is impersonal, an ironic human judge of mankind which recognizes its share in the struggle of the species and therefore mourns while it mocks. Significantly, Johnson's observing self in his writings, like the mediating reason of his psychology or a faculty advisory committee in an American university, has no power beyond exhortation. It is thus very different from the norm, the figure engaged in right action; it approves or condemns, but makes no pretense of willing, since it is not a persona like Swift's Drapier or Pope in the *Epistle to Arbuthnot*. Only in creating the literary work can it be said to perform man's necessary ordering of experience, and Johnson usually allows the labor to be implicit. Sometimes as observer it merely records the contents of the mind at the moment, thereby registering honesty; sometimes it consciously creates meaning, as artist, moralist, or simply dutiful man.

Tending toward these more or less detached masks—these observing selves which survey mankind in England and Egypt as well as from China to Peru—a number of idiosyncratic figures have opened themselves to the influence of the universal: Eubulus of *Ramblers* 26 and 27, who is trying to achieve harmony after a youth damaged by flattery and folly; the girl of No. 55, superior to her mother's eccentric impropriety; Myrtylla of No. 84, who discovers how badly her domestic education in the country has prepared her for civilized life; Pertinax of No. 95, who has succeeded in overcoming an education in cynicism; and the Rasselas group, of which Imlac is preeminent in this respect. All of these figures follow Johnson's favorite narrative pattern, movement from ignorant acceptance of a narrow field of vision to the painful discovery of a boundless, chaotic, challenging world. Like Johnson himself, these observing actors need the whole world of phenomena from which to imagine and evaluate meaning.

Most of Johnson's characters, however, are butts who try shortcuts to the good life, purveyors or personifications of a whole range of trite positions who seek to cut experience to a narrow pattern which they have mastered. Some are selfish, some dedicated, and some Faustian virtuosos of the trivial who are led straight to defeat or madness. All are deluded, like the sentimental, mannered mock-self that Johnson adopted in a letter of October 27, 1777, to Mrs. Thrale, and echoed in one of April 11, 1780: "Now you think yourself the first Writer in the world for a letter about nothing. Can you write such a letter as this? So miscellaneous, with such noble disdain of regularity, like Shakespeare's works, such graceful negligence of transition like the ancient enthusiasts. The pure voice of nature and of friendship" (*Letters*, II, 340–41). Johnson himself disdains regularity and approves negligent transitions and epistolary expression of the true voice of nature and friendship, but he implies here both their easy trivialization and the mindlessness of routinely tossing the phrases together. In contrast with Swift's personae-butts, who nourish the depths of evil behind the shield of the ordinary, Johnson's characters tend to provide harmless, foolish echoes of valid thoughts. For Johnson, unlike Swift, daily life endangers the vigorous man because it offers him no obstacles to battle. Johnson's antiself, the internal tempter whom he projects as his pattern butt, is the sick and weak soul that will grasp any generalization out of despair; he is not the proud, perverse mocker who haunts Swift. Like Shaw's Don Juan, Johnson's good man must repudiate a sentimental trite devil and encourage the striving will.

The Rambler is full of people looking for the fastest delusion to happiness, some enclosed in harmless madness like the man in No. 5 who achieves joy "by a constant practice of referring the removal of all his uneasiness to the coming of the next spring," and others more dangerous to themselves or society. In No. 25, cliché-mongers frighten themselves into torpor with the fancied rigors of intellectual effort, and when in No. 191 Bellaria sees the cowardly folly of her mother and aunts she thinks herself free to embrace fashionable coquetry. Even predatory figures are victims of their own delusions: having developed an ominous repertoire of anecdotes to dominate others, Suspirius of No. 59 has doomed himself to perpetual apprehensions; to gain a collection of maps and dead insects, the zealous virtuoso Quisquilius of No. 82 has sacrificed his human feelings and his money; through obsessive frugality, Mrs. Busy (*Rambler* 138) reduced her children to rustic fools and "a large manor into a farm"; seeking fame as a wit through mockery and tricks, Dicaculus (*Rambler* 174) earned universal dislike. More painfully because more sympathetically, the observer of Seged's tale (*Ramblers* 204 and 205), a recapitulation of main themes in *The Rambler*, shows that action based on self-pleasing theories, no matter how well-intentioned, guarantees its own miserable defeat.

Just as *The Idler* extends the panorama of miscellaneously fragmented people—like the violent Jacobite and Whig pair of No. 10, the frugal housewife of No. 13 who keeps her daughters in sterile slavery in a garret, a bored woman in No. 46 who tortures her maid with riddling orders—many of its papers reflect the patterns of movement and theme that Johnson was concentrating in the contemporaneous *Rasselas*. The letter writer of No. 55, a virtuoso of botany and zoology, wastes time with the princely munificence of Rasselas himself: "Seven years I was employed in collecting animals and vegetables, and then found that my design was yet imperfect." Tim Ranger, of Nos. 62 and 64, shares Rasselas' fundamental problem, how to use wealth and leisure for happiness. Dick Shifter of No. 71, like the young Rasselas, tritely eulogizes nature. Observing a collection of lazy-minded perpetual vacationers, Robin Spritely of Nos. 78 and 83 parallels and elaborates Rasselas' mingling with the pretenders to philosophy in Cairo. Another gathering of deluded characters in No. 92 seems to be an imaginative, specific offshoot of the more generalized novel: Tom Double, who has invented ways of ducking all questions; Will Puzzle, full of easy clichés on politics, who claims to have foreseen everything before it happened; and Ned Smuggle, who makes a secret of everything, including his address. In No. 100, Johnson provides an extreme parody of contemporary moral advice, and of Rasselas' wish to plan his future, in Miss Gentle, who is so eager to lead an orderly life that she regulates the whole day mechanically, so affirmative that she responds indiscriminately to everything. Unlike the travelers of *Rasselas*, each of these butts has settled for one easily manageable part of the surrounding chaos, madly abandoning the chance for wholeness. Except for the observant idlers like Robin Spritely and Mr. Sober (of No. 31), who are well along the road from idiosyncratic to universal self, such characters are frozen within their single aims and attitudes, their abbreviated and farcical humors. Seeing only what is to one side of their noses, they are minimized rather than exaggerated, absurd like Swift's personae-butts without their sinister power to discolor a whole world.

When Johnson brings these projected figures into contact with the world through the conventional rhetorical patterns of his time, he subverts not only their delusive expectations but even the implied promises of the genres themselves. Johnson often thinks in genres— witness the essay on epitaphs in the *Life of Pope*, the pieces on *Paradise Lost* in the *Rambler*, the discussions of Shakespeare's plays—but his frequent attacks on the artificiality of conventions, as in the *Milton*, the *Gray*, the *Pope*, and the *Preface to Shakespeare*, suggest an impatience with traditional forms which his art embodies. Unlike such predecessors in burlesque as Pope and Fielding, he maintains a suspicious superiority to all fictional devices or even artistic conventions because they subordinate and attenuate true experience. In his novel, for example, he deliberately rejected the emotional profits of plot while teasing the reader with its exotic ingredients. As he says in contrasting essayist and fiction writer in *Rambler* 184, the universal self, the guide and truth-teller, must range over all experience for his products; in his limiting capacity as fantasist, the artist works with elements not subject to testing, with the pleasing delusions of the idiosyncratic self. Attempting to grasp public truth rather than merely divert, Johnson pulls the analogies of *The Vanity of Human Wishes* from a wide range of knowledge about man—but only from genuine human experience. Not a bird, or a flower, or a flirting nymph, but a particular man best condenses experience to represent the decline of favorites or the sterility of military grandeur.[30] Avoiding the richness of analogies lest he subvert the hard-won generalization, Johnson even more than Swift imperils the central techniques and effects of poetry.

Combining the expectation of allegory and an extreme artificiality which provokes readers to consider realistic probabilities, the oriental tale provided Johnson with a suitable form for his and mankind's struggle. In such a tale as *Rambler* 65, a description in conventionally lush oriental diction of a day in the travels of Obidah, Johnson can neatly develop his favorite narrative elements: a journeying self, the world's dangers and accidents along the way, and a universal evaluating self (here a hermit) to explain and exhort. Later oriental essays and the novel fill out the pattern or play variations on it. In *Rambler* 190, Morad, the adviser to the Indian emperor, tries to use his own career as a model for his son, but since he is shown to be deluded, the son—like Rasselas after his encounters in the world—must add his adviser's experiences to his own fund of observations. Day after day, the emperor Seged of *Ramblers* 204 and 205 tries to secure a measure of happiness for himself and his court, but like the systems of *Rasselas* all his projects are subverted by chance or by the immutable laws of human nature. Roughly at the same time as the novel, three oriental *Idler* papers come closer to its main patterns. In *Idler* 75 the young intellectual Gelaleddin leaves his small town to seek eminence and returns defeated to find no one interested in him. Ortogrul of Basra (*Idler* 99) tells of the meaninglessness of his old age after he has set himself a pointless goal and achieved it. By contrast, the councilor of No. 101 had spent his life trying to follow a coherent plan and found every part of it foiled by the chaos of events; but by throwing himself into experience, he had derived from the struggle Johnson's one reward, a serene mind. Both the irony inherent in the very use of the oriental tale and its convenient provision of observing and acting selves allow Johnson to modulate from contempt of Ortogrul through amusement at Gelaleddin to pity for Seged and admiration for the energetic old man.

Like *Ramblers* 186 and 187, which anticipate Mark Twain's burlesque of Eskimo loves, *Rasselas* accepts the conventions of the oriental tale—including secret passages, subterranean ways, "unsuspected cavities" filled with treasure, and so on—but uses its simplifications and falsifications to indicate the absurdity of life, not its wonder.[31] Most conveniently, it helps him to expose the barbarism of pastoral life, the swindling philosophical rhetoric of "Life Led According to Nature," and the sterility of harem fantasies. For good measure, he tosses in subordinate burlesques of the genre in Imlac's uneventful voyages in caravans and on oceans, in the abduction and return of Pekuah, in the vacillating hermit and the addled sage. He undermines not only the oriental tale but the very fabric of narrative with irony, making central in the novel not the climactic knot for which Aristotle has prepared his reader but a hilarious, inconclusive wrangle about marriage. But where direct guidance for the conduct of life is at issue, in the incorporated essays on pilgrimages, poetry, piety, madness, marriage, traveling, history, grief, and the workings of the imagination and of guilt, Johnson disdains fictional trifling and raises Imlac to a universal self who can provide accurate and unambiguous generalizations.

Weary of literary conventions but searching for the archetypal in human experience, Johnson even more than his contemporaries relies on the journey of life as his staple narrative pattern, often with special focus on the movement from innocence. Among his surveys of the journey, the allegorical dreams of the *Vision of Theodore* and *Rambler* 102 echo Addison's *Vision of Mirzah* in accepting man's fate as just, but elsewhere the pattern ironically projects Johnson's fantasies of his own career: his return to Lichfield after his mother's death, as he wrote Baretti, was the disappointing, unmarked "journey of a wit to his own town" (*Letters*, I, 140). The voyager's success only aggravates his dissatisfactions, as Johnson said clearly in his great poem: "Fate wings with every wish th' afflictive dart," destruction comes together with fulfillment.

A man's achievements can never match his reveries; and his status among others is at the mercy of their whims and preoccupations. Johnson's reveries of undistinguished and unappreciated return are most directly concentrated in the story of Gelaleddin, the wandering young intellectual of *Idler* 75,[32] but he has a good many parallels, like the impoverished, genteel Zosima of *Rambler* 12 who ventured out in search of employment but found only insults. Following a different branch of the road, Eubulus of *Ramblers* 26 and 27 is attempting to recover from a bad start as a youth lured to London to be a wit. On another, Ruricola of *Rambler* 61 describes young Frolick, a local boy who after seven years in London studying law has returned, the lying hero of many adventures, to universal admiration; a parallel in No. 157, Verecundulus, successfully applied himself to study and then, on his return from the university, was an abashed failure in company; in No. 101, a wit undergoes still another version of this move, scoring an immense conversational success in the coffee houses but disappointing a group expressly gathered at a patron's country house to listen to his talk. Serotinus of No. 165, who "sallied forth into the unknown world" and won a fortune through "industry and knowledge" but impressed very few fellow townsmen by his achievement, even more clearly reflects Johnson's sad awareness that no career can fulfill the imagination's hunger for prominence.

In imaging blunted ambition and loss of innocence in the ambiguous journey, *The Idler* forms a context for the contemporaneous *Rasselas*. As Pertinax of *Rambler* 95 had been confused by the mixing of truth and falsehood which constituted his education in debate, so Dick Linger of *Idler* 21 (as well as his echo Tom Tranquil of No. 73) faces his choice of life uncertainly, because he is one of those whose "imagination is active and resolution weak, whose desires are ardent, and whose choice is delicate; who cannot satisfy themselves with standing still, and yet cannot find a motive to direct their course." In No. 58 a traveler who seeks happiness by a voyage to his childhood home attracts no more notice than Imlac or Johnson. In No. 80 a wise experienced adviser "scarcely expects to be credited" when he tells a young girl on her way to London that "her expectations will likewise end in disappointment." At this point in Johnson's life the *Dictionary* had raised the literary reputation of the author of *The Vanity of Human Wishes* and *The Rambler* to the highest position in the nation, and he knew the greatness of his powers. But while the tone is less somber than in the earlier works, reflecting both his success and the mere satisfaction of survival, his vision of man in the world has not changed.

Rasselas, the most ambitious fictional product of this time of complex self-evaluation, provides Johnson's most elaborate projections of what he saw within himself: several different versions of the idiosyncratic self moving from enclosure out into chaos, grappling to learn the world under the stimulation of the insatiable imagination. After discovering the insufficiency of competing solutions to the problems of life, these projections return to the empty paradise partly to acknowledge defeat but partly also because they have been learning to approach the universal self, to see themselves ironically in the light of man's fate. Having completed extensive social research and considered the adventures of Pekuah and the ready advice of Imlac, the Prince and Princess find what we knew before, that though man can traverse mountains, oceans, and deserts, his philosophies and social systems provide no positions from which to overcome irrational hopes, the conflicting fantasies of others, chance, time, and mortality. But they also learn that receptivity to life allows one to compare one's lot with others', acquire a certain distance from selfish concerns, and see oneself healthily in a human context. When we meet the young Rasselas, he is not only in a Happy Valley but also, emblematically, man in the middle of a bowl of mountains, the isolated center of the world stage; when we leave him, he has learned some caution against his own wishes, and has allied himself with others with whom he will form a society.

The most arresting symbols of the novel—those enclosing hills, the pyramids, and the retreats culminating in the catacombs—solidly concentrate what the evaluating self makes of man's (and Johnson's) journey through life. After accompanying this self on a general observation of domestic and public experience in society, we narrow our gaze to an item in the foreground, the Great Pyramid. Like the one element of overt narrative interest within the long journey, the abduction of Pekuah (which is tied to a visit to the Great Pyramid), here is the whole ironic tale of man's limitations: with absolute power and a world on which to exercise it, the pharaoh could achieve no more satisfying expression of his striving than these synthetic hills. But the pyramids do exist, a monument to the pharaoh remains, like Belinda's lock or the poem describing it. While sallying out to work with the materials that chance to be at hand must be ultimately pointless, such challenging the world, whether with pyramids or dictionaries, is nevertheless the only healthy activity for a mortal creature. Otherwise, Johnson's great private dangers await lesser characters in the novel. Attempting to reach farther, the mind can only manufacture guilt and turn inward to drown in fantasies, like the lonely astronomer's; abandoning its ambitions, it yields slothfully to pastoral barbarism, baronial retirement, fruitless hermitages and monasteries, all forms of the final vision of the catacombs. Men fool themselves and then die, says the universal self of the archetypal journey.

But since men cannot avoid death, they must try to minimize the folly, and for this they must work toward a union of the struggling and observing selves, toward acting at the moment in the light of the accumulated human experience. As always with Johnson, the emphasis within the book has been on taking what is before us, on becoming enough involved in life so that we will not withdraw into madness. Although Rasselas has lost his most extreme illusions, he has acquired experience—"images"—to provide a base of more valid generalizations and guide his reveries; projecting Johnson's sense of himself, he is at the center of a society of close friends, a club with whom to discuss one's yearnings and the course of life. Except for the superficial triumphs of achievement (represented by Imlac and the astronomer) Rasselas has gained what is available in the world. Despite the apparent circularity of the novel, Rasselas, Nekayah, and Pekuah have really changed, have in fact acquired the orientation to experience which for Johnson is education: the acceptance of a developed universal self, the ability to evaluate one's own desires.

By contrast, the people in Johnson's writings who avoid such change are pitiable because they block most of their imaginative avenues for apprehending reality, the sympathetic antennae of the mind which Johnson himself had had to exercise to overcome the partial world provided by bad eyesight and hearing. While they protect themselves from the normal disappointment of failing to achieve the immeasurable, they diminish their strivings to the subhumanly easy and isolate themselves from any but mechanical contact with other people. Within a few weeks in *The Idler*, Johnson provides a typical sample of such aborted selves who try to climb by words into small segments of worlds: in No. 47, Deborah Ginger's husband wants to move from tradesman to town wit by way of theatrical and political clichés; Tom Restless of No. 48 seeks the reputation of learning by echoing coffee-house chatter; the wife in No. 53 "has no language but the dialect of her own set of company. She hates and admires in humble imitation; and echoes the words 'charming' and 'detestable' without consulting her own perceptions"; and Dick Minim of Nos. 60 and 61 pours out a whole graveyard of critical chestnuts. As Imlac illustrates in tritely describing his early hopes or the qualifications of the poet, even the most able idiosyncratic selves cannot be objective enough to see life steadily and in proportion.

In pursuing the only serious human ambition, the wish to grasp and order one's perceptions, such idiosyncratic selves as Rasselas, Nekayah, and Pekuah are far superior to the novel's representatives of truncated systems and to the thwarted selves in the other writings, while the cured astronomer and Imlac approach the evaluating, universal self which understands the world. Action, engagement with the world, is as essential to a full spokesman for man as wide observation. Although Imlac often serves as Johnson's mask of aging teacher, he derives his authority from his own career as actor in life at large. And the book takes its title from the Prince because he is its most important figure: in the move from isolated fantasy to involvement with the outside, as from ignorance to experience, the Prince more than anyone else reflects Johnson's vision of his own career.

For projecting this private ironic vision in public art, Johnson usually sends his representative man on a journey, often from his home and back, symbolically from innocence to ambiguous experience, from blindness in Eden to an unformulable world which comments on that Eden. So far as men can control it, the journey expresses a delusive wish to reverse the doom of man by assuring felicity. The Eden—childhood, dependence, limitation—cannot satisfy man's striving for achievement and involvement; although experience may distract the hunger of the imagination for grandeur, range, and permanence, nothing in this life can satisfy the hunger.[33] Since the evaluative self knows the immense futility of attempting to usurp God's functions and decree the future, to make divine general truths by applying a limited and divided mind to an infinity of confusing data, the journey has to be ironic. Man's obligation to make order in imitation of the divine can never be more than tentatively and partially fulfilled.

Still, striving to overcome obstacles can give a sense of achievement, like Johnson's own; testing oneself to the utmost can call up one's powers and talents and increase one's consciousness of being; and experience for Johnson always offers more hope, more possibilities, more material with which to work, than any withdrawal in an effort to simulate Eden. For Johnson, the idiosyncratic is not the perverse, unchanging devil in man of Swift's moral psychology, but that principle of the moral and appetitive which is distinctively human and distinctively capable of learning and changing. Much more than Swift, Johnson sees this appetitive as more or less alike in all men, capable of forming essential contact among men if it can break out past its fears and protectively limiting organs. If its complement the observing self can examine enough of human experience to provide it with informed recommendations, encouragement, and evaluations, the striving self can will toward health. Since like other Lockeans Johnson tends to see the aberrations of the idiosyncratic self as derived from defects either in its machinery or in the environment, what was evil for Swift looks more like psychological deficiency to him.

In Johnson's view, man's striving self (like Johnson's own) yearns, fails, and broods, but it also provides the basis of feeling, fantasy, and external experience from which man's other self can build its guiding truths. Only through the interaction of imagining self and world can the surveying universal mind discover meaning. The meaning is temporary, dependent on continuing revaluation, in the very long run unmeaning, as pyramids lose their points and language its signification. But for the whole self—the partnership of both the individual self who yet represents the type in his very idiosyncrasies, and the universal spokesman for all of considered human experience— and for its time, as for Johnson and his, such provisional meaning permits a triumph over isolation, sloth, fear, guilt, and chaos.

V

WORDSWORTH

1. The Self as Poet

AS AN ENGLISH protestant and a member of a respectable, middle-class, solvent, close, and substantial family, Wordsworth was rooted in the established order; as a hill-country child and an orphan at an early age, he learned young the characteristics of isolation. Although he, his brothers, and his sister entered adult life as a united group in a good position to contemplate bourgeois careers, his and Dorothy's early letters suggest that the unity was defensive, the orphans' front against a world that had shown itself unreliable. After the death of their parents, William and Dorothy in particular found a new arbitrariness in the authority claimed by grandparents and uncles, an unexpected discourtesy from the world; and the Earl of Lonsdale's refusal to pay what he owed them was confirmation of the world's treachery. As he matured, Wordsworth sought ways to tie both the specially elected poet and the specially damned figure like Lowther to the family of living things from which both had been distinguished. At the same time that his poetry projects a sense of union with man and nature and the divine, like Pope's, Swift's, and Johnson's works it affirms his own uniqueness above the mass. The wonder of being both figures, the typical specimen and the individual, is always before him; as against his predecessors, he observes and is observed in each capacity, forming always a double self which he seeks to unite. While such a sense of multiple identity perplexed by a fear of fragmentation may be characteristic of Wordsworth's time and calling, it seems also to reflect his private response to his early familial and social situation.

Conscious of the seductions of subjectivism, suffering from inexplicable mistreatment by his recognized fellows, Wordsworth found his grand subject in the individual mind's relations to the world outside and within it, the problem made central by Descartes and thrust upon English thinkers by Locke and Hume. And his grand resolution of his and mankind's problem is the integrating, unifying self, the Poet. In Swift's vision, the observant moral being selects the true path despite the assault of chaos; in Johnson's, the psychologically whole man continuously shapes chaos, exercising the will and imagination—on the advice of the observing reason—into valid generalizations upon which to act; in Wordsworth's, the imagining self, the figure creating ties to all that it senses and conceives, becomes the high archetype of the species. For Wordsworth, both the parts of the self and all experience are fused in the highest form of man, which in turn grasps apparent chaos, not as generalizations but as forms of truth, to store in the memory for lifelong spiritual nourishment.[1]

Such a sense of meaning may perhaps be called symbolic realism, as against Swift's fabulism or Johnson's nominalism. Swift invents a mind that sees other people as animals and persuades us that we share that mind; Johnson provides pyramids which he and we know are an illustration of a psychological point, mere chaos if not so used; Wordsworth, intensely cooperating with experience, shows us within that experience actual emblematic shapes or patterns which concentrate undefinable moods or overwhelming passions. In the tempests of Wordsworth's young manhood, for example, his hopes for union and his horror of chaos were brought to a crisis by the French Revolution, which grew into a Form of immense significance in his vision of the mind's development. For decades it remained a major symbol of his central complex of human feelings: hope, fulfillment, disappointment, recollection, and consolation. To contain and fuse his private, conflicting responses to this most unifying and disintegrating stimulus of his age, he needed a poetic lifetime.[2]

But some elements in his character that tied him to the ordinary— and partly animated both his greatest poetry and his dullest orthodoxy—antedated any single event, no matter how momentous, and grew stronger almost irrespective of events. Reflecting his source in the lower bourgeoisie, Wordsworth from his early letters respects the conservative and prudential. Where his turbulent personal involvements permitted, he tried hard to act respectably; where they did not, he evaded but did not rebel. Dorothy wrote that first he thought of being a lawyer, like their father, "if his health will permit";[3] but it wouldn't. He toyed with avuncular recommendations to study oriental languages or prepare for the church, and he more seriously (by January, 1791) wanted to be a traveling companion and tutor. When no chances to play Imlac or George Primrose appeared, he sniffed the possibilities of journalism as a career that would unite income with morality, but again stayed safely on the shore. As soon as he had a reliable (though small) income, he settled on a traditional, and with time even an orthodox and conventional, manner of living—a secular version of Goldsmith's Vicar's—as the best expression of the union of individual and mankind in a vital Form.

Assuming his public role of literary figure, Wordsworth saw himself as a fusion of the respectably general and the proud unique. Anchored in conventionally pure living, he could ascend new heights of imaginative thought for mankind. As a self-conscious innovator, even a revolutionary, he wished to dissociate himself from the literary expectations of his day, like Gray to prepare and attract a special audience: an audience, however, representative of basic humanity unspoiled by artificial pretensions to taste. His revolution, he insisted, was not against the grand English tradition but against contemporary divergence from it; he could rise clothed in the moral and aesthetic sanctity of this tradition above contemporary frippery. Naturally, he was also superior to the fashionable audience, one social version of the recurring dim obstacle—routine, corruption, death—between him and the reality he sought to join. Although he always wanted popular success, by early middle age (May 21, 1807) he wrote as if resigned to the admiration of a moral and intellectual elite: "The things which I have taken, whether from within or without—what have they to do with routs, dinners, morning calls, hurry from door to door . . . endless talking about things nobody cares anything for except as far as their own vanity is concerned. . . . It is an awful truth, that there neither is, nor can be, any genuine enjoyment of Poetry among nineteen out of twenty of those . . . who either are, or are striving to make themselves, people of consideration in society."[4] Such an abandonment of all but the human core implies selectiveness even in his vision of unity. He was a man talking to men, but only a few at a time listened; presumably they in turn would talk to others. Routine lives fall back into the ocean of time; fundamental, archetypal ones rise from it as mountains or tall trees. Seen before Wordsworth's observing eye, the true poet towers above mankind not as a distinct giant but as a grand figure, like a pine or an alp, growing out of a base of populous humanity.

Such organic elitism, along with Wordsworth's equal concern for the individual and general selves, allows him to sense poetic talent as a divine gift. Since it is putatively independent of its possessor, Wordsworth could scorn those who dislike his poetry without suspecting his own vanity;[5] since it is primarily a heightening of universally present qualities, he did not fear the universal self's amused stare. Having made a religion of the imagination—which can bring an immortal concentration of life and meaning in the moment—and of its creation poetry, he assumes through poetry a guarantee of salvation which Swift and Johnson would not even allow the apparent saint. Although the poet possesses this guarantee more surely than others, he does not possess it exclusively or, like the older poeta, separately: Wordsworth cannot effectively imagine himself in this spirit too pure for mankind. The serious poeta appears in Wordsworth's work with some frequency but little intensity, mainly before and after his finest period. In *The Prelude* Wordsworth develops his self-conscious youthful appearance in the part as well-intentioned coxcombry, and in *The Excursion* he smiles when the Solitary adopts its attitudes.[6] For a vision of the large and varied total self, not an idealization of one aspect of it, Milton's and Gray's traditional refining figure is too fragile.

A role more permanently congenial to Wordsworth is the poet as bard, as patriot, teacher, and father, as the leader and representative of his people. He hopes like his illustrious predecessors in the stream of the world's great poets to see something new, to create "a power like one of nature's," to emulate Milton in his noble variety. The poet, he says, sends his special energy through the reader and acts like a natural force to awaken the reader's vitality. In *The Recluse*, Wordsworth aims even beyond Milton, for he seeks a muse to pierce past heaven and earth to the divine truth, to "the Mind of Man." Like Shelley but also like Thomson and Collins, he envisions thereby a feeling and reflecting self, a missioned explorer among the uncertain elements of the mind.

Wordsworth's focus on the self and its responses in the poems is clearly a calculated risk and adventure, a path by which to seek meaning. If he could completely understand himself, he could understand—by their effect on him—other people, living animals and plants, and the divine life of the universe as well. For Johnson and Swift the accumulated experience of mankind offers a standpoint from which to evaluate the partial, acting self; for Wordsworth this self is endless and sufficient, both individual and archetype, yielding more as it is studied more by the general reflecting self. In his fascinating autobiographical letter to Anne Taylor of April 9, 1801,

Wordsworth says that he cannot explain his current techniques and the beliefs of the Preface to the *Lyrical Ballads* as sudden discoveries, for "in truth my life has been unusually barren of events, and my opinions have grown slowly and, I may say, insensibly" (*Early Letters*, p. 327). Besides protecting his private "events," Wordsworth in asserting his mind's organic growth assigns it almost divine autonomy. A few years later, he described himself as living much in the past, fitting his past experience into a vision of an organic whole. He saw himself not as an instrument for ordering phenomena into consistent generalizations but as one microcosm and macrocosm, a representative whole in the fused and living universe. For the older goals of finding the right path among confusion and of creating a new order out of apparent chaos he substituted the reflective and intuitive union of essences.

Like Johnson, Wordsworth insists on facing the vision of the whole man, on generalizing all situations to embrace mankind, on aiming directly at the emblematic and archetypal. But where Johnson excludes idiosyncrasies from his literary rendering of man's condition, Wordsworth finds the subtleties of the individual consciousness centrally representative, because all men have such feelings. What his introspective journey yields to Wordsworth, therefore, is the sensitive aspect of all humanity, and this in turn is essential man. His own events, pruned but not falsified, become emblematic in his reflective poems, although in his fictions he molds autobiographical reveries in the manner of his predecessors. The breakdowns of Swift and Johnson may perhaps be inferred where they are not privately documented; Wordsworth describes his, and makes it a universal accompaniment to the loss of innocence. Since the movements of his soul are holy to Wordsworth, the idiosyncratic self which he examines in his sober narratives becomes a heroic model as well as a representative of man; the observing general self, which in his predecessors could direct a variety of judgments, becomes for him mainly an admirer. It still mediates between the idiosyncratic selves and the reader, but since they are now archetypes it speaks with proprietary reverence.

Wordsworth early realized the danger as well as the advantages of living heavily within his own imagination, as witness his repeated insistence on being open to outer influences. He had difficulty in accepting other people, or for that matter mere otherness, as real. In Cambridge and London, he says in *The Prelude*, he tended to lose himself in fantasies about the passing faces in the crowd, wondering and uncertain about the lives behind them; and in France during the Revolution he felt detached and safe despite the obvious surrounding violence. As Johnson had habituated himself to overcome his isolating deficiencies, so Wordsworth encouraged his tendencies to join with outer symbols of mankind, to reach out in sympathy to his equivalents and complements. It was not immediate awareness of others, as with Burns or Keats, which determined his social conscience or poetic world, but a tendency to turn them into versions of himself or fit them as Forms within his scheme of the world.

Such a limited sense of mankind as a few alternative selves (no doubt in part reflecting his hill-country upbringing and identification with a small group of brothers and sister) was recompensed by immense sensitivity, attentiveness, and delicacy toward those he loved, as Dorothy wrote in 1793. While his inclinations do on rare occasions support the poeta against the insensitive herd, or the man of genius against the dolts, they tend normally toward the straightforward—familial and social. More than Johnson certainly, and perhaps more than the cosmopolitan and gregarious Swift and Pope, Wordsworth makes firm distinctions between those conventionally identified with him—his intimates, his family, the people among whom he grew up and lived, and in some moods the English nation—and the others, the outsiders. Certainly no writer of stature in the eighteenth century is so bloodthirsty as Wordsworth in his patriotism, so capable of denying humanity to whole classes of others.

Although the sensitive poet might despise the routine getting and spending of the larger society and the presumed corruption of distant groups, he needed to be particularly careful to preserve his base in mankind. Sympathetic communication is central in Wordsworth's vision of union: he wrote in 1804 that "absolute solitude and seclusion from the world . . . [is] a great evil"; in *Peele Castle* he repudiates "the heart that lives alone"; and he shows in all his narratives that mental and moral health comes with movement out of the self. Like nature and the universe, society provides influences, emanations of humanity, which are to help the individual to fulfill himself. Wordsworth's connection of self with society seems to begin at Pope's or Johnson's dynamic balance but to evolve far from it: rapturous abandon is properly the quality of the individual alone in nature or in himself, whereas in society man can find the calmer relatedness and consolation, the human sympathies from which to build a larger self. We must have others, as we must have poetry and all relatedness, if not to stimulate intense feeling, then at least to console us for the inevitable pains of loss, guilt, and death.

As observer, Wordsworth sometimes attempts the same distanced, universal view of man that Swift is able to project through dramatic personae or Gray through the carefully shaped *poeta;* but Wordsworth's figures are patently self-analytical or archetypal or both. He never uses the persona like Swift, as the embodiment of complex and detailed human characteristics assumed to be not his own; and he rarely sketches his characters, like Johnson in the periodical essays, as ways of exploring the surface variety of human life and playing it against complex, permanent human nature. In *The Excursion* we can infer from his note that all the men are alternative versions of himself;[7] in *The Prelude*, the poetic self is developed in unexampled precision and sensitivity, with all the other characters acting (quite properly) as stimuli and projections of his sensations; in *The White Doe* and in other developed narratives, the central persons are symbols of moral qualities he sees in himself, while other figures are conventional and public, the chorus of his dramas. Wordsworth makes relatively little use of the dramatic possibilities of the narrator, who is likely to be either himself exploring psychological states—as in *Resolution and Independence* or *Strange Fits of Passion*—or a convenience by which to keep his distance. When he does play the self-conscious narrator, as in semi-comic ballads like *Peter Bell, Simon Lee,* or *The Idiot Boy*, his tone tends toward condescension, which reduces the observed archetype to a fragment of the self. More typically, his narrative personae are routinely appropriate: a shepherd telling children a local story, a young man listening to an old man talk of the forlorn Margaret, a pastor explaining the moral significance of his dead parishioners, a bard evoking the tale of the White Doe from his harp.[8]

When Wordsworth wants to observe the highest human archetype, he presents the Poet bringing union and relevance, like hills or smoke uniting earth and heaven. The poet, he says in both the Preface to the *Lyrical Ballads* and *The Excursion*, connects and communicates all the physical, social, mental, and spiritual fragments for the moment of deepest experience. Although a peddler, a teacher, a pastor, an old man, a baby, or, indeed, anyone can take his turn to show the interrelation of human and divine experiences, only the poet can fuse nature and our minds, in symbolic visions (like the ram and his reflection at the end of *The Excursion*) which tie perception and memory to shared experience and a universe of meaning. Like Wordsworth, pressed almost unbearably by the vitality of images and sensations, the poet—mankind's specialist in imagining—becomes illuminated through their fusion with his conscious observing self. In the tranquillity which follows, he re-creates a unity which he communicates to his readers, evoking in them a response like his own transcendence. Through his creative imagination, the poet saves his essential self from chaos, and also leads his lesser selves—representing the mass of mankind—to unity. Working with others, the poet can hope to provide ennobling and civilizing consolation for humanity.

In his early, great period, Wordsworth as poet could fitfully partake in the triumph of the unified vision over the stubborn chaos of outer mortality and inner guilt: in *The Prelude* or *Tintern Abbey*, the momentary achievement of self-consciousness as purified mind, when the human archetype and the universe meet as peers in a fused imagination. Losing the vision of meaning—in Vaudracour, Michael, the poet of the Intimations Ode, and the Solitary—results from human insufficiency faced with social complexity, the routine of the normal, and the effects of time, chance, and death. While Wordsworth finds in tradition and human experience a ground for hope, it does not provide him with a standpoint for judging man. Rather, he passes by the guardianship and mediation of the universal self to arrive at a more fundamental eighteenth-century moral criterion, nature animated by the divine will. In the long years between or after the intense visions, the poems affirm Wordsworth's consolation in the knowledge that all his acts must be archetypal, that there is no such thing as idiosyncrasy, that all is in accordance with the way life moves. Wordsworth's later total projections of man in the world, such as *The Excursion* or *The White Doe*, seek to subdue pain and guilt by a theology more optimistic than Pope's in *An Essay on Man* and to raise the human archetype to massive grandeur out of refined fragments like the Pastor or Francis Norton. Such a living world exists wholly for the selves which perceive the harmony: the Poet, and the Everyman whom the Poet can animate.[9]

The prime elements in Wordsworth's conception of harmony, as I have suggested, are Wordsworth's characteristic projections, undying Forms of union, newly discovered emblems or archetypes. Offspring of the imagining self and the living world outside it, they affect a condition of consciousness fuller than Johnson's evaluating self abstracting general laws from human experience. Manifesting itself in art, myths, folklore, or religion, Wordsworth's archetypal permits the imagination to rest in the eternally real, to combine the unique and the universal, and to tie the present to the past and the future. And as these Forms, which harmonize in the poet's consciousness with others and yet remain distinct for future nourishment, are projections of Wordsworth's sense of himself and the Poet in the world, they share a family likeness with Platonic ideas, with the visions of religion, and with the personifications and filmy reveries of such predecessors as Collins and Gray. As Johnson had used the symbolic generalization and Swift the persona-butt, so Wordsworth made of the Form his special poetic mechanism to unite the centrally private and the gathered elements of the public. By its means, he could soar and remain on solid land, lead and keep a place in the flock. As with his defense of the ordinary—irreducible human nature, at any time the storehouse for the human archetype without or beneath social artifice—he is always aware of the stable base capable of transcendence.

In Wordsworth's greatest works, such as the Intimations Ode, all of the distinct elements take on archetypal grandeur as Forms. Everything from the opening meadows, groves, and streams to the concluding sunset, acting as an aspect of nature and man as well as itself, combines concrete solidity and the symbolic enlargement characteristic of Wordsworth. Possibly the boy in the mind's eye, both a parallel of the shepherd boy we can see and an earthly adumbration of the children we imagine on the shore of eternity, is most memorably emblematic, but the poet, the boy, and the reader are all images and aspects—like the Solitary Reaper or Michael or the two figures in *Resolution and Independence* or those in the scene above Tintern Abbey—of man's fundamental Form, his eternal situation in the world. That situation is itself an expression of what Wordsworth recognized as his own, analytically elevated in the lyrics and projected at one remove—a distancing which sometimes allows greater frankness—in the narratives. Often Wordsworth's fictions serve to show what would become of him (and of man) if he left his fellows or lost his hope, and often they are hortatory models of union and solace. They usually move from joyous innocence to guilty loss and consolation: the career of his observed, archetypal self evolving above the mass like a mountain out of the plain, like a poet out of mankind. Standing along a slope, the observing self compares and judges, awarding virtue and happiness proportional to the integration of mountain and plain.

2. The Projected Self as Lonely Wanderer

To achieve the fulfillment of individuality and union, man for Wordsworth needs the intimacy of a small circle, an intimacy found most naturally in the home. Without such warm harmony, which comes unconsciously to children and the passionless old, Words-worth's archetypal emanations wander alone and alien in the material world amidst the dangers of "mutually inflamed" passions, the prey of "solitary anguish" in the country and social storms in cities. From this general humanity, therefore, must rise one ideal projection of Wordsworth, the eminent self, the intense and lonely figure who nobly observes life from above, sweeping over space and time from mountains and the heights of memory. Perhaps because the vision of power in man on high tempts Wordsworth throughout his career, his most violent anger is called forth by tyranny: the temptation of total aloofness, the ultimate withdrawal from human sympathy.[10] But even man at his highest, man the saving imaginative teacher of union and relevance, is fragile and vulnerable to outer accident and the psychological groping of adulthood, partly because any local group in which he fits is at the mercy of the larger society and finally of mankind.

Bereft of social nourishment, man frequently appears to Words-worth projected in solitary misery: a stranger in the violence of cities; an outcast ridden by guilt; a mind paralyzed within sight of an earlier goal or damned in despair to its own confines. For such a figure, the degree of guilt or pain is proportional to the dissociation from mankind. Cutting off all the fertile impulses which might lead him from his raw, chaotic fantasies, detached solitude holds the very greatest dangers for the sensitive man. Therefore Wordsworth's repudiation of aloofness, as in the famous *Elegiac Stanzas* evoked by a picture of Peele Castle, tends to be as embracing as Imlac's warning to the grieving Nekayah but vastly more intense:[11]

> Farewell, farewell the heart that lives alone,
> Housed in a dream, at distance from the Kind!
> Such happiness, wherever it be known,
> Is to be pitied, for 'tis surely blind.
> (*Poetical Works*, IV, 260)

Wordsworth's isolated man usually does not wish to live alone; rather, he takes the Form of a distraught wanderer, a stranger out of Eden painfully seeking restoration to himself and his kind. Although the lonely journey itself tended to become more positive as Words-worth aged, on the whole he saw it as ambiguous, always beginning in loss and only rarely leading to union. Perhaps reflecting his shock at the death of his parents or his youthful descent into corrupt soci-

ety from the northern hills, his early wanderers are consistently dis-
appointed and guilty. The heroine of *Ruth*, for example, meets shal-
lowness and vulgarity when she emigrates to America (as does the
Solitary of *The Excursion*), the savage ironies that faced Smollett's
Lismahago and Dickens and Mrs. Trollope rather than the opportunities of Defoe's or Scott's characters. Later in Wordsworth's career,
the sort of consolation for the journey which is suggested in the
Intimations Ode makes some mild amends for the Fall. But neither
his vision of the striving self nor his evaluative self could provide a
return to the Happy Valley.[12] Only at rare intervals could a third element, the intuitively sympathetic imaginative self which fused the
other two in the timeless moment, create a different, new life.

As long as Wordsworth's wandering Form is isolated, he may fill
any of a number of conventional social places. He may be a beggar
or a pedlar;[13] a lone traveler more or less comforted by nature; a
young or inexperienced person sent on a difficult mission; a distraught
woman, with or without offspring; a Cain or Oedipus hating himself
and life, or a reconciled Ancient Mariner; a sailor or soldier in danger
recalling felicity, the archetype of suffering or aging man; a castaway,
man as shipwrecked sailor or earth. Among this projected wanderer's
congenial settings are bewildering moors during storms; difficult but
rewarding mountains; the river of time or of our fate; the tempting
stream of life; the mind as swelling river or sea or ocean; the sea as
eternity. Finally, Wordsworth's wandering Form runs the danger of
mental even more than physical isolation. After the mind's wavering
under stress (which concentrates the associations of guilt and pain),
madness permits this acting self to escape from material horrors to the
ultimate separation of fantasies or suicide. A mind in chaos can sus-
tain no life; like the sick child whose experience informs much of
Wordsworth's poetry, it must be resuscitated from without, restored
to the family by an act of love proceeding from nature, or man,
or God.[14]

Even Wordsworth's early poetry, before Annette Vallon provides
a tidy source of guilt feelings, presents a vision of reflective wandering in search of restoration. In *An Evening Walk*, Wordsworth's first
extended poem, the solitary *poeta* makes the circuit of his world
seeking relatedness and gathering sensations and images (often of
other solitaries) to evaluate, in a pattern found in Wordsworth's
beloved Beattie but cut also by Thomson, Gray, Cowper, and their
models back to Virgil. Emphatically contrasting a forlorn young
widow and children with a placid group of swans at the center,

Wordsworth adds to the conventional social outburst of his day his own special sense of human dislocation. When the moon rises, people's homes come into view for the observer, particularly the single cottage which is most meaningful, the "sole bourne, sole wish, sole object of my way" in which coziness and the emotional warmth of his sister await him.

Images like this isolated cottage high on the side of a hill, the setting sun, a solitary light or star, moon, poet, nation, girl, or shepherd, all recur in Wordsworth's poems, usually though not always with attractive connotations. External symbols tied to the poet's mind, they constitute objective guarantees of his own sensations and therefore his existence, of his relatedness and therefore possible harmony. He is not cast off from mankind like the widow or like the gypsy nursing mother whom the wandering poeta of the *Descriptive Sketches* meets in the Alps. As a contrast to her, this troubled poeta studies the chamois hunter, a happy prelapsarian who in turn symbolizes Adventuring Man, single but organically growing out of his society. In both poems the autobiographical persona, who is decorously not free to act out Wordsworth's fantasies, returns safely after considering the alternatives of sterile and fruitful solitude.

In the disembodied fiction *Guilt and Sorrow*, Wordsworth can safely indulge the pleasingly dreary personal fantasies which had been censored into the fate of the gypsy woman and the chamois hunter. A solitary traveler on Salisbury Plain, man in the stormy vastness of nature, succumbs archetypally under the burden of virtuous intentions and serious crimes. His dream of domesticity ruined by poverty and fraud, he had committed a violent wayside robbery, from which he has been fleeing for years. He swoons at the sight of his own and mankind's fate, a man hanging from a gibbet in the empty plain; comforts a woman also turned vagrant because of fraud; mollifies the violent anger of a father toward his son; and calms the last moments of his long-abandoned wife, whom Providence carts in for the occasion. No doubt his age's gothic frenzy was working in Wordsworth, but it is his sense of himself that informs the vision of the well-intentioned guilty man who can yet offer consolation, sympathy, and relatedness, the poet's gift and man's chief obligation—and who prefigures the function of mingled guilt and experience in opening the way to these qualities in the greater poems. Furthermore, powerful fantasies rising from the struggle with Lowther seem to direct the financial mistreatment of poor people in Wordsworth's early poems, and the two outcasts comforting each other suggest Wordsworth and his sister or Annette—with the wife's arrival, Dorothy *and* Annette—tossed about in a wild and stormy world.

Wordsworth's most substantial juvenile achievement, *The Borderers*, plays more arrestingly with similar fantasies, this time providing men to embody the main alternatives of guilt and betrayed innocence. Dangerous eminences abound, as well as archetypal beggars and scavengers; Oswald the villain is totally alienated by his pride; most of the narrations involve outcasts or outlaws; marauders under the leadership of the hero Marmaduke prey on society; the forlorn Idonea wanders before us on a plain with her father, the blind old Herbert, who dies on a thoroughly blasted heath. As readers have long noticed, Marmaduke, who has been tricked into causing the death, suffers the Ancient Mariner's fate:[15]

> a wanderer *must I* go,
> The Spectre of that innocent Man, my guide. . . .
> over waste and wild,
> In search of nothing, that this earth can give,
> But expiation, while I wander on. . . .
> *(Poetical Works*, I, 225)

As gloomy as Childe Harold and even more satisfyingly guilty, Marmaduke can carry the full measure of Wordsworth's Oedipal anguish.

In other early pieces such as *The Vale of Esthwaite, Fragment of a 'Gothic' Tale*, an untitled fragment "The road extended o'er a heath," *Inscription for a Seat, Incipient Madness*, and *Lucy Gray; or, Solitude*, other traveling selves enact guilty or at least fearful fantasies, the difference in tone or prospects depending on the degree of detachment from society. Such detachment is a matter of viewpoint, and different versions of the self may need different sorts of relatedness to a surrounding society. Where the piece is an abandoned fragment, it tends to be a vision of unqualified struggle; where Wordsworth finished it, he provided for the forlorn at least sympathy and sometimes restorative society. In *The Brothers*, for example, a sailor visiting his native hills appears to the vicar as

> one of those who needs must leave the path
> Of the world's business to go wild alone.
> *(Poetical Works*, II, 4)

After hearing of his brother's melancholy and death, the sailor returns to his trade, purged of the yearning to live again his idyllic youth, accepting as man's fate the wandering isolation of the sea—but as a member of a crew, not Gray's poet*a*. As both brothers, the one at home who pined and died and the guilt-bowed sailor, Wordsworth's projected self declares a peaceful resolution above the understanding of the routine vicar.

Domestic circles like the ones assumed in *The Brothers* or described in *Michael* and the Lucy poems are often broken in Wordsworth's early narratives, as if his fantasies were busy denying what his mind sought to affirm, the possibility of union in innocence to ward off chance and time. As symbols of disruption of the family and even of society, the forsaken women who swarm through his poems derive from a tradition as old as literature and particularly strong in the sentimental novels and poems of his time and that period immediately preceding it.[16] Nevertheless, their highly charged and frequent recurrence suggests a special responsiveness to them in Wordsworth's mind. No doubt biographers since Legouis' discovery of the affair with Annette are right to stress her significance, but *An Evening Walk* and *Salisbury Plain* (the original of *Guilt and Sorrow*) indicate an earlier concern with such fantasies, perhaps deriving from the loss of home and mother suffered by the boy off to school and intensified by her death when he was seven.

One way to repudiate the guilty fantasies of forsaken women is to project the journey from home of the weak or childish, and therefore blameless, self, the unprepared innocent. In Wordsworth's poems this pattern involves enough figures to constitute a small genre of its own. Like Goldsmith's George Primrose these become both echoes of the picaresque tradition and ironic commentaries on it. One archetypal striving self, the Blind Highland Boy, arouses the evaluating narrator, our substitute, to bring the ambiguities into the open. Isolated by his blindness, in a society isolated in its mountains, the boy reaches out to the unknown:

> Yet he had many a restless dream;
> Both when he heard the eagles scream,
> And when he heard the torrents roar,
> And heard the water beat the shore
> Near which their cottage stood.
> (*Poetical Works*, III, 90)

Although he delights in his freedom on the river and bitterly resents the rescue which ends his dream, that dream of freedom has been leading him to imminent and certain destruction. In time, the narrator implies, he would be reconciled to his temporary and ignorant security like man generally,[17] an unchanged Rasselas tended by equally ignorant servants.

More usually, Wordsworth's young adventurers drown in experience. When *Michael's* Luke is sent off on a mission, like Lucy Gray and the Idiot Boy and Ben the Waggoner he fails, presumably through a combination of his own innocence and the power of the elements opposing him; like Marmaduke and the hero of the much later *Dion* (1816), both also corrupted by evil guides, he is forced into permanent exile. All of these unprepared innocents, concentrated in the blind beggar of *Prelude* VII, reflect that side of Wordsworth and every man which complains of the eternal unexpectedness of sin. Although like Thomson and Johnson he affirmed the adventure into life, like Cowper he saw that God—or the universe, or Nature—must share the responsibility.

If solitude implies not guilty alienation, as with Oswald or Napoleon,[18] or the mistreatment of innocence, but distinct identity rising out of a nourishing society, it provides an avenue by which the human spirit can perform its most fruitful work. *London, 1802* celebrates Milton the ideal poet-patriot, raised as a star, isolated by moral eminence rather than willfulness or guilt, to guide the nation of the average. Poem XVIII of the same group, on national independence and liberty, sees England as the single remaining light in Napoleon's darkened Europe. Similarly, in No. XXVII,

> . . . We are left, or shall be left, alone;
> The last that dare to struggle with the Foe.
> *(Poetical Works*, III, 122)

Such heights of virtue are held also by individual heroes, as with Prussia's Schill, a meteor in Part II, No. XIX, whose name will remain fixed like a star for posterity. Even in the absurd victory ode over Napoleon, Wordsworth seems compelled to introduce a dominating solitary, St. George, to support his happy English folk. In Nos. XXXVI and XXXVIII of the "Memorials of a Tour on the Continent, 1820," Wordsworth himself, like Thomson and Goldsmith before him, climbs to the height of imagination to survey and transcend his experiences. Assuming the position of poet as imagining man, Wordsworth can mediate between past and present, between the ordinary life of mankind and empyrean transcendence. In contrast to such typical satirists on high as Churchill and Byron, he climbs a hill to show his fellows the way, not attack them.

As the solitary acting selves grow into Forms before the poet's reflective gaze, they develop nimbuses of meaning. In *Yew-Trees*, as in the Ode and elsewhere, Wordsworth focuses on a single tree as an archetype of life, a link through generations with the sensations and recollections of individual people. The girl in *The Solitary Reaper*, like the old man of *Resolution and Independence*, is an archetype of man's enduring identity: uniting the species, humanity's eternal song reaches from the unrecorded millennia of civilizing agriculture through her at work in the fields to the heart of the poet.[19] Indeed, whenever Wordsworth successfully communicates sympathy for a human solitary, whether in Michael, Margaret, Emily Norton, Peter Bell, or their dozens of analogues, he makes him a symbolic tie to the reflective self, to the reader, and to all of man's experience. Confronting the universe, the representative solitary man in the Intimations Ode concentrates this side of Wordsworth's vision. Standing amid the actual or recollected accretions of life, he asks what meaning they offer him and what effect he has on them, to what extent they exist irrespective of him and to what extent he creates them. He asks, that is, for the Solitary Reaper's song to be made intelligible, for an answer to his questions and Job's. The answer—the poem itself—is the universe's revelation to man mediated through the poet.

In *The Prelude* the poet's mind, perhaps the ultimate archetype for striving man, nakedly glows before us and him in the world, affirming independence and seeking relatedness. By examining with intense clarity the developing swell of this consciousness, the poet hopes to achieve the fusion of his selves in an act of the imagination, a triumphant individual power that brings man to partake of the universal harmony and removes him from time. His present observing self leads us to a level above the normal and shares with us enlightened judgment of his earlier self; in moments of special intensity, as on Snowdon, it unites us with that self.

The recollection to which we are directed pictures representative visions and movements of any man's life, beginning with the famous breeze that permits the acting self to float on life's river and to travel the seas and continents of the mind. High on his slippery rock in Book I, the young Wordsworth surveys a strange world to which, advancing past the poets of the eighteenth century and the author of *An Evening Walk* and *Descriptive Sketches*, he will relate himself. Exchanging his Cumbrian eminences for Cambridge and its shallow secular plain in Book III, he descends symbolically as well as literally, yielding some distance to the primal fall.[20] At the end of Book IV, he rejects that muddy society to pour himself into delirious France, for the while completely and unreflectively responsive to the feelings and excitements of his intimates: an idiosyncratic self alive to men and women as the child had been alive to nature. But such complete social immersion, like the twig's floating on the river, minimizes man. Seen from the reflective distance, he is merely one of a swarm of lost strangers, like the blind beggar among the London masses in whose explanatory placard

> was a type,
> Or emblem, of the utmost that we know,
> Both of ourselves and of the universe. . . .
> (VIII, 617–19)

By contrast, Book VIII contains the famous affirmative vision of the shepherd and his dog rising out of the mist, the imagination's revelation to the solitary Wordsworth that independence and social relatedness are possible for man.

Such a vision, meaningful as the Solitary Reaper is meaningful, still does not show how Wordsworth himself can constitute pure meaning; he must clearly bring his own divided consciousness before the reflecting self and achieve their union. Therefore he starts afresh, as he says, in Book IX. Returning to a more detailed observation of the days in France, he finds himself and his fellows related in far more complex ways than he had earlier admitted. Beaupuy, for example, rises before his vision not only as the admirable lover of freedom, but also as an egalitarian aristocrat—like the poet, an apparent solitary dedicated to social relatedness. Vaudracour and Julia, so long an undiscovered code for Wordsworth and Annette, directly symbolize the personal caught up in the struggles of society and destroyed by them. In this whole French sequence and in the retrospect on it—the France of Book IV seen from the viewpoint of experience—Wordsworth shows himself both the involved friend and lover and the stranger with primary ties at home. After the betrayal of the hopes of France by English reaction, he was therefore doubly isolated, divorced by the Channel from his principles and Annette, and separated from his countrymen by his principles and emotional allegiances. While his fellow Britons prayed for victory, perhaps

> I only, like an uninvited Guest
> Whom no one own'd sate silent, shall I add,
> Fed on the day of vengeance yet to come?
>
> (X, 273–75)

Although he does not speak of his reconciliation with English con-
servatism, here, in the worst pain to which he can admit, is its
beginning. Desire for the communion of his fellows outweighed the
allegiance of this solitary to the ideals and people and delusions of
the Revolution, but this conversion from youth begot breakdown,
not serenity.

Only a fusion transcending both the struggling young self and
the evaluating older one could provide mental health, a fusion to
which he travels by the guiding image of the voyage. His mind had
moved smoothly to its proper development, he says early in Book XI,
except "when Spells forbade the Voyager to land" (XI, 49). And
Book XIII, the symbolic summary, opens with his trip westward
through Wales, to the top of Snowdon among all the Forms. There,
the archetype of the human mind in the glow of imagination, he is
an echo of the shepherd made conscious of his nature and function,
and a union of all the human conditions in the poem. The highest
imaginative reason has been his subject; the living mind is a river
which he has traced

> From darkness, and the very place of birth
> In its blind cavern

through its wandering that leads out into the total union of man,
nature, and the universe as

> The feeling of life endless, the great thought
> By which we live, Infinity and God.
>
> (XIII, 173–84)

He leaves us with the vision of the healed, transcendent, fused, and
creating self in a unified, living world, which he and we, as observers,
can pronounce the human ideal. The narrating self, like the saints in
Dante's paradise, is merely a cheerful part affirming the glory of the
imagining whole, a perfect mediator between our reflecting selves
and the universe around us. Opposing the vision of the lonely striving self beset on its moors by outer and inner chaos stands not a

universal reasoning and evaluating spokesman of humanity but a greater figure that subsumes them both: the towering, imagining mind on the mountain, a sovereign eminence more strongly anchored than Blake's or Shelley's in the world of striving man.

Like the autobiographical and occasional poems, Wordsworth's substantial fictions derive their shapes and major symbols from his fantasies of solitude, mediation, and union. The villain Oswald of *The Borderers* is a philosopher of alienation, of lonely dominance, one response of Wordsworth to betrayal and detachment from a natural social context, just as the hero Marmaduke is a seduced and entangled self which seeks reunion and serves, in moving always around the edges of society, as a stimulus to moral thought in its members. Similarly, Wordsworth's secularization in Cambridge, his fall from high living, provides the pattern for *Michael*'s Luke, indeed for all who abandon nature and the secure family for social diversions. Even the wagoner Peter Bell, a willing solitary rover in woods and on water, constitutes a close analogue, almost a burlesque, of the fallen poet who used to wander lonely as a cloud. All the notable personages in *Peter Bell*—the corpse, the ass, the dead man's son, the widow and her other children—and incidental elements like the offstage Methodist congregation have the one function of registering on Peter's sensibilities and making him responsive, drawing him to his fellows as the daffodils drew the poet to earthly life. Riding with the ass and corpse, Peter symbolically repeats his career and also reflects on it through his awakened universal self:

> *Now*, turned adrift into the past
> He finds no solace in his course. . . .
> (*Poetical Works*, II, 374)

As in *The Pilgrim's Progress* and *The Divine Comedy*, Peter has followed the conversion archetype of shocked awakening in middle life to God's messenger. His new religion, however, is sympathetic withdrawal into humble life.

The White Doe of Rylstone, Wordsworth's most complex fictional shaping of the world, builds largely on the symbolic projection of fantasies of isolation, echoing some elements of the Wordsworth family in the poet's youth. The main figures—the Doe, Francis, Emily, and old Norton—are wanderers in a charade of man's purpose and fate on earth. A "Fair Pilgrim" set off from human society, a missioned spirit of hope and grace, the Doe acts as intermediary for man and the divine, like the shepherd boy of the Intimations Ode or Peter Bell's summoners or the poet's inspired visions. In the persons of Francis and Emily, man struggles through chaos and sorrow for transcendent union; but within their circles they too are saving spirits who bring love and relatedness and life. When Francis is abandoned by his father as every man must be, his world (like Marmaduke's before him) briefly becomes a phantasm, a tottering dream (ll. 419–25). But since he persists in working to associate his rebellious father and his forlorn sister with the human rebirth around them, he regains meaning and harmony: after the sentencing of his father and brothers, Francis is reunited with them and accepted as their guide. Emily, whose world is shattered by her brother's guiltless death, returns to responsiveness and sanity by the agency of his surrogate the Doe, which does for her what babies do for other forlorn women in Wordsworth's poems: setting a pattern for dreadful exploitation by the Victorian novelists, Wordsworth gives Emily the moral and psychological rewards of maternity without affecting her virginity.[21] A luminous Una surviving Elizabethan turmoil, she is to be, like Dorothy for her brother William or like a poem for us, a mediator, a tie to the past and to the life of the world.

In his monumental *Excursion*, Wordsworth undertakes to move man from the hardness of Peter Bell or the confused despair of Emily into relatedness with others, to lure the archetypal solitary self and its neutral reflection, our representative the narrator, into social communion. Climbing a hill to open the poem, like Dante on his famous way to discovery, the narrator soon meets in the Pedlar both his instructive Virgil and his mediating Beatrice. As the poem makes clear, the Pedlar, a professional bringer of relevance and civilization, has been eager to form ties with everyone he has met; he has become the embodiment of the feeling intellect, the creative and sympathizing solitary rooted in his society rather than the sterile, detached, analytical reasoner. Like the reflecting self of *An Evening Walk* or *Descriptive Sketches* the heir of the eighteenth-century tradition from *The Spectator* to *The Task*, he provides a vantage for observation and panoramic sweep; but he is a unifying element in the archetypal mind, not a poeta.

The willful Solitary, the cautionary example and divisive mental element to whom the Pedlar conducts the narrator in Book II, appears after a funeral and is himself attracted to death. His domestic joy has gone with his children and wife, and a second attempt to hope and live through involvement in the French Revolution has been blasted. Despite the Solitary's experience, the Pedlar—the element of hope and social fruitfulness in the mind—urges him once again to leave his despairing thoughts and move into life. For stimulus and consolation the Pastor, a second reflecting and evaluating self, a sober and pious brother Imlac who adds religion's support to the Pedlar's vision of sympathy in nature and humanity, leads the other three in Books VI and VII through a survey of human journeys. Among these, a rejected suitor triumphs by willing the record of his love to his beloved; a miner walks "THE PATH OF RIGHTEOUSNESS"; a promising youth decays into a popular singer; a strong-minded woman bears a dissolute son; another mother is abandoned by her child's father, and dies after it to the mournful satisfaction of the listeners. The Pastor's message of consolation is community, a divinely inspired order whereby men naturally live and die in clear relationship to each other: a sermon like Edward Young's *Night Thoughts* deriving the theme of Gray's *Elegy* from the evidence in *Rasselas*.

In the remaining books, Wordsworth restates and expands the theme of community, the only hope against the encroaching, depressing, isolating, fragmenting march of material science and industry. Carrying the soberly joyous, mutually encouraging group of friends, their boat in Book IX assumes its traditional place as the emblematic medium of man's excursion through the variety of life:

> Right across the lake
> Our pinnace moves; then, coasting creek and bay,
> Glades we behold, and into thickets peep,
> Where couch the spotted deer . . .
> . . . till a natural pier
> Of jutting rock invited us to land.
> *(Poetical Works*, V, 305)

By the end of the poem, the Solitary, whose conversion to hope and humanity has passed a great stage under the care of his visitors, agrees to join them for another day. With the aid of other men and the free gifts of nature and time, the innocent, inspired, relating, and loving self has moved toward healing union with its pained, struggling, experienced other self. Through the excursion the group grows out of the sickly confining self but keeps roots within the fortress of mountains, the church, and England—a consoling spot of brightness amidst the gloom of nations, civilization's hope. The whole movement of the poem develops a vision of the serene and harmonious mind, consoled for loss and death, at rest in beauty in the universe; and the harmony implies a coming fullness of the individual, a sympathetic but very distinct identity, not submergence within the mass.

The ideal here is still *Tintern Abbey*'s or the Intimations Ode's, but discursive, analytical complexities have modified the intensity of the gaze into the life of things. Having found and accepted his place among people, Wordsworth seems to have lost the compelling need to image his exact, ambiguous position as poet. The move from aloof, traditional *poeta* in the early poems to organic representative of man in his highest condition was quick, and the awareness of this organic position as mediator animates the great period of his poetry. But as in the Ode Wordsworth says the loss of the imagination is his guarantee of immortality, so acquiring solidity seems to have cost him the poetic vision. Descending to communion in political and religious orthodoxy, he paid away the heights of imaginative mediation.

3. *The Projected Self: Division and Union*

Reflecting the sense of division which is one subject of *The Prelude* and provides whatever vitality exists in *The Excursion*, Wordsworth's poetry characteristically assumes a pattern of alternative possibilities. Although the moral weight attached to the elements varies with time and theme and genre, Wordsworth seems to create this twinning arbitrarily, even compulsively, from the fruitful swans and desolate people in the middle of *An Evening Walk* to the balancing of recollected and present scenes, of contrasted pairs of travelers, churches, visions, and social orders in the *Musings Near Aquapendente* of almost fifty years later. Sometimes he can keep the alternatives viable in an encompassing poetic world, as in the antithetical *Expostulation and Reply* and *The Tables Turned*, each of which is in turn a dialogue between opposing views: in the first, between a complex of action and reading on one hand and a "wise passiveness" on the other; in the second, between nature and the intellect, which here includes both science and art.[22] Usually, however, Wordsworth lacks the negative capability to rest in uncertainty; even where he refrains from formal conclusions, as in developing the different psychological conditions of himself and Dorothy in *Tintern Abbey* or the two careers of *The Brothers*, he seems to suggest a fusion into a higher meaning in the world of the poem which itself reflects the larger imagining mind. And his more elaborate reflective works do formally seek to move from division to integrity. *The Recluse*, his sketch for *The Prelude*, focuses mainly on the poet's need to reconcile the oppositions within himself and between himself and the outside world. In the longer, greater poem, Dorothy, Wordsworth's complement and companion in *The Recluse*, is like Coleridge importantly paired with him; and the lesser figures—the solitary veteran, the companions on the walking tour and on the climb up Snowdon, Beaupuy, the shepherd—appearing in separate episodes, are separately related to him. All of these people are primarily evidences that the outer world exists; they are mediating elements to feed the imagination and help it fuse the affirmative, aspiring self and the pained, despairing, guilty self in glowing union.

A number of the narratives involving twin selves appear to be animated by censored versions of urgent internal demands, and they often turn on the question of where to assign guilt. Such guilt may be evidently general and universal, incurred by all men who leave innocence and therefore most acute for poets, who are guardians of the fresh imagination. In *To H.C., Six Years Old* and the Intimations Ode, for example, a child appears as the acting alternative self of the poet who apostrophizes it, living in weightless visions and projecting his fears for the fate of poets and the imagination in the world.[23] In *Michael*, one fantasy of a hidden Eden maintained at the cost of a lost self competes with another fantasy of dangerous wandering in the world of experience. Peter Bell, penetrating to the recess, looks through the corpse and the ass to a private darkness, like a horrified Dimmesdale or Kurtz. Much later in *The Egyptian Maid* Merlin, the poet as guilty magician, brings an alternative personification of the pure imagination to Arthur's court in atonement for a grave sin.

Often, however, the pain appears to be more concretely rooted in the outer events of Wordsworth's life. *The Brothers*, for example, seems to indulge fantasies of Wordsworth's death as a punishment of his brother John and any other relatives who had abandoned him, and condemns them to guilty wandering; because of another sailor's drunken turbulence in *The Waggoner*, the hill-dwelling, respectable Ben—a comic projection of the poet as mediator and civilizer—loses his livelihood. Ten years after John's death, the old fantasies recurred in *Artegal and Elidure*, although this time division ends in union.[24] *She Dwelt among Untrodden Ways* and *I Traveled among Unknown Men* are as likely as *A Slumber Did My Spirit Seal* to reflect, as Coleridge suggested of the last, an imaginative terror at the thought of the death of Dorothy, of anyone else for whom Wordsworth could think himself responsible (like Annette Vallon or her daughter), or finally of his own childhood self. *Strange Fits of Passion*, even more than the other Lucy poems, again shows Wordsworth aware of the psychological mechanism by which one dreams the death of the beloved as an exercise in guilt, which is washed out by the discovery that she is well. In *Vaudracour and Julia*, Wordsworth's alternative self not only can blame older figures for the mistreatment of the beloved, but he has been tricked by them into the great guilt of killing a man—as if Wordsworth were saying, "This is what I should have had to do to remain with Annette." I do not insist on the sanctity of any of these diagnoses; I argue only that the people in Wordsworth's narratives, like Swift's personae and Johnson's characters, plausibly reflect the author's fantasies about himself.

When Wordsworth divides the self into figures of different ages, he tends to project the conditions of his formative years, often in terms of the change from innocence to experience. If one of his young men yields to corruption, he has been tempted by an older man: both a fashionable pattern, as in Byron and Shelley, and the echo of a permanent call from Genesis and Sophocles through Milton.[25] In the fictions, Wordsworth often follows patterns which blame his elders for his losses. The loathly-hag folktale *Goody Blake and Harry Gill*, for example, effectively generalizes some of his moral-psychological assumptions but is in appearance a long way from autobiography. When Goody Blake cuts pieces of young Harry Gill's hedge for firewood—when she attempts to steal warmth for her cold age—he rebuffs her, incurring the guilt which determines his subsequent life. His guilt has, moreover, brought with it the chill of age, an implied equivalence which affects such quintessential poems as the Intimations Ode. In *The Borderers*, naked fantasies about young Marmaduke's corruption by the evil, potent, older stranger Oswald play also with Oswald's youthful fall and suggest an inevitable cycle.[26] Luke's seducers in swinging London were presumably companions of his own age; but old Michael, himself innocent and incomplete like his sheepfold, has allowed his lamb to stray among them unguarded. Echoing the same attitudes, *The White Doe of Rylstone* opposes the virtuous Francis and his father over the fundamental issue of religion. Whereas the father waves the bloody Catholic banner of the dead past, the son affirms the new dispensation, which is certified by God through the Doe as the faith to mediate organically between tradition (the living past) and man's future. The old man's courage and his absolute fidelity to an ideal, aspects of intentions innocent as Michael's, somewhat mitigate his guilt; but the youth and his sister are completely blameless. As in *Vaudracour and Julia*, the old and what they represent cause the misery of the young; as in *Michael*, nothing can prevent the separation defined by time and change; as in *Simon Lee the Old Huntsman*, nature supports the victory of the young over the old.

Where autobiography might have been inferred by his contemporaries, Wordsworth moderated the projection of unorthodox attitudes, but he did not blot them out. In the mildly fictional *Excursion* he made much of the superior wisdom of the old Pedlar and the authoritative Pastor, but yet provided the Solitary with vigorous rejoinders. Wordsworth never wrote the continuation which was to refute the Solitary's objections and fully socialize—and age—him: as the permanently rebelling aspect of Wordsworth's mind, he should not and could not be suppressed. In the Intimations Ode, Wordsworth looked directly at his contrasting elements of youth and age, and found there a forlorn balance, a therapy for loss in age, a consolation for what adult experience makes of youth's innocent magic:

> Hence in a season of calm weather
> Though inland far we be,
> Our Souls have sight of that immortal sea,
> Which brought us hither,
> Can in a moment travel thither,
> And see the Children sport upon the shore
> And hear the mighty waters rolling evermore.
> (ll. 162–68)

Like social classes and psychological and moral states, youth and age form divisions, alternative conditions of being, which are incomplete as poles but can at certain times be fused in the glorious triumph of the imagination which Wordsworth pictured in *The Prelude*. Such fusion is the goal of his poet and his poem.

If the pattern of division and alternation often forms the way into a poem by Wordsworth—the proposition—union is the resolution to which it leads. As so often with Wordsworth's fellow romantics, union is his favorite symbol and ultimate vision, his fulfillment as man and poet and his intuition of God's purpose. He gropes for it directly in his lyrical and reflective poems, projects it in the parables at the core of his narratives,[27] mourns its loss in the Intimations Ode and elsewhere, and tries to rebuild it from its elements, as in *The Prelude*.

Since all things are aspects of the One and of each other, nature and human experience everywhere offer Wordsworth symbols or agents of the union. All intense hopes and promises, for example, are versions of each other and of the one Form of the soul's expectations from life. The utopian dream of the French Revolution is no more or less the bright vision burst by the light of common day than is the youthful promise of John Wordsworth; and both are early glories lost to the maturing poet along with the child's unlimited imagination, of which they are a part. Every union of brother and sister, parent and child, man and wife, or friend and friend constitutes the same symbol of all human intimacy, the universal Form of love. Among so many, certain recurrent elements in nature are particularly convenient images of the union of all things, some like the rainbow and the river having been divinely selected for the purpose. The confluence of streams as a symbol of the grandeur of time and natural growth forms a major structural device in *The River Dudden*, the *Ecclesiastical Sonnets*, and *The Prelude*; throughout the poetry, lifting mist and fog suggest the removal of blemishes to make union manifest; mountains and caves, the serene hidden pool, and the still moment often image the harmonious mind; world-filling sound announces harmonious union, as does the quiet ascent of smoke from fireplaces, to blend with the air and tie man to the sky.[28] The features of Wordsworth's native landscape, like the features of his human involvements, become elements in his recurrent attempts to catch the Form of relatedness and union.

Even the frequent parallels of humble and grand in Wordsworth's nature poems (from *To a Daisy* of 1802 to *The Contrast: the Parrot and the Wren* of 1825) reflect genuine alternative selves which he wants to resolve, rather than simple exercises in revenge like Smart's fables. Although Wordsworth's respect for the ordinary may derive, like Smart's identification with it, from his class, Wordsworth's middle origin makes mediation congenial. Examples of his wish to show the high as rising normally from the low in all areas of experience could be cited almost interminably, from the Preface to the *Lyrical Ballads* to the poems of his old age. In Book VII of *The Prelude*, for example, he speaks of the vast amount of the ordinary at the base of life, which yet forms the source of the more profound feelings:

> not to be despis'd
> By those who have observ'd the curious props
> By which the perishable hours of life
> Rest on each other, and the world of thought
> Exists, and is sustain'd.
>
> (VII, 491–95)

Like Wordsworth's ideal of diction that fuses the noble and the ordinary, the poet mediates among men by bringing them relatedness, whether by making them feel for others like themselves or by representing them at their highest in communicating with a living universe.

Wordsworth's move from the conception of unity as synthesis, which had been Pope's and Johnson's, to the sense of organic fusion came early in his poetic career. In *An Evening Walk* the persona is still concerned with making harmony of what he sees, with weaving the figure of himself as poeta with such visual and emotional elements as day merging into night, the swans' procession, and the sinking widow with her dying children. Like the poeta of *The Seasons* or Collins' *Ode to Evening*, he also shapes the distant, mingling sounds and the visions, landscapes, and prospects into a solemn blend appropriate to vague and melancholy sensations, and he responds sympathetically to scenes which he reflects but does not create:

> No purple prospects now the mind employ
> Glowing in golden sunset tints of joy,
> But o'er the sooth'd accordant heart we feel
> A sympathetic twilight slowly steal. . . .
>
> (*Poetical Works*, I, 34)

But by the time of *My Heart Leaps Up When I Behold*, Wordsworth's more characteristic and more romantic vision of unity concentrated in one natural element was already confirmed. The leaping of the heart is man's directly intuitive, involuntary affirmation of unity with a living universe that has called to him. Attached to the vision, of the arch in the heavens and the poet successfully yearning toward it, are all the essential elements of fullness: man called by nature outside him and responding; the self integral over the span of its existence; man uniting with other men, through a universality of which the Bible is witness; and man united by natural piety to what-ever is divine in the universe.[29] The poet seems to stand alone with the rainbow, the emissary of man striving toward union with the emissary of the world. Unlike Manfred or Prometheus, he is the average man raised to intensity, an impassioned mediator rather than a sole aggressive divinity.

Wordsworth's great early poem on the theme of unity, which intensely draws together most of its strands, is *Lines Composed A Few Miles above Tintern Abbey*.[30] Through a lyric form in itself new and yet growing organically from the earlier ode, he brings us to see his imaginative vision at the end of the strophe and antistrophe, and in the epode shows himself the glowing mediator between another person and all the elements of the universe. In the first long move-ment, he suggests that time, which divides him from the self that last looked from this spot, paradoxically unites him with that and other former selves through memory. The steep and lofty cliffs before him recall his past and "connect/ The landscape with the quiet of the sky," and the blended farmhouses show that man lives here in har-mony with nature. As the poet's surveying mind recollects a later stage in the past, he realizes that his unconscious response to the scene has led him to mystic experience of the One, a sense of living intensely in and through the universe. After such awareness, he can open the second movement of the poem (lines 58–111) with a feel-ing for the future as well as the present effect on him of the natural scene. His various selves, his various stages of response to nature and man, are fused by his present awareness of the Wye. Nature's sounds now convey to him the whole melancholy music of the universe, the grandeur beyond sensation alone, arousing

> a sense sublime
> Of something far more deeply interfused,
> Whose dwelling is the light of setting suns,
> And the round ocean and the living air,
> And the blue sky, and in the mind of man:
> A motion and a spirit, that impels
> All thinking things, all objects of all thought,
> And rolls through all things.
>
> (*Poetical Works*, II, 262)

But again, and even in exaltation, he is a mediator above all, a man willingly tied to the humanity of which Dorothy is his present representative. In the structural equivalent of the epode, Wordsworth senses his former self in his sister's voice and "the shooting lights" of her "wild eyes"; therefore, like the scene, and with the help of the scene, she binds him to his past, to herself as another human being, and to nature. He urges her to give herself to the influence of nature, so that later

> when thy mind
> Shall be a mansion for all lovely forms,
> Thy memory be as a dwelling-place
> For all sweet sounds and harmonies,

she will remember him with thoughts that in turn will solace her amidst the pains of life. Even if he is away then or dead, she will recall this intensely unifying moment, his holy joy in it, and (in an echo of the opening) his feeling that after many years of absence, the elements of the scene were dearer to him "both for themselves and for thy sake!"

Wordsworth not only says that he has been intimate with the One in this poem, but he demonstrates it, in the composition of scene and thought and in the symbolic placing and moving of the actors: under the feelings and ideas, he shows us first himself drinking in the natural picture; then, himself examining his mind, reflecting, and returning to the outer world again; finally, himself fervently addressing his wild-eyed sister and affirming the intimate union of their response to meaningful nature and its formal emanations.[31] Astonishingly, he evokes from the place and their two persons a sense of the self-contained harmony of nature, of the responsive harmony within the poet of his past and present and future, of the harmonious tie between the unity within him and the unity without, of the union of himself and his sister through their identical actual and imagined emotional states (his of the past and hers now, hers of the future and his now), and of the living union which he asserts of all beings in the universe, a union apprehended by the creative, imagining self which can hold all his world suspended in the moment. Under and through the passionate perception and thought, the image of humanity striving successfully toward unity in and with nature forms the symbolic core of Wordsworth's vision.

As *My Heart Leaps Up When I Behold* and *Tintern Abbey* imply and the poems on distraught women affirm, the human mind badly needs an external focus, an anchor in the outside world, to prevent its drift from reality and union. Natural phenomena like a rainbow or a tree can act as emissaries and stimuli; but a human being like Dorothy or the old Cumberland beggar or Lucy can more directly perform the poet's function of bringing new awareness through the sympathetic imagination. Under the properly stimulating imaginative circumstances, as in *Resolution and Independence* or *The Solitary Reaper*, any figure can be such a healing symbol of unity even without formal communication. On a calm morning after a stormy night, in the midst of pleasant sights on the road, the poet of *Resolution and Independence* inexplicably feels depressed. At this point he meets a leech gatherer, an emanation of the universe who unconsciously unites life and death, waking and sleep, time and eternity, man and nature; and the poet regains harmony. Like the stored spot of serenity that enshrined the daffodils, the old man has been perceived and transformed by the imagining self, a power allied to nature's. He will be available at future times as a vision of man at home in the world, to reconcile the poet to his life.[32] In *The Solitary Reaper*, the imagining power overcomes the differences of time, place, sex, and occupation to fuse the history and quality of man into a moment out of time, where it blends with the essence of the nightingale and the cuckoo and the Hebrides. It ties the highland girl to "battles long ago" and to "Arabian sand" and transforms her song, unintelligible to the discursive reason, into the voice of mankind. Traveling alone, Wordsworth sees a vision of striving man rising out of mankind's eternal average plain, and experiences with it identification and union. The poem does not have the complexity of sensation, the ecstatic detail and concretely weighted thought of *Tintern Abbey*, but it stands in simple, intense fullness as Wordsworth's most successful emblematic vision of humanity, the sort of general truth which Thomson, Gray, and Johnson sought and only partially found.

All of *The Prelude* pursues this same world sense which can heal the self and make it occasionally capable and always aware of total relatedness. Necessarily, this elaboration of *Tintern Abbey* projects the loss of innocence and its transcendence, the movement from a primitive Eden and the return to a greater, consciously grasped Eden.[33] As against Johnson and Gray, whose earthly paradises are kind delusions encouraged by the supervisors of youth, and as against Goldsmith and Sterne, who have lost Eden forever along with childhood,

Wordsworth in *The Prelude* celebrates a faint, uncertain, inconstant, but vastly hopeful reconciliation of the songs of innocence and those of experience. The sense of the imagining self—incorporating, observing, and transcending the idiosyncratic and universal selves—permits Wordsworth a new, tentative hope for earthly harmony. I emphasize the tentativeness, for while he often delights in the restoration of harmony, he is everywhere, even in *Tintern Abbey*, sensitive to its loss. The change implies an elegiac sorrow for the aching joys and dizzy raptures and grassy splendors, the essence of the lost youth for which one can only seek a gentler compensation. Consolation is his lasting offer, not ecstatic rebirth. He is greatly an elegist, a singer of the past and the bits of recompense that we have for its loss, a portrait painter of the spirit in sunset: the author of the Intimations Ode.

4. The Elegiac Self: Mourning and Consolation

Since Wordsworth's subjects are visionary innocence and the retrospective sense of loss and consolation, he is a poet of spring and fall, transition and relatedness, not often of desolation or brilliant sunshine. Against eroding time and chance, he usually affirmed the triumph of harmonizing recollection that binds the present to the long human past, the return of individual events not to Pope's sterile turbulence but to a living sea. In his fullest vision, the self seeks a union which is based on sympathy of the aged with the yearnings of youth: not the observation of a distinct idiosyncratic by a distinct universal, but the living moment when fallen reflective man and acting, dreaming youth come together. Both are universals; both are anchored in concrete sensations; both are distinct and yet organically related in a larger imagining self which encompasses also their tie to the universe. Before the eye of the mature reflective poet is the struggling self, luminously at home in youth, doomed by experience to division, wandering, and guilt, and redeemable by a hope that works through the imagination.

The individual event, the single life, the inspiring moment, the dreams of youth, and the exalted prospects for mankind are alternatives of the same spot of time which outwardly must pass in an early burst, but which leaves a recurrent sense of meaning to console the reflecting mind. Sometimes in the poems this mind must summon the valid experience from the bounded and ordered world of memory so that it can evaluate the struggling lives that it has known. Generally, the consoling intimation of meaning derives from that which remains, whether a mental image like Emily Norton or a physical relic like the graves of *The Excursion*, the stones of Michael's sheepfold, or the weeds of Margaret's ruined cottage. In the Intimations Ode and elsewhere, life is the very spark of memory, that which is extra, above the material or routine. The recompense for loss is memory; the worst loss, forgetting what is lost.[34]

From the beginning of his career, Wordsworth sees external nature and the memory as primarily stimuli to the self's creation of meaning, purveyors of images to relate the self to its own past and to the collective human past, particularly through its awareness of loss and consolation. The short lyrics, which focus on one emotion, tend to derive it from such sensations. *To a Sky-Lark*, for example, praises the bird largely because its song pulls the poet from despondency to the hope of recompense. In *To the Cuckoo*, which Wordsworth catalogued under the intense "Poems of the Imagination," the bird's song not only recalls his boyhood responses but stimulates him to recreate them:

> O blessèd Bird! the earth we pace
> Again appears to be
> An unsubstantial, faery place;
> That is fit home for Thee!
> (*Poetical Works*, II, 208)

It has restored the world of his imagination, of which as always he feared the loss. In *The Two April Mornings* and its companion piece *The Fountain*, Old Mathew suffers the sensation which is at the core of the later Ode, the fear of losing the sense of loss:[35]

> "My eyes are dim with childish tears,
> My heart is idly stirred,
> For the same sound is in my ears
> Which in those days I heard.

"Thus fares it still in our decay:
And yet the wiser mind
Mourns less for what age takes away
Than what it leaves behind."
(*Poetical Works*, IV, 72)

From the rainbow and Lucy to the prosy rivers and sunsets of Wordsworth's later sequences, his short poems center on symbols which evoke through memory the eternally related pair of elegy—mourning and rebirth.

The surveys and narratives elaborate this union of loss and recompense through the use of more varied projections of the self. In the two early poems, for example, the melancholy poeta responsive to evening, sunset, and the gloom of age luxuriates in a vague sense of deprivation: *An Evening Walk* and *Descriptive Sketches* are full of *weltschmerz*, sensations of lost vitality, and reflections on the brevity of man's day on earth, for which the uncertain antidote is human sympathy. In Wordsworth's richer poems the element of retrospect in the narrator's position, as in *Guilt and Sorrow* and *Michael*, seems to emanate from the conception of memory as both judge and shaper of meaning.

Meaning ultimately resides in the reflecting mind, where intensity has been smoothed and modified but not destroyed by removal from the pressures of incoherent circumstances. Even if the mind can no longer raise itself by the creative imagination to a sense of the emotion beautifully ordered by recollection, at least it can sympathetically see into the life of things and bring back its vision. One such reconstituted perception, *Michael*, centers in human problems intensely developing in a hidden recess, circumscribed and ordered for the tranquillity of the perceiving mind. Wordsworth bring us "from the public way" in the first line, to the hollow within the mountains and its emblematic ruins, promising that the story will "delight . . . a few natural hearts" and prove useful to poets who will be alternative versions of himself. In the actual tale, the embodiment of Michael's hopes dissolves in "evil courses," but this loss of his second self, his imaged youth, carries some indefinable consolation, the "comfort in the strength of love." Reaching out of the tale, the memory of serene love and hope resides in the crumbling sheepfold, which awakens sympathy and evokes human meaning in the minds of the narrator and others who knew the shepherd. The narrator, in turn, provides the poem itself; like Pope's *Rape of the Lock* or Gray's *Elegy*, the poem is a frail memorial to stimulate not the reader's acceptance of any moral orthodoxy but his sense of sharing man's eternal lot.

Like *Michael, The White Doe of Rylstone* memorializes human passions rising from insoluble problems, mourns the extinction of a family and a way of life, and yet finds a weight of consoling meaning in the awareness of the past. As all life is engulfed by time, the rebel Nortons have been swallowed centuries ago by storm and change. With them has gone the religion of the Banner, a brilliant dream which had to yield to more soberly fruitful qualities, as the early splendor had to pass from the poet of the Ode, and the utopian visions from *The Excursion*'s Solitary:

> The lordly Mansion of its pride
> Is stripped; the ravage hath spread wide
> Through park and field, a perishing
> That mocks the gladness of the Spring!
> (*Poetical Works*, III, 331)

Like Peter Bell, Emily comes to a new and calmer life, her sufferings fused with nature's consolation. At the time of the story, only the Doe remains, the visible sign of divine recompense, the memorial of violence resolved, combining within herself the functions of the old leech gatherer, Michael's sheepfold, Peter Bell's ass, and the Ode's lone tree and flower, the birds and rainbow and daffodils, indeed all the stimuli to man's reconciling mind. Victorious over the Banner and confirmed by the ruin of the priory and by nature as God's emissary, she is a token of the transmutation of the turbulent past into sober hope. The positiveness, even the cheeriness, of the orthodoxy limits our responses, whereas the sheepfold lets us range indefinitely; she speaks to a benevolently run protestant society, whereas Michael's world included all theologies and none.

In *The Excursion* Wordsworth designed the Solitary to be a large tragic archetype that subsumes all the other painfully experienced moral agents in the narratives; in contrast with Michael ambiguously saved by the purity of his life, and Emily and Francis Norton stamped with God's official seal, the Solitary can find in our world a psychological medicine available to all. Beginning with the mysteriously consoling story of Margaret, social and individual dislocations are seen as aspects of each other, of the central archetype of man's cyclic hope and disappointment. As Margaret and the Solitary have in the bitter course of life lost their early dream, so their whole society has been increasingly enslaved by the material intellect at the expense of areas of vital communion. Wordsworth and the Wanderer insist that the social loss lies in the passing of such local customs as chanting funeral processions, not in the destruction of delusive dreams about the instantaneous brotherhood of man (Book II, 546–52). Against the Intimations Ode's faith in a general social responsiveness as some recompense for the loss of the private imagination, in *The Excursion* men can invest their hopes in specific and therefore slight measures like state-supported rudimentary education.

But even the Wanderer's ecstasies at the prospect of universal literacy (IX, 290 ff.) cannot wholly destroy Wordsworth's main thesis and vision, that all hopefulness is a mark of human promise. Rebuilding and attaching to the French Revolution all the yearning visions which had been shattered by the deaths of his wife and children, the Solitary had given an earnest of his willingness to be drawn out of himself, to be saved by a less delirious but more constructive faith in improving society. Without unrealistic expectations but with prospects of usefulness and sympathy, he is likely to rejoin the human community, as the lonely mountain hamlets—his parallels—are the seminal elements that join in a free England which itself constitutes the vital hope for continuity and union of an enslaved world. Characteristically, the visions of lake, ram, hills, and nation, the underlying movement from aloofness to community, far outweigh the specific thesis. Consolation, as always in Wordsworth, comes from a sense of totality and understanding, not from argument.

While *The Prelude* also relates the social to the individual, Wordsworth's direct aim is lyrical rather than epic; his song is the crisis in the poet more than the program for society. His shocked response to the reign of terror and to England's role in destroying the dream of political liberty creates an overwhelming vision of the pained, dissociated self, which he makes no pretense of patching with programs of social uplift. As in the Intimations Ode, his great fear is betraying the gleam of the poetic imagination, the private ability to create unity and meaning. Suitably beginning the poem with the unexplained feeling of rebirth, he finds a recurrent, mysterious pattern of intensity and deprivation, which has moved in him from the loss of the first magnificence after early infancy:

> For now a trouble came into my mind
> From unknown causes. I was left alone,
> Seeking the visible world, nor knowing why.

> The props of my affections were remov'd,
> And yet the building stood, as if sustain'd
> By its own spirit!
>
> (II, 291–96)

He attempts to trace the "unknown causes" within himself, and to discover the conditions under which the trouble could recurrently be healed, but as in *Resolution and Independence* the moods are ultimately mysterious, part of the nature of man which ties him to other men and to the universe. Therefore the poem is hopeful, singing restoration and not despair; through love and the imagination—private and inherent qualities whose social application he leaves to others—he has been able to achieve the true recompense for the early loss, its transcendence in unity and relationship.

Wordsworth's most concentrated expression of reveries of loss and recompense is his *Ode on Intimations of Immortality from Recollections of Early Childhood*, his age's great elegy for the passing of youth, innocence, vitality, and imagination.[36] As a single tree and a field in stanza iv remind the poet taking stock of himself in the world, he has lost his exultant feelings, the visionary gleam, the glory and the dream, the transforming imagination of the happy shepherd boy before him and the six-year-old prophet dreaming of immense possibilities. In stanza ix begins the true consolation, the awareness that after the inevitable loss of the child's creating imagination and the private ecstasy, the adult has two compensations: the faith, guaranteed by the ache of longing, that they are natural to the soul and will shine clear even after the loss of droning earthly life; and human sympathy, the ability to grow out of the self to share a vision for all mankind.

Above all, though the adult can no longer live in the unity unconsciously like the shepherd boy or invent it like the six-year-old at play, he can symbolically participate in it through his understanding:

> The Clouds that gather round the setting sun
> Do take a sober colouring from an eye
> That hath kept watch o'er man's mortality;
> Another race hath been, and other palms are won.
> Thanks to the human heart by which we live,
> Thanks to the tenderness, its joys, and fears,
> To me the meanest flower that blows can give
> Thoughts that do often lie too deep for tears.

In losing the gleam, he has suffered all the losses to which all mortals are subjected by time and chance. Through understanding he has reached the grand consolation: meaning, the assurance of relatedness with all things that live, have lived, and shall live. Characteristically, the figure extended before us is divested of solitary radiance, but he gains in its place the recognition of immortal relatedness. As an archetypal acting self, he is doomed to the ordinary and the mortal; as the self that remembers and reflects, he can at once merge with what he was in the triumphant past and stand with mankind in awareness of man's significance. The consolation, therefore, includes the idea of growth to something valuably harmonious, not restoration to an earlier pinnacle. Nothing can bring back the ecstatic transcendence, the dominance of the individual imagination over all conditions of life; but a tranquil and continuous sense of harmony is no small recompense for intermittent ecstasy.

Mediating between us and the Poet of the Intimations Ode—and *The Prelude* and other lyrics—posed before the world is the self writing the poem, in his turn an agent of relationship and understanding. This reflective self is not a norm like Swift's implied self, or the universal sympathizing, all-experiencing self of Johnson, but a spokesman for collective adult man reporting on the mystery and wonder of developing human consciousness. Like the Swiftian norm, the reflective self is responsible for pointing out all the most complex and subtle, as well as direct and powerful, evidences of the human phenomenon before us. But he looks with admiration, with more than Johnsonian sympathy, since the struggling self before him gropes to recapture its grandest condition, union of feeling, thought, and imagination.

Responding intensely to experience with sensations of guilt and loss, with a horror of submergence in dead chaos, man in this vision can arrive at a blankness emptier than Gulliver's and more absurd than Rasselas', but through imaginative sympathy he can instead fuse sensations of his radiant past with awareness of the condition of others. Unlike Thomson and Johnson, two earlier voyagers committed to the outside world, Wordsworth in his poems symbolically retreats to a base in the past and the Cumberland hills. But as against Fielding, Smollett, Goldsmith, and Dickens, whose substitutes often return— escape—to an ideal country home, he pursues a goal of sympathy and union through contemplation, understanding, meaning. The observing, reflective self is the mediating element in the poet, whether narrating fictions about alternative selves or directly relating the acting self to the reader, as the acting poet mediates among men now, the external world of nature, and man of the past and the future.

For Wordsworth the basis of harmony is an awareness within the self of its own alternative impulses; from that can come sensitivity to life and integrity outside, both in man and in the rest of the universe. Pain and evil are separation—that is, the isolation of a part of the self from the remainder of that self and of all selves. The innocent self, which lives most purely and intensely in the transcendent imagination, discovers otherness and the mortality of separation and discontinuity when it moves into the world of time. As he ages, therefore, man must seek understanding, sympathy, relatedness—the virtues of the mature self whose evaluative function has been swelled by the remains of the imagination—in place of the radiant vision. Or rather, as an outgrowth of the vision, man can respond so organically as to incorporate a sense of the imagination's effects in memory and feed the hopes of the self with that sense. For the spontaneously inventive imagination the adult substitutes the recollection and recognition of symbolic Forms from which the poet as quintessential man can derive meaning for all men. As Wordsworth at the foot of Rydal Mount could interpret the peaks and the shepherds to readers in cities, so his poetic imagination could unite him to the universe, and his reflective self could relate his illuminated moments to his general course of life. The vision which once was, always remains for consolation, for assurance of the vitality of the self and the world. While individual joys and pains are swallowed up in the sea of time, they have also been infused into the Forms of human renewal through the archetypally human mind, and they remain always available for discovery and dissemination by the poetic imagination.

That this vision of the role of the self in the world is based on Wordsworth's experiences the perceptions and admissions of *The Prelude* make brilliantly clear. Equally characteristic, and developed in various degrees of self-consciousness throughout his writings, are a sense of guilt and isolation, a need for outer human contact, a yearning for eminence imaginatively and yet prudently modified by an affinity for the base of the ordinary, and a search for future guarantees in a lost past. For all of these attitudes and orientations Wordsworth's biography provides ample evidence; and for some of them at least, so does the pressure of a bewildered time that urgently sought a new order.

VI

THE AUTHOR'S SELF
AND ITS TIME

1. Man in the World

IF I HAVE been conducting a moderately fair examination, it is clear
that a writer's vision of both man and the world is seriously affected
by how he sees himself. Whatever he intensely and originally imagines
reflects his habitual sense of his moral and social condition. To order
the immensity of data, for example, a writer's sense of himself acting in the world may lead him to seek one right way or a variety
of equally right ways, to aim for tentative affirmation or a triumphant
certainty, to wish for a selection, a synthesis, or a fusion of meaning.
His advice to withdraw into pleasures and fancies within the self, or to
move outward; his view of evil as a perversion, a negation, or an
antithesis of the good; his idea of the function of art; his uses of
universally available narrative patterns (the journey, the Fall) or
situations (climbing mountains, struggling or sauntering among
crowds) or metaphors (from nature, from current science)—all seem
bound with, even emanating from, his nature and projected destinies
as they fill his reveries.

Although society provides contemporaries like Pope and Thomson
with similar intellectual contexts (for example, the divinely ordained
chain of being, Newtonian astronomy, uniformitarianism, decorum
in genres) and subjects (for example, the civilizing process, the spread
of empire, contemporary manners, psychology), even they imagine
very different worlds. For Pope, the surface of life is a chaos consisting of the vital few amidst vast numbers of the dead and worthless: a traditional satirist's world, it is true, but in his day and place

peculiarly suitable for a crippled, middle-class Catholic poet with aristocratic friends and Tory sympathies. His moral and artistic code assumes a divine artist above all distinguishing between dross and the rare living gold; man at his grandest, respectfully emulating Him, shapes a world of order through exclusion and discrimination. Under the jarring massive surfaces, however, lies a vision in no way indebted to genre, a world where the delicate and elegant approximate the ideal harmony, as the recently invented calculus approached truth by minute increments. Where an uncompromising moralist like Swift urges right action, direct and vigorous cleaving through chaos along God's well-advertised expressway, Pope exalts civilized equilibrium, a world where physical, social, and psychological forces are held in dynamic tension through the artist's shaping and selecting vision. Out of a quite different orientation, Thomson sees himself in a world of treasure everywhere available among the worthless slag to reward the devoted seeker. For such a vision, no attitude is more natural than the ironic duality of *The Castle of Indolence*, where the escapist fancy is repeatedly invaded by the daylight needs of art and industry; and no form is more appropriate than *The Seasons*' bastard georgic, privileged to plunder all traditions from Virgil's and Milton's to the *Metamorphoses* and the Italian novelle and the missionary's travel diary.

Period, politics, intellectual orientation, and even literary tradition may affect the terms of an author's discourse, but they go a very little way in explaining the differences among the writers on the themes that recur throughout history. Theoretically willing to subordinate their idiosyncratic selves to man's highest traditions, Swift and Pope are properly classical, universalist, and cosmopolitan, whereas Wordsworth (in this respect echoing Fielding, Sterne, and the sentimentalists) argues for a sequence of loyalties from the responsive idiosyncratic self outward by degrees to the family, the community, and the nation. But to resolve the conflicting demands of the individual and society, the writers follow the direction of temperament or self vision: Swift and Wordsworth are fascinated by the possibilities of individual power, Pope is attracted though not held, and Johnson has ironic doubts. Pope offers dynamic balance, but Swift and Wordsworth join to exalt their individuals, using society largely as context. For Johnson, aware that even his extraordinary abilities could only marginally outdo others, individuals tend to stand out from their background, but not to dominate the scene: when allowed full growth, they can all imagine with formless grandeur but accomplish little.

Since for memorable writers form is imagination's plastic tool, genre can only partially explain such differences in stance; as pamphlets on colonial government, Swift's *A Modest Proposal* and Johnson's *Taxation No Tyranny* share nothing but effectiveness. Despite the diversity of genres or of other formal molds like personae, a writer's identity, or idiosyncrasy, or fundamental literary personality seems to lie in the characteristics and patterns of movement and response of his projected actors. Under the qualities of the individual and local context, of the particular mad persona of any one work, the same wild elements range in openness from the Yahoo and the author of the *Directions to Servants* to the comparative sophistication of Gulliver and the Modest Proposer—elements carefully removed from Swift's universal, humane norm. Especially characterizing Swift are his recurrent guilt and expectation of death, his fear of disappointment combined with passionate ambition, and his sense of injury, betrayal, and abandonment, all of which appear in private letters, even in the midst of success in the *Journal to Stella*, and underlie the movement and rhetoric of his most elaborate works. Such orientations, attitudes, tendencies, or self-conceptions—I contend for a stance toward self and the world, not for psychological or sociological labels—can not only affect preferences in tone, but can also inform a variety of tones, as well as a variety of genres. The attitudes that I see combining in Swift clearly support his bent for derision, but they also suit him as dogmatist. Suspicious of the chaos of the imagination and of contemporary society, he was yet fascinated by it as an arena for the mocking advocate of the low. To overcome the final chaos of death he indulged reveries of eminence, of coming to a high point in this life and in the memory of succeeding generations, which he mocked in visions of the mad projectors and accepted soberly as preacher of single, clear truths. Stemming the opposing waters of cranky individualism and mere conformism to authority, the decent Drapier or Church of England Man or Dean of St. Patrick's—the sane poet and the quickened minister—follows the divinely cloven path.

Like Swift, Johnson loved to proffer oddities, idiosyncrasies, and fanciful grotesqueries, which he formally invited the universal reader to compare with normality. But where Swift's orthodoxy sought a single received truth among the clotted lies, Johnson's mind was intensely empirical, determined on making truths only out of actual experience. Forced into introspection by damaged sight and hearing and therefore especially responsive to contemporary Lockean emphasis on the problem of isolation and communication, Johnson is a psychologist even more than a moralist. Wherever he turns, he notices the mind's fluidity and uncertainty, its often unconscious tendencies to maintain indolence by feeding on accepted and therefore outmoded theories. In pilotless mental drift lies the greatest danger, and yet there are no sure guides; in a vision like Cowper's, whom it confirmed in madness, he sees that man must make absolute moral choices with a fluid mind in a plastic universe. Perhaps as a consequence, his recurrent subject, youth's passage from hopeful innocence to disappointment and knowledge, combines idiosyncratic absurdity with general inevitability, and his tone fuses sympathy and therapeutic irony. If life is a grim joke full of impossible decisions, any attempt to go on deserves some kindness. Heartily desperate, Johnson urges us to fill the mind, which is all that we can know for certain, to keep at bay its own chaos as it wrestles to make order of outside chaos.

In contrast with Swift, for whom the truth awaits anyone who repudiates pride, Johnson sees man as constantly tempted by delusive shortcuts to truth. For Swift, groups of people are mobs made up of prideful, jostling, ambitious lunatics; for Johnson, eccentrics pathetically seeking mental ease. Characteristically, the delusion of Johnson's figures takes the shape of his own danger: yielding the will in order to follow obsessively a part of reality, accepting a simple formula like a vacationer bound to rural clichés or an author bound to a genre. While Johnson himself uses genre as a way in to examine a literary work, he tends to deprecate its arbitrary and therefore facile formality, thereby clearing the way for Coleridge's objections to pouring new poems into old bottles. Since the fundamental movement of his own imaginative writing reflects his sense of expectation cut short or contravened, the subverted form fits it best. Instead of indolently borrowing clichés, one must struggle to wrest from reality the general truths on which to act, one must be ready with all one's forces for the intellectual needs of the moment. Constantly fighting off chance and the rigidity of death, Johnson through his projected figures argues the mental duty and urgent need combined, to find reality and act upon it.

Like Pope, Wordsworth is intensely aware of specialness, of separateness, at the same time that he sees the highest good as union. But where Pope could ground in prevailing philosophies a sense of separate identity within a universal harmony, Wordsworth was forced to develop his own conception of a glowing self fused with a universe alive in all its parts. Reflecting his early secure immersion in the world of nature and his own sensations, Wordsworth sees man as beginning in ecstasy, from which he is weaned into the dull world of the commonplace. To the favorite narrative pattern of Thomson, Pope, Goldsmith, and Johnson—the move from innocence—Wordsworth adds a major element which merges his own experience with the contemporary currents of evangelicalism and romanticism: the heightened consciousness which is consolation for loss and guilt. When the sequence is complete, the archetypal wanderer through life—Wordsworth in the Ode, or Peter Bell, or Emily Norton—accepts grief and transcends pain; otherwise, the character is doomed to continuing guilt or madness, although like Margaret or Michael his story may provide consolation to others. Recollected in tranquillity, such consolation may justify the sin and loss entailed by living and dying—the whole of man's lot. Wordsworth's *Excursion* and *Prelude* are, consequently, like Milton's two epics, new affirmations of the worth of living. His elegiac vision of the recompense (especially in the Ode)—the conscious, sympathetic imagination—transcends sin and guilt by universalizing them and incorporating them into his unity; his whole body of poetry recurrently assures man—a projection of the sensitive orphaned boy who had to leave his hills—that human union does, after all, make up for disillusion and individual death.

Besides infusing their idiosyncratic selves into personae or fictional actors, the writers whom I have considered often play with the possibilities of their social roles, which they tend to make symbolic of man's condition. Perhaps because Thomson was the most detached of these poets, the least used to projecting visions of his private self, he is for that reason most precise and representative in recording the problem of the poetic self in his *Castle of Indolence*. Smart as the psalmist, Gray and Goldsmith and Cowper as bards and poetae and stricken deer, Blake as social prophet of the privately imaginative life, all assume roles that elaborate on the vision analyzed in *The Castle of Indolence*. In each case, the poet is man in the world written large, selected to feel most sensitively the pressures from reveries and fantasies within and from social needs without. In Thomson's fable the selves are divided, objectified, and opposed: the imaginative, delusive, Faustian, and yet inwardly drawn magician against the soberly universal spokesman for fertility, social justice, fulfilling sympathy. Thomson's success with the temptation to drown within the imagination and his relative failure in the self-admonitory second canto suggest again that poetic intensity rises most naturally from the poet's self-centered reveries.

More steadily fascinated by himself than Thomson was, Pope sees in the balance of his qualities as private human being and as poet an opportunity to use himself as material for an artful life as well as for poetry. Not only can he receive sympathy and applause for his fortitude in bearing the long disease of his life, but its very pains can justify the traditional satirist's power, privileges, and responsibilities. Since he saw himself primarily as poet, he discusses and portrays the poet and his creation from the *Essay on Criticism* to the Satires and *The Dunciad*, and he shows them symbolically from *The Rape of the Lock* to the artful universe of *An Essay on Man*. Through the early *poeta* and the recurrent fragile beings from the sylphs on, he projects his more private vision of the childlike, elegant, dainty self in art. In his later work, he tends to combine in the public author the satirist and something of the patriotic leader, the teacher, and even, in *The Dunciad*, the prophet. Pope's man is at his best the delicate and imaginative artist, whether he builds a poem, a state, or a world; at his worst, he is the gross fumbling artists of *The Dunciad* or the traitor to the civilized ideal like Atticus or Sporus. Thriving on success and opposition, Pope's public self more and more embodies his private fantasies of eminence in his age.

Like Pope and Wordsworth, Swift shows a strong sense of public activity as teacher and literary entertainer, describing himself only partly in jest as attacking the world in *Gulliver's Travels* and expecting it to take heed. From the Hack to the Modest Proposer, his public projections of symbolically flawed man are all writers. To their ordinary deficiencies as members of one time and place and of all times and places, they add the special characteristics of writers— abnormal vanity, relatively accessible fantasy lives, and a willingness to pay anything for originality. Man writing, he shows, is man thrusting himself forward, assuming a stance justifiable only as self-defense against evil or as the protection of those in his care: the roles in which Swift privately saw himself and which he publicly developed in normative personae like the Drapier. The atheistic and superficial Hack claims all life and thought as his province, but particularly religion and learning; without ever thinking past surfaces, Gulliver, the Modest Proposer, and Simon Wagstaff presume to advise us on human nature, political economy, and the social intercourse of reasoning creatures. In the promulgation of lay sermons and in the art of authorship, burlesques both of Swift's norms and his own sober functions, he sees his central vision of human folly. Observed ironically by his wiser universal self, different versions of his partial self are his models for perverse folly.

Through the scholars and poets that recur in his brief narratives and exempla, the publicly self-conscious author of *The Vanity of Human Wishes*, the Prefaces to *Shakespeare* and the *Dictionary*, *Rasselas*, and the *Lives of the Poets* provides emblems both of man's persistent attempt to communicate with what is outside him and of his inevitable defeat. These majestic teachers imagine their social value at levels beautifully illustrative of human delusiveness. In their doomed wish for happy action, Johnson's authors may see clearly, but still they struggle like Rasselas, letting life go by while they ponder how to use it. Although the Imlacs among them are better off than other people because the moving toy shops of their minds are better stocked with images, they cannot triumph over time or the immense temerity of the human imagination. Seeking fame in an ephemeral world, Johnson's poets, editors, and scholars, like all other men, attempt to shine socially, deprecate other careers, fight over trivial notices, and pronounce clichés as grand discoveries: symbols all of the vanity of human wishes.

Wordsworth is not so fascinated as Swift and Johnson by the vision of himself as writer, perhaps because he saw his function as bringing meaning to the individual reader rather than to society. He sees his public self as sometimes poeta, sometimes bard, sometimes teacher, sometimes member of a select professional guild. In some moods, he appears to himself an extraordinary man, endowed with a special gift; but since the gift is at God's arbitrary disposal, such a view restores him to archetypicality as a man chosen like every man to represent human possibilities. The poet for him is thus a more intense version of all men, a figure like his characters rising seriously out of his species to become a Form, an intelligible Solitary Reaper. Since his grand function is imaginative relationship and his grand ideal intense unity, Wordsworth does not deal with the sorts of conflicts between private and public self reflected in Pope, or in the Victorians. Speaking sympathetically even as bard, he needed to feel no estrangement from a satiric world; confident of the socially cementing value of his poetry, he had no Tennysonian qualms about the relevance of art.

No doubt the varying positions among these writers can be assigned to intellectual currents streaming through England or western Europe or the world in sharply distinguished periods of time; but only if we diminish their creations to historical documents. Over the period of time from Swift's odes to Wordsworth's death, the effect on literature of evidently changing world orientations is neither clear nor easily predictable. For example, everything I have said is consistent with the view that the late seventeenth century's ordered world yields to a vision of at least temporal disintegration in an age of sensibility, which in turn leads to Romantic synthesis. Examining social institutions, Wordsworth seems to join Swift in yearning for a return to an older archetype, though he wants organic growth rather than total reform; in the trough of confidence between them, Johnson lacks faith in continuity, in an orderly frame or organic growth or careful preparation, neither accepting the intuitive certainty of Swift's truth nor anticipating Wordsworth's recurrent elemental forms. More "modern" than either, he finds man's moral and psychological condition always tentative, always demanding improvement but never stable. But for every writer we must significantly qualify the generalizations of the *zeitgeist*. Swift's conservative certainty is constantly at odds with his own subversive urges, urges which he saw as thrusting to social dominance in his time. Johnson affirms order in the divine mind whatever the dance of plastic circumstance, and insists that the human mind can and should continuously attempt to create order even as he laments its incapacity to succeed. In the midst of ecstatic vision Wordsworth fears delusion, and in retrospect he finds despair more easily than tranquillity.

Wherever we look, our authors demonstrate the truism that anyone long worth reading transcends the formulas by which we attempt to define the literature of his time. Using another of the major indices of shifts in viewpoint, we can see a general development from a largely objective focus in Swift to a largely inner one in Wordsworth, by way of Johnson's balancing concern to keep feeding his mind with materials from without; but the very cruxes of their literary work—the characters of the Hack and Gulliver, the role of external nature, the primacy of generalizations—controvert fashionable ticketing. Another coherent scheme of literary-philosophical history would rightly find in Swift clear distinctions between reality and illusion, in Johnson gloom over the easy blurring of these distinctions, in Wordsworth a deliberate wish to efface them; but such a history can only call paradoxical Swift's familiarity with the short step to insanity, Johnson's construction from it of an ethic of engagement, and Wordsworth's fear that the imagination can delude. Their writings force these phenomena of feeling and thought on any careful reader; for the ultimate causes, one needs to guess psychosomatically, like Walter Shandy, or rest in Toby's conclusion that God made them that way. Looking at the writings, and at the writers, we can at least say that unimpeachable historical generalizations still seem to be distant.

Another truism, that powerful art builds on tension, gathers support from the writer's necessary application of the modes and attitudes of his day to his demonstration of their necessary insufficiency. All three major figures center their visions on paradox: for Swift, the emptiness of sober harmony without a quickening spark of the perverse; for Wordsworth, the apparently static ideal of intimacy within a family circle and the antithetical ideal of organic growth which in the narratives disrupts such union; for Johnson, the impossibility and yet the urgency of making order of chaotic experience. In expressing these paradoxes, Swift and Wordsworth created fictions to portray aspects of the self in ways which might otherwise have been closed off by the internal censor: the perverse visions of Swift's projectors, the guilty sex-associated wanderings of Wordsworth's characters. Johnson used fiction's shield less than they, partly because it was the very exercising of the imagination—the relaxing of controls over it—which he found most dangerous. He could show the lonely, grotesque, guilt-crazed astronomer or the defeated adventurers in life, but the next stage of psychological stripping (fantasies of a linen-dressed harem, for example, or of death and damnation) was too wild for free exposure in art, whether as yahoos or as abandoned mothers.

Genre, like period, interacts with the distinctive vision of the individual writer. Pope and Swift show us condemnable butts, visions of their perverse selves and ours which must be kept down for the sake of social stability. But Johnson's universal self, even when it sneers, accepts its share in human delusion. By Johnson's time, the primacy of Shaftesburian-latitudinarian imaginative sympathy was an accepted moral truth, as witness his casual explanation in the *Life of Cowley* for the metaphysical poets' failure to achieve greatness: "As they were wholly employed on something unexpected and surprising they had no regard to that uniformity of sentiment, which enables us to conceive and to excite the pains and the pleasure of other minds; they never enquired what on any occasion they should have said or done, but wrote rather as beholders than partakers of human nature; as beings looking upon good and evil, impassive and at leisure; as Epicurean deities making remarks on the actions of men, and the vicissitudes of life, without interest and without emotion" (*Lives*, I, 20). In Johnson's satire, the moralist's repudiation of the evil self has yielded to the sympathy of the psychologist, who for personal as well as for intellectually popular reasons joins his fellows in seeking mental health. Even the author of *The Vanity of Human Wishes*, Johnson's most olympian universal self, ends by participating tearfully in the sorrows of deluded man. Within the same large genre, we are a long way from the dread indignation of *A Modest Proposal* or the disgust of *The Dunciad*; while a different generation no doubt contributed to the change, perhaps it did so chiefly by providing encouraging climates for other temperaments.

Another genre, lyric poetry, allowed writers like Goldsmith, Gray, and Cowper to express the conviction of isolation without onus through the poeta. Wordsworth, developing greater confidence in the poet's centrality among men, grows from the separateness of the poeta to an assumption of the solidly centered, complex archetype of the Ode and *The Prelude*. After the universes of theology had been damaged by science and organicism, after the military ideal had fallen for Englishmen with the rise of Napoleon, after the statesman and patriot king had been sneered away by a century of party politics, the aloof, especially sensitive and suffering poeta could be turned into society's savior, the archetype of creative man, the essential provider of meaning and relevance in Wordsworth's *Preface*, in Shelley's *Defence*, and generally in the major poems of their day. The poet as poet has his social place in the Intimations Ode, as he does not in Gray's *Elegy* or Goldsmith's *Deserted Village*. Like the other elements working from without on the poet, a generic spokesman helps· to shape his self-image but is also shaped by it, selected and adapted to express the world conceived through an individuated stance.

Poor in paradoxes and surprises, I am left with the view that time, genre, and personal orientation encouraged Swift's dominant qualities as moralist, Johnson's as psychologist, Wordsworth's as poet. Growing up amidst the violent religious, political, and economic dualities that were forced on any Irishman of the seventeenth century, Swift inhabits an imaginative world of lunatic assaults which any sane man must sense and repel to live decently. In such a world, where a path between mad and vicious extremes has been provided by Revelation and the traditions that form the universal self, an eccentric course evidences blind, irresponsible pride. Rising from a gentler but less defined society as a brilliant boy without health, money, or position, in a turmoil of mild Jacobitism at home and benign whiggism nearby, with no truths sufficiently clear or sufficiently resisted to seek identification with one's exclusive self, Johnson develops a world full of temptations to draw man from the battle for personal meaning: a vision in which every man is more or less lost in sloth but where the degree of effort against the ultimate defeating incoherence determines the relative sanity. And Wordsworth, a child in the secluded northwest, finding meaning in the close family, the enfolding hills, the few local human archetypes, in a middle spot between the shepherds and the magnate Lowther, between the living siblings and the dead parents, conceives the good of fusing in one's consciousness all the people of the Lake country, and in turn other English country people, city people, other nations, and the dead of the past and the crowds yet to be born. Reflecting their special circumstances and self-views, Swift characteristically focuses on the chaotic concrete, the crack in the ordering of life, which can be both the trapdoor to destruction for the careless good man and the warning of the deluded's systematic hell; Johnson seizes the general, a temporary platform to hold on to; Wordsworth gazes at the point of union for two or more kinds of world.

Although the nature of the individual imagination and its tie to the course of human life remains a mystery (as I rather expected it would), I think this look at Swift, Johnson, and Wordsworth demonstrates its entanglement with the reveries about the self and the world. In arguing for a division into a projected acting self and an observing self, I do not propose an end for literary investigation, though it fits neatly into our fashionable approaches to psychological, sociological, and even theological views of the self. Rather, such an assumption may be a fair beginning from which to approach a more congenial subject for the critic. If, as I think, literature achieves meaning and stature from its vision of man running his career in the universe, then the writer's handling of his central selves can lead us to what gives individuality and universal application to that vision.

2. *The Contrasting Selves*

At different times, in different genres, and for apparently different reasons, writers from Swift through Wordsworth—and possibly from Homer through Bellow—exhibit an ambivalent sense of separation from their fellows which they project in visions of man acting out his solitary life before the gaze of an observing self. Paradoxically, such a sense ties them not only to each other but also to mankind. Splitting the self in two has always permitted an author to see the course of individual life, ruminate over its general laws—"nature" in its main eighteenth-century meaning—and use the conclusion to understand and judge the unique acting self. Writing itself is, after all, a form of this duality; the writer necessarily engages in a "criticism of life" when he puts on paper his vision of man in action.

In shaping the art of the writer, the imagination naturally seems to give life to themes and movements that bring the single acting self and the representative of fellowship, the observing self, into some sort of mutual awareness. Where the writer sees himself as *poeta*, his sense of alienation governs his conception of the poetic world, so that Gray's bard acts and imagines before a degraded society and Thomson's saving artist cannot feel for his indolent, imagination-drugged companions, but both share the values of observing civilized humanity. More generally, the persistent sense of separated and merging selves coexists with haunting notions of wholeness disintegrating, of harmony aborted, of the good faced by the crumbling of evil, of life attracted to and subverted by mortality; and it partakes in the other famously explored dualities of spirit and matter, fantasy and realism, the fanciful (or the imaginative) and the natural.

Observer and observed persist through literature, but they exhibit different characteristics in different writers, serving indeed among the determinants of uniqueness; in the relative attractiveness of, say, action and serenity we can see both changing conditions and special individual stances. Swift's civilized observing norm and crazy actor reflect the same duality as Wordsworth's brilliantly fulfilled actor and quiet, elderly observer, but not at all the same conception of man's nature and needs. For both, as for Johnson and other writers whom I have discussed, the self often projected before us has left the ordinary course of life. But Swift's is a ludicrous monster thrust out of the sea of time, while Wordsworth's rises as a mountain uniting water and sky, a benign source and instrument of human unity.

Since the writer seems to project his own idiosyncrasies into the complex acting self, we can be guided toward his vision of man's condition by what we learn of his sense of himself. Observing the tendencies of his conjured spirit, Swift finds in the madhouse a suitable arena for man's plotting and rhapsodizing; the uncertain or frustrated voyage persuades Johnson's ordinary idiosyncratic selves of the vanity of human wishes, while his more fearful figures escape from this truth into madness; and Wordsworth's voyagers wander in search of lost intensity or solace. Reflecting the pattern of self-centered reverie, some of these acting selves serve as cautions and models not only for the reader but for the author as well. Swift reproves his own tendencies to fly off in wild visions, to think he can alter all human behavior through projects like an academy to reform language, to fit mankind into ideal political or religious systems, to save man from man's barbarous elements. Through homilies or exempla about life's plastic folly, Johnson everywhere burlesques his own wish to arrive at general truths as well as his struggle for intellectual prominence. Wordsworth shows the dangers of isolation, prosiness, and the loss of vision. Furthermore, even the ages of the acting selves tend to reflect the changing self-directed reveries of their creators, particularly where fiction can give the illusion of censorship. Although some symbolic visions of mankind, like the solitary girl, recur throughout Wordsworth's career, his acting self generally grew old along with him, moving from a young Marmaduke through a mature Peter Bell to an old Merlin of *The Egyptian Maid*. Swift's main figures even more sharply echo his own stages of life—a young Hack in the *Tale*, a middle-aged Gulliver or Drapier, and elderly Simon Wagstaff, Footman, and Modest Proposer. Perhaps because Johnson's youthful imaginings are not preserved, the one movement of his idiosyncratic selves, from innocence to disappointment or withdrawal, reflects middle-aged sympathy for his own and mankind's loss of youth.

Through the projected natures and relations of the two selves, the three writers imagine their differing worlds, which also differ in ways consistent with changing attitudes around them. As universal norms, Swift's and Johnson's observing selves treat their acting subjects with superiority and sympathy, respectively, throughout their authors' careers; Wordsworth's observers, however, tend to vary their tones with his age and the development of his theory of imagination as relatedness. For Swift, the childless heir of the classical-Christian tradition, the universal self knows and reveals an existing true world, while the idiosyncratic self creates a prison in which to gibber. Discerning only one true path in morals, religion, politics, language, Swift advises repudiation of the divisive special self, or at least its incorporation within the universal. His great successors advocate a more or less equal union of selves through Lockean sympathetic understanding—Johnson for mutual enlightenment and action, Wordsworth for a fused harmony capable of illuminating itself and the rest of the world. In Johnson's division, the idiosyncratic self struggles in an aimless world to find a guide in the only Lockean truth, the present contents of the mind, while the universal observer mourns the absurd ache. Since Johnson relies for serenity on continuous induction based on the most extensive gathering of specific data, he regards the idiosyncratic—which does the gathering—not as the perverse but as the normal. And for Wordsworth, the observing self merely corroborates the acting self's development of the fusion, the new union with an eternal living world.

In Wordsworth's vision, the acting self unifies the elements within the poem, while the observing self explores ties to the acting self and to us. Perhaps as a consequence, Wordsworth recurrently imagines a new imagining self which fuses the other two or holds them in suspension, an analogue of his search for a redemption, a new life, whereas Swift and Johnson, separating distinct selves, seek a clearer understanding of our ordinary sublunary life. Wordsworth's and his century's admiration for the acting self looks at first like a simple preference for tragedy as against the comic or satiric identification with the norms of universal society, but genre here seems more to serve than determine the vision of man in the world. Although in the satires of Swift and Pope the idiosyncratic observed self is condemned, in Johnson's, sympathy joins the derision, and the observed self conspicuously partakes in our universal delusiveness; moving a step further, for the romantics the observer may be no more social or universal than the actor, and in such clearly nontragic works as *Kubla Khan*, *The Blind Highland Boy*, or *Don Juan* we sympathize with the separated, acting self. Swift's program to purge the self of evil, Johnson's (and Sterne's and Goldsmith's) sympathetic irony, Wordsworth's yearning for imaginative growth, are all reflected in the interrelations of the selves or derived from them. At the very least, such conceptions are consistent with the moral and religious passions, psychological tolerance, and revolutionary utopianism notable in their respective times.

Although the separation of the literary self into the suffering and the observant, the idiosyncratic and the universal, is neither unique to the literature of one time nor constant throughout it, a sharp distinction between mutually illuminating selves seems particularly prevalent, characteristic, even deliberate in the literature of the eighteenth century, a time whose epistemology depended on perception and reflection and whose popular theology and moral psychology repeatedly balanced the aloof and the warmly involved. No doubt

Chaucer laughs at himself a bit in his famous Prologue, Donne theatrically admires his involvement in the act of love, and Milton projects his own ego on the grandest of all screens—if my guess about the workings of the imagination makes sense, they would seem obligated to do so. Furthermore, the doubleness is, no doubt, generic—such amused self-consciousness as Johnson's projecting Rasselas and even the figures struggling with human wishes may be expected in comedy. But aside from suggesting their authors' awareness of their own absurdities, Tom Jones and Charles Primrose in acting before the evaluating authors united with the reader are more likely to appear in the eighteenth century than before or after. Even in drama, sententious observers crowd in on observed sufferers; where Hamlet's or Lear's companions had to deal with their actions, Dorimant's and Mirabell's, Cato's and George Barnwell's evaluate them endlessly. When two central figures appear in narrative, one like Abraham Adams, Robert Lovelace, or Rameau's nephew is likely to act (or caper) before the observing other, in a manner very different from the collaborative absurdity of a Bouvard and Pecuchet or the complementary fullness of a Bloom and Dedalus.

To judge also by Wordsworth and his great contemporaries, diverse selves appear in relation to a variedly conceived world for diverse personal reasons, but the literary period has its part in shaping the imagination's grasp of the elements in the self. As against the visions of earlier writers, for Wordsworth and the other romantics the observing self is usually sympathetic and often subordinate to the actor. One of Wordsworth's triumphs is to share the discovery of his own projected nature with us and persuade us that at our best we are identical in kind if not in degree: that in his highest qualities and powers, man is a poet. Such a view of the special self as generic, of the sensations of the single consciousness as representative, permits the apparently direct, unformalized projection of the idiosyncratic self in poetry. To such a self which strives and above all imagines, dreaming visions that surround it with a living universe, we respond with emulous respect. Should the dream be catastrophically exploded, as with the guilty and forlorn, the dreamer is to be loved and not scorned. Rasselas means well, but he is absurd and doomed because that is man's fate in a world beyond his control; even if struggling is useless and love a delusion, because Childe Harold and Don Juan struggle for control and, through love, imagine beauty they are good.

Coleridge's acting and observing selves are somewhat different from Wordsworth's, but they relate to each other like his. As might be

expected, Coleridge's poetic selves, more consistently than Wordsworth's, are victim as well as sinner—that is, the ambiguity of guilt
more insistently thrusts at his imaginative vision of the world and
more powerfully demands transmutation into poetic symbols. This
can be seen in what he called his conversation poems—for example,
*The Aeolian Harp, This Lime Tree Bower My Prison, Frost at Mid-
night, Dejection: An Ode*; in them, he regularly contrasts a rueful,
guilty, almost sluggish observer and a momentarily vitalized acting
self. Inevitably, his great symbolic poems project the same imaginative view of the self in the world. Kubla Khan, sitting in his castle
and hearing the river's tumult and the ancestral voices prophesying
war, shows creative and apprehensive qualities like those of the self
with which his poem ends, the figure yearning for imaginative possession. In *The Ancient Mariner*, Coleridge develops an elaborate
world around the guilty victim, achieving the effect of nightmare
strangeness particularly through the sense of observation by a confederacy of normative selves: the argument, the glosses, the shipmates,
the various symbolic deities, the gambling pair and the spirit voices,
the concluding moral. Through the tale frame he provides a vision of
a superlatively potent acting self accounting for his course of life
amid a variety of uncontrollable moral forces—his sinful experience—
to a listening average man, while we watch the two acting out their
respective frenzy and responses. It is something like the Imlac-
Rasselas situation, something like Cowper's John Gilpin before the
amused narrator, and something like the Grubaean Hack–normative
universal self; but we are to feel awe, respect, and pity, not contempt. In *Christabel* as in *The Ancient Mariner*, Coleridge projects
in his acting self a sense of an early encounter with evil for which
there was no preparation or outside aid. Such moral symbols as the
power over Christabel given to Geraldine and the snake around the
heroine's neck (like the albatross around the Mariner's) emphasize
the interrelation of good and evil, the ambiguity that surrounds any
action in a fallen world, as what seems to be pantheistic inspiration
in *The Aeolian Harp* is a distorted vision of the working of orthodox
Christianity. Idiosyncratically accepting guilt and blaming God, Coleridge joins his contemporaries to delight in the self which has lived
luminously.

Shelley's apparently different acting self, which repudiates guilt as
a mass delusion, aims at a similar fascination. Asserting man's right
and need to throw off the darkness of matter and live with divine
intensity, Shelley admires the striving self, the element which has

sought and intermittently achieved spontaneous and independent participation in the spirit that animates the world. By the end of the *Hymn to Intellectual Beauty*, for example, the recording self has been minimized, absorbed into the inspired agent of the spirit of Intellectual Beauty, the self which can serve as an archetype, prophet, and model for mankind. The famous apostrophes to natural beings or elements, such as the *Ode to the West Wind*, *Mont Blanc*, and *To a Skylark*, move to project as an actor the self which prays for the free spirituality of the wind or the bird. In Shelley's most elaborate vision, *Prometheus Unbound*, the noble archetypal self stands forth as man free and loving, an object of admiration for a variety of observing choruses: when man overcomes his tendencies toward dominance all men will be free and equal to each other and to the sentient universe, and formal anarchy will be universal harmony. In Shelley's visions, pain, change, and death are reserved to a figure *here*, a reflecting self in a swamp of material routine, while the ideal, noble, and free qualities are concentrated in the projection of an acting archetype across the screen of the world—whether of a past self temporarily inspired, a natural element symbolic of such human inspiration, or a mythic and joyous man.

For the romantics generally, the self that seeks transcendence, the acting and aspiring self, is more alive than its observer and therefore superior to it. The Shelley who screams or faints in the poems is still, like Prometheus, a bringer of light (or a lamp, to borrow Abrams' famous metaphor) offered to our admiration, not to our Swiftian scorn or Johnsonian pity. Dickens' universal narrator in *Bleak House* is as pessimistic as the voice of *Rasselas*, but not at the expense of Esther Summerson, whose striving goodness cannot be defeated by life or death. Although Gray's Eton College boys are merely victims heedless of their doom and Fielding's Adams and Jane Austen's Miss Bates are objects of derision, innocence can save a Scott or Dickens or Thackeray figure from both evil and ridicule. Like Burns in his creation of Holy Willie, Dickens can set up figures to be feared and hated, but they are immediately perceived as potent fragments, not Swiftian butts or Johnsonian cowards.

All times contribute to the archetype of man struggling across a world panorama, and writers generally observe that archetype, but the writers at any one time tend to shape the visions of acting self, observing self, and world in ways that are closer to each other than to those of other periods. Although Wordsworth's poet experiencing intimations of immortality, Shelley's Prometheus, Byron's Manfred,

Coleridge's Mariner, and Keats's spirit rising from a darkling grove differ intensely from each other, their relationships with the observer help to form a unifying distinction for their time. Against Swift's and Johnson's acceptance of the observer's world of common sense, the great romantics all offer transcendence, though they understand it differently: Wordsworth breathing elegiac hopes; Coleridge suspicious of demonic possession; Shelley prophesying earthly redemption and the ultimate brilliance of death; Keats drawn to the intense paradoxes of ecstasy and pain; Byron suspicious of ecstasy as delusion but with no viable alternatives. Whatever remains obscure to the critics, it seems clear that the writer's vision of himself molds his creation of appetitive man in ways that we can define, and that his age significantly shapes the relations between that aspirant and the collective observer that unites us with the writer.

NOTES
and
REFERENCES

Journal Abbreviations in Notes

ECS	*Eighteenth Century Studies*
EIC	*Essays in Criticism*
ELH	*Journal of English Literary History*
ELN	*English Language Notes*
ES	*English Studies*
HLQ	*Huntington Library Quarterly*
JAAC	*Journal of Aesthetics and Art Criticism*
JEGP	*Journal of English and Germanic Philology*
JHI	*Journal of the History of Ideas*
L&P	*Literature and Psychology*
MLQ	*Modern Language Quarterly*
MLR	*Modern Language Review*
MP	*Modern Philology*
PELL	*Papers on English Language and Literature*
PMLA	*Publications of the Modern Language Association*
PQ	*Philological Quarterly*
REL	*Review of English Literature*
RES	*Review of English Studies*
SAQ	*South Atlantic Quarterly*
SEL	*Studies in English Literature*
SIR	*Studies in Romanticism*
SP	*Studies in Philology*
TSLL	*Texas Studies in Literature and Language*
UTQ	*University of Toronto Quarterly*

Chapter I

1. *The Letters of Samuel Johnson*, ed. R. W. Chapman (Oxford: Clarendon Press, 1952), II, 79.
2. *Collected Letters of Oliver Goldsmith*, ed. Katharine C. Balderston (Cambridge: Cambridge University Press, 1928), p. 39.
3. Review of *An Essay on the Writings and Genius of Pope* (1756) in *Works of Samuel Johnson* (London: Pickering, Talboys, & Wheeler, 1825), II, 42.

Chapter II

1. See Bernard N. Schilling, *Dryden and the Conservative Myth* (New Haven: Yale University Press, 1961), *passim*, esp. p. 10; for a discussion of images as guides to the theories of an age, see M. H. Abrams, "Archetypal Analogies in the Language of Criticism," *UTQ*, 18 (1949), 313–27, and, of course, Professor Abrams' *The Mirror and the Lamp* (London: Oxford University Press, 1953).
2. For the brilliant paper which used the *Arbuthnot* to set off the current discussion of rhetorical stance as against personality, see Maynard Mack, "The Muse of Satire," *Yale Review*, 61 (1951), 80–92; a recent able argument that "the voice heard within the long speeches came from the throat of Pope himself" is Irvin Ehrenpreis's "Personae," in *Restoration and Eighteenth-Century Literature*, Carroll Camden ed. (Chicago: University of Chicago Press, 1963); Professor Mack somewhat modified his position in "*Secretum Iter*: Some Uses of Retirement Literature in the Poetry of Pope," in *Aspects of the Eighteenth Century*, ed. Earl R. Wasserman (Baltimore: Johns Hopkins Press, 1965), pp. 207–43. For a fine recent study of this poem, see J. Paul Hunter, "Satiric Apology as Satiric Instance: Pope's *Arbuthnot*," *JEGP*, 68 (1969), 625–47.
3. Cf., among many other possible works on the recurrence of archetypes, Northrop Frye's *Fables of Identity: Studies in Poetic Mythology* (New York: Harcourt, Brace, & World, 1963) and his more famous

Anatomy of Criticism: Four Essays (Princeton: Princeton University Press, 1957); Albert Guerard, Jr., "Prometheus and the Aeolian Lyre," *Yale Review*, 33 (1944), 482–97; Geoffrey H. Hartman, "Romanticism and 'Anti–Self-Consciousness,' " *Centennial Review of Arts and Science*, 6 (1962), 553–65; Peter L. Thorslev, Jr., "Wordsworth's *Borderers* and the Romantic Villain-Hero," *SIR*, 5 (1966), 84–103.

4. Such a figure is suggested in Robert C. Elliott's stimulating chapter on "The Satirist Satirized," in his *The Power of Satire: Magic, Ritual, Art* (Princeton: Princeton University Press, 1960), pp. 130–222.

5. For the drama critic, see Johnson's disposal of the unities of time and and place in his *Preface to Shakespeare*; for a typical assumption of "double vision" on the part of one influential critic, Lord Kames, see Alex Page, "Faculty Psychology and Metaphor in Eighteenth-Century Criticism," *MP*, 66 (1969), 237–47; for the famous examination of Boswell's "divided vision," see Bertrand Bronson's "Boswell's Boswell," in his *Johnson and Boswell: Three Essays*, University of California Publications in English, Vol. 3, No. 9 (Berkeley and Los Angeles: University of California Press, 1944), pp. 399–429.

6. Pope's tendency to play roles and manipulate the image of himself has been noted by many scholars dealing with his letters. See George Sherburn's introduction to Pope's *Correspondence* (Oxford: Clarendon Press, 1956), I, xiv–xv; Rosemary Cowler, "Shadow and Substance: A Discussion of Pope's Correspondence," in *The Familiar Letter in the Eighteenth Century*, ed. Howard Anderson, Philip B. Daghlian, and Irvin Ehrenpreis (Lawrence: University of Kansas Press, 1966), pp. 34–48. Maynard Mack, "A Poet in His Landscape: Pope at Twickenham," in *From Sensibility to Romanticism*, ed. Frederick W. Hilles and Harold Bloom (New York: Oxford University Press, 1965), p. 3, speaks of Pope's amusement in referring to his small size, and his *The Garden and the City* (Toronto: University of Toronto Press, 1969) finely handles Pope's conscious sense of himself; Donald J. Greene, " 'Dramatic Texture' in Pope," in *From Sensibility to Romanticism*, ed. Hilles and Bloom, p. 33, refers to "the mock-naive role he is so fond of playing" in the Horatian imitations; Paul J. Alpers, in "Pope's *To Bathurst* and the Mandevillian State," *ELH*, 25 (1958), 23–42, sees Pope as carefully posing himself in the poem. For the tradition and nature of the poeta, see Amy Louise Reed, *The Background of Gray's Poetry* (New York: Columbia University Press, 1924), p. 40 ff.

7. For a discussion of the current interest, see Geoffrey Tillotson, ed., *Rape of the Lock and Other Poems*, Twickenham Edition (London: Methuen, 1940), p. 279. For stimulating discussions of the poem, see Brendan O'Hehir, "Virtue and Passion: The Dialectic of Eloisa to Abelard," in *Essential Articles for the Study of Alexander Pope*, ed. Maynard Mack (Hamden, Conn.: Archon, 1964), pp. 310–26; and

Murray Krieger, " 'Eloisa to Abelard': The Escape from Body or the Embrace of Body," *ECS*, 3 (1969), 28–47.

8. For the literary form as imitation of the character of a mad and venal figure, I am indebted to Ronald Paulson, *Theme and Structure in Swift's Tale of a Tub* (New Haven: Yale University Press, 1960). On Pope's reconciling extremes, see Maynard Mack's introduction to the Twickenham Edition of *Essay on Man* (London: Methuen, 1950); Ernest Tuveson, *"An Essay on Man* and 'The Way of Ideas,' " *ELH*, 26 (1959), 368–86; Martin Kallich, "Unity and Dialectic: The Structural Role of Antithesis in Pope's *Essay on Man*," *PELL*, 1 (1965), 109–24; Martin Kallich, "The Conversation and the Frame of Love: Images of Unity in Pope's *Essay on Man*," *PELL*, 2 (1966), 21–37.

9. For discussions of the necessary contrast of vice and virtuous norm in formal verse satire, see Mary Claire Randolph, "The Structural Design of the Formal Verse Satire," *PQ*, 21 (1942), 368–84; Alvin B. Kernan, *The Cankered Muse: Satire of the English Renaissance* (New Haven: Yale University Press, 1959), pp. 13–15; Howard D. Weinbrot, "The Pattern of Formal Verse Satire in the Restoration and the Eighteenth Century," *PMLA*, 80 (1965), 394–401; Philip Pinkus, "The New Satire of Augustan England," *UTQ*, 38 (1969), 136–58; Edward A. Bloom and Lillian D. Bloom, "The Satiric Mode of Feeling: A Theory of Intention," *Criticism*, 11 (1969), 115–39.

10. For perceptive discussions of the complexities of theme and contrast, see Cleanth Brooks, "The Case of Miss Arabella Fermor," in his *Well Wrought Urn: Studies in the Structure of Poetry* (New York: Reynal & Hitchcock, 1947); Reuben Arthur Brower, *Alexander Pope: The Poetry of Allusion* (Oxford: Clarendon Press, 1959), p. 144 ff.; Earl R. Wasserman, "The Limits of Allusion in *The Rape of the Lock*," *JEGP*, 65 (1966), 425–44.

11. Cf. Maynard Mack, " 'The Shadowy Cave': Some Speculations on a Twickenham Grotto," in *Restoration and Eighteenth-Century Literature*, ed. Camden, p. 70, on the "apocalyptic mutterings," the sense of loss of the civilized ideal, throughout Pope's poetry; Ricardo Quintana, " 'The Rape of the Lock' as a Comedy of Continuity," *REL*, 7 (1966), 9–19, on "the way in which the concept of change permeates the poem" (p. 10); Rebecca P. Parkin, "The Role of Time in Alexander Pope's *Epistle to a Lady*," *ELH*, 32 (1965), 490–501, on "the urgency occasioned by the passing of time" in the poem (p. 490).

12. For a detailed examination of this journey, see Aubrey L. Williams, *Pope's Dunciad: A Study of Its Meaning* (London: Methuen, 1955); for its form, see Alvin B. Kernan, *"The Dunciad* and the Plot of Satire," in *Essential Articles*, ed. Mack, pp. 726–38.

13. For a discussion of the contrasting themes, see A. D. McKillop's Introduction to his edition of *The Castle of Indolence and Other Poems*

(Lawrence: University of Kansas Press, 1961). Except for *The Seasons*, for which I use the J. Logie Robertson Oxford Standard Authors edition of Thomson, this is the text cited.

14. Cf. Alan Dugald McKillop, *The Background of Thomson's Seasons* (Minneapolis: University of Minnesota Press, 1942), p. 39; Ralph Cohen, "Spring: The Love Song of James Thomson," *TSLL*, 11 (1969), 1107–82.

15. Cf. Ralph M. Williams, "Thomson and Dyer: Poet and Painter," in *Age of Johnson* (New Haven: Yale University Press, 1949), pp. 209–16; McKillop, *Background*, p. 18.

16. Cf. Ralph Cohen, "Thomson's Poetry of Space and Time," in *Studies in Criticism and Aesthetics, 1660–1800*, ed. Howard Anderson and John S. Shea (Minneapolis: University of Minnesota Press, 1967), pp. 176–92.

17. Christopher Smart, *Jubilate Agno*, ed. W. H. Bond (Cambridge, Mass.: Harvard University Press, 1954), pp. 131, 139, 141. For the circumstances of Smart's writing this work, see Arthur Sherbo's authoritative *Christopher Smart: Scholar of the University* (East Lansing: Michigan State University Press, 1967), pp. 122–63.

18. For Smart's intense response to the physical world, see D. J. Greene, "Smart, Berkeley, the Scientists, and the Poets: A Note on Eighteenth-Century Anti-Newtonianism," *JHI*, 14 (1953), 327–52.

19. *Collected Poems of Christopher Smart*, ed. Norman Callan (Cambridge, Mass.: Harvard University Press, 1950), p. xlv. All references to Smart's poems except the *Jubilate Agno* are to this edition.

20. Cf. Robert Brittain's Introduction to his edition of Smart's *Poems* (Princeton: Princeton University Press, 1950), pp. 59–61.

21. Dennis, in Willard Higley Durham, ed., *Critical Essays of the Eighteenth Century* (New Haven: Yale University Press, 1915), pp. 147–251; for painting as well as the other arts, see Brewster Rogerson, "The Art of Painting the Passions," *JHI*, 14 (1953), 68–94; Walter John Hipple, *The Beautiful, the Sublime, and the Picturesque in Eighteenth-Century British Aesthetic Theory* (Carbondale: Southern Illinois University Press, 1957), p. 305.

22. For more developed discussions of Goldsmith's and Gray's personae, see my "The Family-Wanderer Theme in Goldsmith," *ELH*, 25 (1958), 181–93; "The Broken Dream of *The Deserted Village*," *L&P*, 9 (1959), 41–44; and *Thomas Gray* (New York: Twayne, 1964).

Chapter III

1. Cf. Bertrand A. Goldgar, "Satires on Man and 'The Dignity of Human Nature,'" *PMLA*, 80 (1965), 540: "One special form of *argumentum ad hominem* used against satirists of man is the charge that their generalizations reveal only what they have gained from self-knowledge, that their portrayal of mankind is only a reflection of their own character. Shaftesbury had declared that those who have hard thoughts of human nature are at least no hypocrites, for 'they speak as ill of themselves as they possibly can'"; see also Herbert Davis, "Swift's Character," in *Jonathan Swift: A Dublin Tercentenary Tribute*, ed. Roger McHugh and Philip Edwards (Dublin: Dolmen Press, 1967), pp. 1–23; Irvin Ehrenpreis, *Swift: The Man, His Works and the Age*, 2 vols. (London: Methuen, 1962, 1967), *passim*, esp. II, 276, on the basis of Swift's comic satire: "It will appear that psychologically the hidebound moralist is the necessary origin of the prankster, yet that as a literary accomplishment the prankster's work must be read in isolation from the moralist's"; Robert C. Elliott, *The Power of Satire: Magic, Ritual, Art* (Princeton: Princeton University Press, 1960): "The 'I' of *A Tale of a Tub*, that egregious modern, avid after conquests and systems, is removed from Swift by the whole great range of the irony. Similarly, the 'I' of *A Modest Proposal* is a horrible parody of Jonathan Swift, Dean of St. Patrick's. These are Swift's anti-selves. But in a way the anti-self implies complement; and the folly, even the cannibalism of the projector of the *Modest Proposal* are symbolically the folly and cannibalism of Swift himself (and of ourselves insofar as we read properly).... There is a sense ... in which 'I' is I and, to revert to the *Travels*, Swift is Gulliver: giant and pigmy, bemused admirer and victim of scientific idiocy, lover and hater of man—purveyor and target of satire" (p. 222); W. B. Carnochan, "The Complexity of Swift: Gulliver's Fourth Voyage," *SP*, 60 (1963), 23–44: "Swift's treatment of Gulliver stems directly from his own ambiguous attitude toward satire, its usefulness and its motivations; his mixed sympathy and contempt for his created character indicate deep uncertainties about himself and his chosen art" (p. 32); W. B. Carnochan, *Lemuel Gulliver's Mirror for Man* (Berkeley and Los Angeles: University of California Press, 1968): With aging, "Swift's growing self-awareness is reciprocal with the growing sense of himself as a comic actor on the world's tragic stage, while at the

same time he is an observer of the action. Explicit self-dramatization in the later satires gives us frequent glances of the Dean in a third-person view, and some of these are very much like the third-person view of himself as Lemuel Gulliver" (p. 111); C. J. Rawson, "Gulliver and the Gentle Reader," in *Imaginary Worlds*, ed. Maynard Mack and Ian Gregor (London: Methuen, 1968), pp. 51–90: "The *Tale* has a vitality of sheer performance which suggests that a strong self-conscious pressure of primary self-display on Swift's own part is also at work; the almost 'romantic' assertion of an immense (though edgy, oblique, and agressively self-concealing) egocentricity. Swift's descendants in the old game of parodic self-consciousness are Romantics of a special sort, like Sterne and (after him) the Byron of *Don Juan*" (pp. 51–52).

2. *Letter to Viscount Molesworth*, in *The Prose Works of Jonathan Swift*, ed. Herbert Davis, Louis Landa *et al.* (Oxford: Blackwell, 1939–), X, 82.

3. Cf. Ricardo Quintana, *The Mind and Art of Jonathan Swift* (London: Oxford University Press, 1936), p. 57: Swift felt a "dualism cleaving society into two groups, one made up of the cultivated few, the other of the mass of mankind. Consistently he distinguished between these groups, assigning to the former the onerous obligation of preserving through precept and example the decencies, graces, and rationale of civilized life; to the latter the duty of obedience to superior authority"; cf. Ehrenpreis' view that Sir William Temple was the representative of the Christian humanist ideal who is the norm played against the speaker of *A Tale of a Tub* (*Swift*, I, 190).

4. His response to his position often blends resentment, a sense of his essential superiority, and what Clarissa Harlowe called her "punctilios," an insistence on all one's social prerogatives. In the *Journal to Stella* (ed. Harold Williams, Oxford: Clarendon Press, 1948), for example, he writes ebulliently of a warm welcome from a duke's daughters (Sept. 20, 1710); of triumphs among the ministers (Nov. 10); of being too proud to claim credit for the first fruits (Nov. 24). On February 7, 1710–11, he reported a serious quarrel with Harley, who had casually treated him like a hireling rather than an aristrocratic equal. He had sent Swift a fifty-pound note for writing the *Examiners*, and Swift had returned it angrily: "I absolutely refused to submit to this intended favour, and expect further satisfaction" (I, 182). As a writer, Swift combined the earlier ethos of genteel amateurism with a heightened suspicion of political patronage: "I am sorry I sent you the Examiner; for the printer is going to print them in a small volume; it seems the author is too proud to have them printed by subscription, though his friends offered, they say, to make it worth five hundred pounds to him" (II, 399). Ehrenpreis describes Swift as a member of the admin-

istrative class in Ireland (*Swift*, I, 71); for the seventeenth-century attitude toward the socially aspiring figure, see Ronald Paulson, *Satire and the Novel in Eighteenth-Century England* (New Haven: Yale University Press, 1967), pp. 36–41.

5. *The Poems of Jonathan Swift*, ed. Harold Williams, 2nd ed. (Oxford: Clarendon Press, 1958), I, 17–18. This is my text for all Swift's poems.

6. *The Correspondence of Jonathan Swift*, ed. Harold Williams, 5 vols. (Oxford: Clarendon Press, 1963), I, 9.

7. His letters from Ireland often play on the themes of his relatively obscure life pattern and the danger of prominence. On July 18, 1717, he wrote in characteristic imagery to Atterbury: "I am in a hopeful situation, torn to pieces by pamphleteers and libellers on that side the water, and by the whole body of the ruling party on this; against which all the obscurity I live in will not defend me" (*Correspondence*, II, 279; cf. letter to Ford, February 16, 1718–19). As he grew older, the self-pity and even the anger were likely to be modified by amusement at the expense of his own striving pride, as shown in a letter to Pope of July 8, 1733. In *The Fictions of Satire* (Baltimore: Johns Hopkins Press, 1967), Ronald Paulson sees Swift's self-portraits in the apologias of two kinds, "before the fall and after, or before the 1714 retreat to Ireland and after" (p. 196); earlier, he says, Swift appears as a wit, a courtly gentleman, "an amused observer of folly," but from *The Author upon Himself* "there are two notable changes: his influence on the ministry and participation in greatness are emphasized (perhaps over-emphasized), and, second, he has now become the 'pursued' ...," (pp. 196–97).

8. For information on Swift's career as a churchman, I am indebted to Louis A. Landa, *Swift and the Church of Ireland* (Oxford: Clarendon Press, 1954).

9. Cf. *A Letter, Concerning the Sacramental Test* (1709), and letters to the Earl of Oxford, November 27, 1724 (*Correspondence*, III, 41), to Lady Worsley (*Correspondence*, IV, 79), and to Pope (*Correspondence*, III, 289).

10. For example, "Mr. secretary had too much company with him to-day; so I came away soon after dinner. I give no man liberty to swear or talk b——dy, and I found some of them were in constraint, so I left them to themselves" (*Journal to Stella*, I, 273).

11. Cf. Herbert Davis, "Swift's View of Poetry" (1931), rpt. in *Fair Liberty Was All His Cry: A Tercentenary Tribute to Jonathan Swift, 1667–1745*, ed. A. Norman Jeffares (London: Macmillan, 1967), pp. 62–97, on Swift's deliberate antipoetizing; Maurice Johnson's *The Sin of Wit* (Syracuse: Syracuse University Press, 1950) says of Swift's poetry what Ricardo Quintana rightly saw as Swift's general view of romantic illusion in "Situational Satire: A Commentary on the Method

of Swift" (1948), rpt. in *Studies in the Literature of the Augustan Age*, ed. Richard C. Boys (Ann Arbor: George Wahr, 1952): "The only myth genuinely embraced by Swift is the myth that there are no myths..." (p. 264).

12. See, for example, *Correspondence*, III, 87, 102, 117, 382; IV, 138, 336; V, 46.

13. For the dangers, particularly of mechanism, see Martin Price, *Swift's Rhetorical Art* (New Haven: Yale University Press, 1953), esp. pp. 81, 104–5; John M. Bullitt, *Jonathan Swift and the Anatomy of Satire* (Cambridge, Mass.: Harvard University Press, 1961), p. 144; Kathleen Williams, "Restoration Themes in the Major Satires of Swift," *RES*, 16 (1965), 258.

14. Cf. Price, p. 78; William Bragg Ewald, Jr., *The Masks of Jonathan Swift* (Oxford: Blackwell, 1954), pp. 13–23; Edward M. Rosenheim, Jr., *Swift and the Satirist's Art* (Chicago: University of Chicago Press, 1963), 60 ff.; Ronald Paulson, *Theme and Structure in Swift's Tale of a Tub* (New Haven: Yale University Press, 1960).

15. Barry Slepian, "The Ironic Intention of Swift's Verses on His Own Death," *RES*, 14 (1963), 249–56, argues fairly plausibly that the poem is an extended exercise in self-mockery; Marshall Waingrow, "*Verses on the Death of Dr. Swift*," *SEL*, 5 (1965), 513–18, modifies Mr. Slepian's thesis.

16. Ronald Paulson seems to me right in suggesting that Swift's satires fuse the grand rhetorical traditions of Juvenal and Horace—like Juvenal, Swift has the vision dominate our awareness and like Horace, he removes all mediators between ourselves and the object of satire (*The Fictions of Satire*, pp. 29–30, 129–222); for other views of the distinctions in stance of the Roman satirists, see Philip Pinkus, "The New Satire of Augustan England," *UTQ*, 38 (1969), 136–58, and W. B. Carnochan, "Satire, Sublimity, and Sentiment: Theory and Practice in Post-Augustan Satire," *PMLA*, 85 (1970), 260–67.

17. See Richard I. Cook, "The Uses of *Saeve Indignatio*: Swift's Political Tracts (1710–14) and His Sense of Audience," *SEL*, 2 (1962), 287–307.

18. Cf. Louis Landa on the *Letter to a Young Clergyman*: "It is characteristic of Swift that he chose to write from the point of view of a layman, a gentleman of the world, in the same tone that he had adopted in his religious pamphlets of 1708" (*Prose Works*, I, xxiv).

19. *Prose Works*, IX, 85–86. For a discussion of the context of this piece, see George P. Mayhew, *Rage or Raillery: The Swift Manuscripts at the Huntington Library* (San Marino: Huntington Library, 1967), pp. 37–42. Swift had written to Jane Waring, on May 4, 1700, that one qualification he would expect in her as his bride was a readiness "to engage in those methods I shall direct for the improvement of your

mind, so as to make us entertaining company for each other, without being miserable when we are neither visiting nor visited" (*Correspondence*, I, 35–36).

20. See Richard I. Cook, " 'Mr. Examiner' and 'Mr. Review': The Tory Apologetics of Swift and Defoe," *HLQ*, 29 (1966), 143.

21. For a discussion of this situation in the work of one younger contemporary, see "The Enclosed Self," in my *Fielding's Moral Psychology* (Amherst: University of Massachusetts Press, 1966), pp. 1–19.

22. Cf. Paulson, *Theme and Structure in Swift's Tale of a Tub*: "One of the comic elements in the portrayal of the Grub Street Hack is his unabashed sacrifice of everything else for the effect of the moment— his willingness to collapse an argument for the sake of the delicious details; or, in short, his casuistry" (p. 28). See also the discussion by Ehrenpreis of the *Argument* [*against*] *Abolishing Christianity*, in his *Swift* (II, 276–97), and Robert H. Hopkins, "The Personation of Hobbism in Swift's *Tale of a Tub* and *Mechanical Operation of the Spirit*," *PQ*, 45 (1966), 372–78.

23. George P. Mayhew has found that Swift, like his Simon Wagstaff, kept a notebook with jottings of current expressions; see his *Rage or Raillery*, p. 152. These similarities are further discussed by David Hamilton, "Swift, Wagstaff, and the Composition of *Polite Conversation*," *IILQ*, 30 (1967), 281–95.

24. I cannot pretend to disentangle my interpretation of *Gulliver's Travels* from the varied and ingenious discussions of the past three decades or so, particularly in the works that I have cited by Quintana, Elliott, Price, Paulson, Rosenheim, and Ehrenpreis; in Kathleen Williams' seminal *Jonathan Swift and the Age of Compromise* (Lawrence: University of Kansas Press, 1959); and in essays scattered through journals (like the 1962 *REL*) and in those collections already cited and in those by Milton P. Foster, *A Casebook on Gulliver among the Houyhnhnms* (New York: Crowell, 1961); John Traugott, ed., *Discussions of Jonathan Swift* (Lexington, Mass.: D. C. Heath, 1962); Robert A. Greenberg, ed., *Gulliver's Travels: An Annotated Text with Critical Essays* (New York: W. W. Norton, 1961); Ernest Tuveson, ed., *Swift: A Collection of Critical Essays* (Englewood Cliffs: Prentice-Hall, 1964).

25. Cf. Clarence Tracy, "The Unity of *Gulliver's Travels*," *Queens Quarterly*, 68 (1962), 597–609, and J. Leeds Barroll, "Gulliver and the Struldbruggs," *PMLA*, 73 (1958), 43–50.

26. Cf. W. B. C. Watkins, *Perilous Balance* (Princeton: Princeton University Press, 1939), p. 6: "The nearest equivalent in the Augustan Age to expression of the most profound sense of tragedy, expressed by the Elizabethans in drama, is not to be found in the work of the dramatists, but at times in Pope, primarily in Swift, though neither

ever wrote tragedy in dramatic form"; Irvin Ehrenpreis, in *The Personality of Jonathan Swift* (London: Methuen, 1958), argues that Swift followed a tragic pattern in his writing of history (p. 69).

27. In No. 28 of *The Examiner*, Swift even describes himself in strongly animalistic language, saying that he has and needs a great deal of material because "I feed Weekly, two or three *Wit-starved* writers, who have no other visible Support; besides several others, who live upon my Offals. In short, I am like a Nurse who suckles Twins at one Time, and hath besides, *one or two Whelps* constantly to draw her Breasts" (*Prose Works*, III, 86). Like the horse, the spider was available for different emotional evocations of man's condition—always grotesque and painful but not, as in the famous section of the *Battle of the Books*, always repellent. In the vigorous *Proposal for the Universal Use of Irish Manufacture*, the author speaks of how he always pitied Arachne's suffering for her victory in spinning over Athena and compares Ireland to the spider and England to the vengeful goddess (*Prose Works*, IX, 18). For contemporary uses of the spider-and-bee image and their reflection in the *Battle of the Books*, see Kathleen Williams, "Restoration Themes in Major Satires of Swift," p. 261; Ernest Tuveson, "Swift and the World-Makers," *JHI*, 11 (1950), 54–74; Ehrenpreis, *Swift*, I, 233–35.

28. On September 9, 1710, he wrote to Archbishop King: "Upon my Arrival hither, I found myself equally caressed by both Parties, by one as a Sort of bough for drowning men to lay hold of; and by the other as one discontented . . ." (*Correspondence*, I, 173); his *Journal to Stella* entry of the same day cheerfully echoes the image (I, 5). On March 4, 1710–11, he uses a conventional image to note for Stella that the ministry was in great danger of shipwreck (I, 206); on October 1, 1711, he described himself to King as "a Man floating at Sea" in no position to plan his future until he can get ashore and "rest, and dry himself, and then look about him" (*Correspondence*, I, 262); cf. also his letter to Ford on January 6, 1718–19 (*Correspondence*, II, 310), and succeeding letters. For an illuminating discussion of the prevalence of madness as a subject for scientific and literary speculation in the eighteenth century, see G. S. Rousseau, "Science and the Discovery of the Imagination in Enlightened England," *ECS*, 3 (1969), 108–35, esp. 123–26. For Swift on the attacked hero, see Kathryn Montgomery Harris, " 'Occasions So Few': Satire as a Strategy of Praise in Swift's Early Odes," *MLQ*, 31 (1970), 22–37.

29. For a discussion of Swift's Irish background, as for all biographical matters, see Ehrenpreis, *Swift* (in this case, Vol. I, Pt. I).

30. For an acute discussion of Swift's use of the clothing image, see Paulson, *Theme and Structure in Swift's Tale of a Tub*, pp. 157–58, 177.

31. Cf. Price, *Swift's Rhetorical Art*, p. 46: "The heart of the poem is the

treatment of metamorphosis, which no longer confirms a spiritual quality by giving it proper embodiment but rather makes the new embodiment another vehicle for the same commonplace qualities."

32. Such an attitude is perhaps to be expected of a man in his twenties, as in a letter to Thomas Swift of December 6, 1693: "My self was never very miserable while my thoughts were in a Ferment for I imagine a dead Calm to be troublesomest part of our Voyage thro the World" (*Correspondence*, I, 13). But he appears still to mean it a quarter century later when complaining to Bolingbroke that "a lower kind of discretion and regularity... seldom fails of raising men to the highest stations, in the court, the church, and the law" (*Correspondence*, II, 332), where they remain long in power while geniuses fall soon.

33. In a famous letter to Pope of September 29, 1725, he wrote that he disliked crowds or groups of people, "but principally I hate and detest that animal called man, although I heartily love John, Peter, Thomas, and so forth" (*Correspondence*, III, 103); some examples of his contempt for clichés appear in the pious phrases in *Baucis and Philemon*; the fashion of hunting husbands in *To Lord Harley, on his Marriage*; the normal routine of clergymen in London, in *The Author upon Himself*; routine courtesy instead of humanity, in *The Sickness*; and romantic phrases, in *Phillis, or the Progress of Love*. Most perceptively, John Traugott in "Swift's Allegory: The Yahoo and the Man-of-mode," *UTQ*, 33 (1963), 1–18, observes that "as in idiom so in any mundane conventionality—clichés, cant, faddish philosophies, nominal pieties, daily habits, manners, even popular literary forms— Swift was only too likely to see allegories of whole attitudes toward life" (p. 3). Hugh Sykes Davies, "Irony and the English Tongue," in *The World of Jonathan Swift*, ed. Brian Vickers (Oxford: Blackwell, 1968), pp. 129–53, adds usefully that "the trite and threadbare horrified him the more intimately because he felt them to be so dangerous a travesty of his own deepest intuitions, ruining the past which he cherished by lifeless and automatic repetition" (p. 135).

34. In *Tatler* No. 230 Swift examines the effect of *"Ignorance, and want of Taste"* in hastening *"the continual Corruption of our English Tongue"* (*Prose Works*, II, 174), with ominous implications for English civilization. In *The Importance of the Guardian Considered* and *The Publick Spirit of the Whigs* he finds in Steele's work an apt illustration of all the moral ills which a corrupt language can exhibit; cf. *Preface to the Right Reverend Dr. Burnet* (*Prose Works*, IV, 57); *Polite Conversation* (*Prose Works*, IV, 107); letter to Henry Clark, December 12, 1734 (*Correspondence*, IV, 274).

35. Mayhew has a most informative chapter on this word play in his *Rage or Raillery*.

36. E. San Juan, Jr., "The Anti-Poetry of Jonathan Swift," *PQ*, 44

(1965), 387–96, and A. B. England, "World Without Order: Some Thoughts on the Poetry of Swift," *EIC*, 16 (1966), 32–43, comment on the apparent chaos of Swift's poetic world.

37. His ideas are, of course, important, well worth the study they have elicited in many of the works cited above, most notably those by Quintana and Miss Williams; for other useful examinations of Swift's thoughts in the context of his time, see Ehrenpreis' biography; the Tuveson and Hopkins essays cited above; various articles by Louis A. Landa—for example, "Jonathan Swift and Charity," *JEGP*, 44 (1945), 337–50, and "*A Modest Proposal* and Populousness," *MP*, 40 (1942–43), 161–70; Paulson's study of the gnostic influence on the *Tale*; George Wittkowsky, "Swift's *Modest Proposal*: The Biography of an Early Georgian Pamphlet," *JHI*, 4 (1943), 75–104; Z. S. Fink, "Political Theory in *Gulliver's Travels*," *ELH*, 14 (1947), 151–61; the ancients-moderns controversy in Miriam Kosh Starkman, *Swift's Satire on Learning in A Tale of a Tub* (Princeton: Princeton University Press, 1950), and her recent reevaluation of the relations between genre and moral statement in "Swift's Rhetoric: The 'overfrought pinnace'?" *SAQ*, 68 (1969), 188–97; theology in Philip Harth, *Swift and Angelican Rationalism: The Religious Background of A Tale of a Tub* (Chicago: University of Chicago Press, 1961); and psychology in Charles Peake, "Swift and the Passions," *MLR*, 55 (1960), 169–80.

38. Although critical emphasis, following Leavis, has been on Swift's intensity, some very effective scholars have noticed his playful vigor. See, for example, Louis A. Landa, "Jonathan Swift: 'Not the Gravest of Divines,'" in *Jonathan Swift*, ed. McHugh and Edwards, pp. 38–60; Louis A. Landa, "Jonathan Swift," in *Literature of the Augustan Age*, ed. Boys, pp. 177–97; Bonamy Dobrée, "The Jocose Dean," in *Fair Liberty Was All His Cry*, ed. Jeffares, pp. 42–61, and Herbert Davis, "Swift's View of Poetry," pp. 62–97, in the same collection; George Mayhew, "Swift's Bickerstaff Hoax as an April Fool's Joke," *MP*, 61 (1963–64), 270–80; "Swift and the Tripos Tradition," *PQ*, 45 (1966), 249–61; and his *Rage and Raillery*.

Chapter IV

1. *Diaries, Prayers, and Annals*, ed. E. L. McAdam, Jr., with Donald and Mary Hyde, Vol. I of the Yale Edition of the Works of Samuel Johnson (New Haven: Yale University Press, 1958), p. 38; see also entries for September 18, 1768 (p. 119), April 7, 1776 (p. 257), and September 18, 1780 (pp. 301–2).

2. James Boswell, *Life of Samuel Johnson, LL.D.*, ed. George Birkbeck Hill, rev. L. F. Powell (Oxford: Clarendon Press, 1934), I, 446.

3. From different perspectives, others have, of course, argued that Johnson's quirks or neuroses were responsible for aspects of his ideas; for example, Arieh Sachs, "Samuel Johnson on 'The Vacuity of Life,'" *SEL*, 3 (1963), p. 357, reasoned that Johnson could turn "his personal distress of melancholy, guilt and indolence" into general, universal systems: "Indolence became 'vacuity,' the obsessive 'chain of sin' became 'habit,' neurotic fantasy became 'imagination,' and these notions were tied together in generalizations about mankind that on the whole are distinguished by their striking pertinence." Cf. Bertrand H. Bronson's seminal "Johnson Agonistes," in his *Johnson and Boswell: Three Essays*, University of California Publications in English, Vol. 3, No. 9 (Berkeley and Los Angeles: University of California Press, 1944), pp. 363–98; and Herman W. Liebert, "Reflections on Samuel Johnson," in *Samuel Johnson: A Collection of Critical Essays*, ed. Donald J. Greene (Englewood Cliffs: Prentice-Hall, 1965), pp. 15–21.

4. Writing to Thomas Warton on February 1, 1755, he says that he is unsure what reception he will have when he swims ashore to the publication of the *Dictionary*, "a Calypso that will court or a Polypheme that will eat me. But if Polypheme comes to me have at his eyes." *The Letters of Samuel Johnson*, ed. R. W. Chapman, 3 vols. (Oxford: Clarendon Press, 1952), I, 61. On his amusement when attacked, cf. *Life*, IV, 127.

5. See also *Diaries*, pp. 20–21; *Life*, I, 66; IV, 34.

6. For a few examples of Johnson's awareness of his competitiveness, see *Life*, V, 34, on his matching himself with Burke, and also *Life*, II, 450; his delight in succeeding as a boy in school, *Diaries*, p. 17; the price for *London* based on Whitehead's fee for a worse poem, *Life*, I, 124; awareness of his comparative superiority over an early competitor who had stayed at Oxford, *Life*, I, 272; his pleasure in meeting an old friend with whom he had no need to compete, *Letters*, I, 346.

7. Cf. letter to Hill Boothby, December 30, 1755: "It is again Midnight, and I am again alone. With what meditation shall I amuse this waste hour of darkness and vacuity. If I turn my thoughts upon myself what do I perceive but a poor helpless being reduced by a blast of wind to weakness and misery" (*Letters*, I, 78); cf. *Diaries*, July 22, 1773, p. 159.

8. Even his most self-condemnatory remarks, as in a letter to Baretti of June 10, 1761, can be followed by expressions of persistent hope: "Of myself I have nothing to say, but that I have hitherto lived without the concurrence of my own judgment; yet I continue to flatter myself, when you return, you will find me mended" (*Letters*, I, 134).

9. "I remember he once observed to me, 'It is wonderful, Sir, what is to be found in London. The most literary conversation that I ever en-

joyed, was at the table of Jack Ellis, a money-scrivener behind the Royal Exchange, with whom I at one period used to dine generally once a week'" (*Life*, III, 21).

10. *Letters*, I, 59–60; cf. his letters to Lucy Porter and to Joseph Simpson (*Letters*, I, 120 and 127) on the death of his mother.

11. *Letters*, I, 370; cf. also his letters to her of June 11, 1775; July 15, 1775; November 12, 1781; and July 3, 1783.

12. Samuel Johnson, *The Lives of the English Poets*, ed. G. Birkbeck Hill, 3 vols. (Oxford: Clarendon Press, 1905), II, 206.

13. *The Rambler*, ed. W. J. Bate and Albrecht B. Strauss, Vols. III–V of the Yale Edition of the Works of Samuel Johnson (New Haven: Yale University Press, 1969), V, 93; see also his letter in the *Universal Visiter* of April, 1756, rpt. in *The Works of Samuel Johnson*, 9 vols. (Oxford: Talboys and Wheeler, 1825), V, 357–62, on the low condition and nature of authors.

14. For various estimates of the degree of irony, see C. R. Tracy, "Democritus, Arise! A Study of Dr. Johnson's Humor," *Yale Review*, 39 (1949), 294–310; Alvin Whitley, "The Comedy of *Rasselas*," *ELH*, 23 (1956), 48–70; Mary Lascelles, "*Rasselas* Reconsidered," *Essays and Studies*, n.s. 4 (1951), 37–52; Agostino Lombardo, "The Importance of Imlac," in *Bicentenary Essays on Rasselas*, ed. Magdi Wahba (Cairo: Société Orientale de Publicité, 1959), pp. 31–49; Geoffrey Tillotson, "Imlac and the Business of the Poet," in *Studies in Criticism and Aesthetics, 1660–1800*, ed. Howard Anderson and John S. Shea (Minneapolis: University of Minnesota Press, 1967), pp. 296–314; Martin Kallich, "Samuel Johnson's Principles of Criticism and Imlac's 'Dissertation upon Poetry,'" *JAAC*, 25 (1966), 71–82; Sheridan Baker, "*Rasselas*. Psychological Irony and Romance," *PQ*, 45 (1966), 249–61. I may add that Johnson was working on his Shakespeare edition at this time and was no doubt neck deep in eulogies of Shakespeare as universal guru.

15. *Letters*, II, 80; cf. *Idler* 44 for similar opinions. In discussing Johnson's psychological views, I am inevitably indebted to such standard studies as Bronson's, cited above; Joseph Wood Krutch, *Samuel Johnson* (New York: Harcourt, Brace, 1944); W. B. C. Watkins, *Perilous Balance* (Princeton: Princeton University Press, 1939); James L. Clifford, *Young Sam Johnson* (New York: McGraw-Hill, 1955); and Walter Jackson Bate, *The Achievement of Samuel Johnson* (New York: Oxford University Press, 1955). Of more specialized relevance would be W. K. Wimsatt's standard discussion of Johnson's diction as expressing his ideas, *Philosophic Words: A Study of Style and Meaning in the Rambler and Dictionary of Samuel Johnson* (New Haven: Yale University Press, 1948); Donald Westing, "An Ideal of Greatness: Ethical Implications in Johnson's Critical Vocabulary," *UTQ*, 34 (1965), 133–45; Arieh Sachs, *Passionate Intelligence: Imagination and*

Reason in the Work of Samuel Johnson (Baltimore: John Hopkins Press, 1967); Paul Kent Alkon, *Samuel Johnson and Moral Discipline* (Evanston: Northwestern University Press, 1967); Robert Voitle, *Samuel Johnson the Moralist* (Cambridge, Mass.: Harvard University Press, 1961).

16. *Letters*, II, 429; see also *Ramblers* 59 and 60, in which sympathetic communication is affirmed both ironically and straightforwardly.

17. Cf. his comment in his *Life of Sydenham* (1742): "There is no instance of any man, whose history has been minutely related, that did not, in every part of life, discover the same proportion of intellectual vigour" (*Works*, VI, 406).

18. He gave up his own options reluctantly, as witness his considerable activities as adviser on the law and as author of Chambers' law lectures, which are examined in E. L. McAdam, Jr., *Dr. Johnson and the English Law* (Syracuse: Syracuse University Press, 1951). In his *Life of Dryden*, Johnson again implied the existence of a core of general mental power: "His compositions are the effects of a vigorous genius operating upon large materials" (*Lives of the English Poets*, I, 457).

19. In his *Vision of Theodore* (*Works*, IX, 162–75), he cast the Habits in the role of soul-destroyers; cf. Bate, p. 40; Sachs, "Vacuity of Life," p. 360.

20. See his letter to Boswell of August 21, 1766 (*Letters*, I, 190); *Diaries*, pp. 133–34; his comment on *Love's Labour's Lost*, I, 147–50: "Biron amidst his extravagancies, speaks with great justness against the folly of vows. They are made without sufficient regard to the variations of life, and are therefore broken by some unforeseen necessity. They proceed commonly from a presumptuous confidence, and a false estimate of human power." *Johnson on Shakespeare*, ed. Arthur Sherbo, Vol. VII of the Yale Edition of the Works of Samuel Johnson (New Haven: Yale University Press, 1968), p. 267.

21. *Johnson's Journey to the Western Isles of Scotland, and Boswell's Journal of a Tour to the Hebrides with Samuel Johnson, LL.D.*, ed. Alan Wendt (Boston: Houghton Mifflin, 1965), p. 116. Cf. Johnson's description of a stormy journey in a coach along a river, in a letter to Henry Thrale of October 23, 1773 (*Letters*, I, 382). On August 20, 1774, he notes that Carnarvon Castle is immensely greater than Beaumaris: "To survey this place would take much time. I did not think there had been such buildings. It surpassed my Ideas" (*Diaries*, p. 204); in the Little Trianon, on the other hand, "The rooms at the top are small, fit to sooth the imagination with privacy" (*Diaries*, p. 243).

22. Cf. *Rambler* 5, which begins by saying that we should enjoy what nature offers us in spring but then insists on changing to allegory,

advising youth "to make use at once of the spring of the year, and the spring of life."

23. Samuel Johnson, *Rasselas, Poems, and Selected Prose*, ed. Bertrand H. Bronson (New York: Holt, Rinehart, & Winston, 1958), p. 522.

24. A very similar, though more limited, point was to be made in *Idler* 63, only a few months later: *The Idler and The Adventurer*, ed. W. J. Bate, John M. Bullitt, and L. F. Powell, Vol. II of the Yale Edition of the Works of Samuel Johnson (New Haven: Yale University Press, 1963), pp. 196–98.

25. Cf. Sachs, *Passionate Intelligence*, particularly the chapter on vacuity; see also Bate, *Achievement of Samuel Johnson*, esp. p. 40.

26. Cf. *Life*, III, 294; see also Stuart Gerry Brown, "Dr. Johnson and the Religious Problem," *ES*, 20 (1938), 1–17; J. H. Hagstrum, "On Dr. Johnson's Fear of Death," *ELH*, 14 (1947), 308–19.

27. Cf. Northrop Frye's description of the "literature of process" of the second half of the eighteenth century in his "Towards Defining an Age of Sensibility," *ELH*, 23 (1956), 144–52.

28. As Clifford points out in *Young Sam Johnson*, p. 149, Johnson began keeping a diary in his twenties: "Part of the compulsion, no doubt, came from his tendency to morbid introspection. But the strict self-discipline imposed by a diary was part of a recognized evangelical, methodistic pattern. There was always a strong Calvinistic strain in his religious convictions." Katherine C. Balderston, "Doctor Johnson and William Law," *PMLA*, 75 (1960), 382–94, argues that William Law's *Serious Call* may have affected Johnson by, among other things, its insistence on self-examination (p. 388).

29. For Johnson's political views, see Donald J. Greene, *The Politics of Samuel Johnson* (New Haven: Yale University Press, 1960), particularly the brilliant concluding chapter, "A Recapitulation and Some Reflections," pp. 231–58.

30. Among the more interesting discussions of the poem are Clifford, pp. 319–20; Bate, pp. 23, 92 ff.; David Perkins, "Johnson on Wit and Metaphysical Poetry," *ELH*, 20 (1953), 200–217; Susie I. Tucker and Henry Gifford, "Johnson's Poetic Imagination," *RES*, 8 (1957), 241–48; Mary Lascelles, "Johnson and Juvenal," in *New Light on Dr. Johnson*, ed. F. W. Hilles (New Haven: Yale University Press, 1959), pp. 35–55; Edward A. Bloom, "*The Vanity of Human Wishes*: Reason's Images," *EIC*, 15 (1965), 181–92; A. D. Moody, "The Creative Critic: Johnson's Revisions of *London* and *The Vanity of Human Wishes*," *RES*, 22 (1971), 137–50.

31. On Johnson's use of the genre in *Rasselas*, see esp. Gwin J. Kolb, "The Structure of *Rasselas*," *PMLA*, 56 (1951), 698–717; and Mary Lascelles, "*Rasselas* Reconsidered"; for a plausible argument that he may have been considering a *Rasselas*-like work as early as the time of *The*

Rambler, see Donald M. Lockhart, " 'The Fourth Son of the Mighty Emperor': The Ethiopian Background of Johnson's *Rasselas*," *PMLA*, 78 (1963), 516–28; also Arthur J. Weitzman, "More Light on *Rasselas*: The Background of the Egyptian Episodes," *PQ*, 48 (1969), 42–58.

32. "He told me that the character of *Sober* in the Idler, was by himself intended as his own portrait; and that he had his own outset into life in his eye when he wrote the eastern story of Gelaleddin": Mrs. Piozzi, *Anecdotes*, in *Johnsonian Miscellanies*, ed. George Birkbeck Hill (New York: Barnes & Noble, 1966; a rpt. of 1897 Clarendon Press ed.), I, 178.

33. Johnson's argument is discussed amusingly in Emrys Jones, "The Artistic Form of *Rasselas*," *RES*, 18 (1967), 387–401; more convincingly, in Mary Lascelles, "*Rasselas* Reconsidered."

Chapter V

1. Albert S. Gérard, *English Romantic Poetry: Ethos, Structure, and Symbol in Coleridge, Wordsworth, Shelley, and Keats* (Berkeley and Los Angeles: University of California Press, 1968), p. 3, says that "if one impulse can be singled out as central to the romantic inspiration. it is the Sehnsucht, the yearning toward the absolute, the aspiration to oneness and wholeness and organic unity, the dream of perfection"; Robert Langbaum, "The Evolution of Soul in Wordsworth's Poetry," *PMLA*, 82 (1967), 265–72, points out that for this purpose of union "memory becomes in Wordsworth the instrument of the associative or transforming power" (p. 270); Georges Poulet, "Timelessness and Romanticism," *JHI*, 15 (1954), 3–22, sees two ways of achieving movement from imprisonment in the present that are meaningful to Wordsworth, the evocation of the past through an odor or a sound and the intense absorption in the present which makes of the moment eternity; Jonathan Bishop, "Wordsworth and the "Spots of Time,'" *ELH*, 26 (1959), 45–65, examines the cluster of associations with memory that the phrase holds for the poet; and Geoffrey H. Hartman, *The Unmediated Vision* (New York: Harcourt, Brace, & World, 1966; a rpt. of the Yale edition, 1954), had argued convincingly for "the image and sound of universal waters" as the goal of all meaning for Wordsworth's imagination (p. 43).

2. An attitude that Hazlitt found fundamental in the writings of his contemporaries, as M. H. Abrams says in "English Romanticism: The

Spirit of the Age," in *Romanticism Reconsidered: Selected Papers from the English Institute*, ed. Northrop Frye (New York: Columbia University Press, 1963), pp. 26–72.

3. To Jane Pollard on August 6, 1787, in *The Early Letters of William and Dorothy Wordsworth (1787–1805)*, ed. Ernest de Selincourt, 2nd ed., rev. Chester L. Shaver (Oxford: Clarendon Press, 1967), p. 7.

4. *The Letters of William and Dorothy Wordsworth: The Middle Years*, ed. Ernest de Selincourt (Oxford: Clarendon Press, 1937), I, 125–26.

5. For example, he wrote to Catherine Clarkson in December, 1814, that if a friend of hers could read some of *The Excursion*'s pathetic parts unmoved then she was a bad person: "Could the anger of Ellen before she sate down to weep over her Babe, tho' she were but a poor serving maid, be found in a book, and that book said to be without passion, then, thank Heaven! that the person so speaking is neither my Wife nor my Sister, nor one whom (unless I could work in her a great alteration) I am forced daily to converse with." *Middle Years*, II, 620.

6. John E. Jordan, in "Wordsworth's Humor," *PMLA*, 73 (1958), 81–93, speaks appropriately of the "mock-heroic strain, this ironic tongue-in-cheek tone" of these passages (p. 88).

7. *The Poetical Works of William Wordsworth*, ed. E. de Selincourt and Helen Darbishire, 5 vols. (Oxford: Clarendon Press, 1949–66), V, 373–76. This five-volume edition and de Selincourt's Oxford Standard Authors edition of *The Prelude* (1805 text), rev. Helen Darbishire (1960), are my texts for Wordsworth's poetry.

8. For more appreciative responses to Wordsworth's use of personae, see Stephen Maxfield Parrish, " 'The Thorn': Wordsworth's Dramatic Monologue," *ELH*, 24 (1957), 153–64; "Dramatic Technique in the *Lyrical Ballads*," *PMLA*, 74 (1959), 85–97; Neil H. Hertz, "Wordsworth and the Tears of Adam," *SIR*, 7 (1967), 15–33; Frederick Garber, "Point of View and the Egotistical Sublime," *ES*, 49 (1968), 409–18.

9. According to a variety of critics, most emphatically René Wellek in his "Romanticism Reconsidered," in *Romanticism Reconsidered*, ed. Frye, p. 110, the concept of a living world is one of those fundamental to the romantic vision.

10. In the *Guide to the Lakes*—to pick a completely unemotional example—after the introductory chapter, Wordsworth undertakes to give a view from above of the whole prospect of the Lakes: it is a favorite observing position from the *Descriptive Sketches* to the 1850 *Prelude*.

11. J. D. O'Hara, "Ambiguity and Assertion in Wordsworth's 'Elegiac Stanzas,' " *PQ*, 47 (1968), 69–82, presents a radical but plausible argument that the poem repudiates both the imagination and nature as isolating elements; Alan Grob, "Process and Permanence in *Resolution*

and Independence," *ELH*, 28 (1961), 89–100, thinks that both that poem and the *Elegiac Stanzas* are "poems of renunciation, statements of the unsuitability of nature's holy plan as a model of human conduct" (p. 90).

12. But since wandering is man's archetypal lot, Wordsworth sometimes sees it as encouraging, as in *To a Skylark* (1802), in which his long and difficult journey is cheered with hope of the afterlife when he hears the lark's call. *The Danish Boy* (1799) describes a boy who has run away from his passionate and violent society, but his escape has cost his vitality; *The Pilgrim's Dream; or, the Star and the Glow Worm* (1818) again deals with a wanderer, who is here forbidden to rest in a castle but has a cheering dream while he is under a tree. Wordsworth, by the way, was familiar enough with *Rasselas* to describe a mountain area in his *Guide to the Lakes* as "a spot like the Abyssinian recess of Rasselas" (London: Henry Frowde, 1906, ed. Ernest de Selincourt), p. 48.

13. Cf. *The Old Cumberland Beggar* and the old man and small child of *The Two Thieves*, whose function, like that of nonhuman emanations of the universe, is to arouse responsive feelings in ordinary people and thus raise them above the insensitivity of daily getting and spending.

14. Cf. Hartman's apt phrase for Wordsworth's expectation of nature as a "principle of generosity" (*Unmediated Vision*, pp. 20–26).

15. For some cogent discussions of central archetypes in the play, see Albert Guerard, Jr., "Prometheus and the Aeolian Lyre," *Yale Review*, 33 (1944), 482–97; Geoffrey H. Hartman, "Romanticism and 'Anti–Self-Consciousness,'" *Centennial Review of Arts and Science*, 6 (1962), 553–65; Peter L. Thorslev, Jr., "Wordsworth's *Borderers* and the Romantic Villain-Hero," *SIR*, 5 (1966), 84–103.

16. Among Wordsworth's more prominent forsaken women are those in *The Complaint of a Forsaken Indian Woman* (1798); *Her Eyes Are Wild* (1798); *The Thorn* (1798); *September 1, 1802*; *The Sailor's Mother* (1802); *The Emigrant Mother* (1802); *Beggars* (1802); *The Forsaken* (1804); *The Affliction of Margaret* (1804); *Vaudracour and Julia* (1804); *The Force of Prayer* (1807); *Song at the Feast of Brougham Castle* (1807); *Maternal Grief* (1813); *The Armenian Lady's Love* (1830); *The Widow on Windermere's Side* (1837). Gérard, discussing *The Thorn* in his *English Romantic Poets* (pp. 64–88), cites various critics on the frequency of the abandoned-mother-and-child theme as a reflection of the Annette Vallon affair.

17. *The Italian Itinerant, and The Swiss Goatherd* (1821) has some of this adventurous ambiguity, contrasting the active wanderer who could make a vigorous life among people with a poor abandoned boy doomed to isolation and ignorance.

18. The lofty solitary is at the extreme of evil in No. I of Part II of the "Poems to National Independence and Liberty," in which a single voice proclaims rule over Greece, drowning out the others—but it is the voice of the alienated tyrant. In No. VI the tyrant is again the destructive solitary, presumably as against the constructive, unselfish eminence which poets normally adorn.

19. In No. IV of the "Memorials of a Tour on the Continent, 1820," *Incident at Bruges*, a voice sings to a harp from a convent, with something of the effect of the Solitary Reaper, evoking from the "passing Stranger" sympathy for another archetype, the eternal captive.

20. R. A. Foakes, *The Romantic Assertion: A Study in the Language of Nineteenth Century Poetry* (London: Methuen, 1958), speaks of Wordsworth's descriptions in *The Prelude* of his "descent to the plains of Cambridge" (p. 68) and "ascent of Snowdon" (p. 73) as clearly symbolic; and Wordsworth's pervasive symbolism in *The Prelude* (and elsewhere) is assumed and finely explicated by Herbert Lindenberger, *On Wordsworth's Prelude* (Princeton: Princeton University Press, 1963) and by Geoffrey H. Hartman, *Wordsworth's Poetry, 1787–1814* (New Haven: Yale University Press, 1964).

21. In *The Somnambulist* (1828), an abandoned girl is temporarily restored to happiness by the assurance of union with another person; after her death, her guilty lover is to spend the rest of his life in solitary atonement, like Marmaduke and Vaudracour. For useful analyses of the themes of *The White Doe*, see Elizabeth Geen, "The Concept of Grace in Wordsworth's Poetry," *PMLA*, 58 (1943), 689–715; Helen Darbishire, *The Poet Wordsworth* (Oxford: Clarendon Press, 1950), p. 157; Ellen Douglas Leyburn, "Radiance in *The White Doe of Rylstone*," *SP*, 47 (1950), 629–33; James A. W. Heffernan, "Wordsworth on Imagination: The Emblemizing Power," *PMLA*, 81 (1966), 389–99.

22. M. H. Abrams, "Structure and Style in the Greater Romantic Lyric," in *From Sensibility to Romanticism*, ed. Frederick W. Hilles and Harold Bloom (New York: Oxford University Press, 1965), pp. 527–60, speaks of Wordsworth's technique of "double awareness" from *Tintern Abbey* to *The Prelude*, his device of balancing an earlier with a present view (p. 533); Parrish, "Dramatic Technique in the *Lyrical Ballads*," examines Wordsworth's experiments as dialectic; Anne Kostelanetz, "Wordsworth's 'Conversations': A Reading of 'The Two April Mornings' and 'The Fountain,'" *ELH*, 33 (1966), 43–52, sees the poems as essentially dramatic in their opposition of valid viewpoints; Florence G. Marsh, "Wordsworth's *Ode*: Obstinate Questionings," *SIR*, 5 (1966), 219–30, finds that poem built on a dual pattern.

23. Among other suggestions of Wordsworth's projection of his own fantasies in his poems, H. W. Garrod, *Wordsworth: Lectures and*

Essays, 2nd ed. (Oxford: Clarendon Press, 1927), says of *The Excursion* that "its nine books introduce us to three heroes; and each of them is Wordsworth himself" (p. 25); Hugh L'Anson Fausset, *The Lost Leader: A Study of Wordsworth* (New York: Harcourt, Brace, n.d.), assures us that "the Emily who had hoped for the success of the Catholic cause, who had been heart-broken by its failure, but had escaped 'that most lamentable snare/ The self-reliance of despair,' was of course the poet who had survived the French Revolution" (p. 413); Z. S. Fink, "Wordsworth and the English Republican Tradition," *JEGP*, 47 (1948), 107–26, sees Wordsworth in *The Prelude* meditating fantasies of leading France out of chaos (p. 121); Chapter VII of Lindenberger's *On Wordsworth's Prelude*, dealing with Wordsworth's relationship to his characters, is full of apt perceptions of the ways in which Wordsworth based his characters, particularly his solitaries, on himself, so that they all become "projections of his own self, his hopes, fears, and depths of despair and they receive only so much characterization as Wordsworth needs to portray his own subjective states" (p. 212); R. C. Townsend, "John Wordsworth and His Brother's Poetic Development," *PMLA*, 81 (1966), 70–78, argues convincingly that John is the model for Leonard in *The Brothers*; Hugh Sykes Davies, "Another New Poem by Wordsworth," *EIC*, 15 (1965), 135–61, engagingly guesses that *A Slumber Did My Spirit Seal* is not a Lucy poem but a vision of the poet in a kind of trance.

24. In *A Tradition of Oker Hill*, two brothers, and in *Ellen Irwin*, two suitors are balanced; cf. also *The Italian Itinerant and the Swiss Goatherd* for contrasted wandering and stationary figures.

25. The only recollection of early childhood which Wordsworth provided his nephew was of his surliness when confronted with a slight by authority: Christopher Wordsworth, *Memoirs of William Wordsworth* (London: Edward Moxon, 1851), I, 9. Dorothy records a few youthful conflicts with his grandparents and uncles: for example, *Early Letters*, pp. 3–4 and p. 100, which also include his difficulties with his brother Richard, who as the eldest might claim some authority. As an inevitable complement and balance, Wordsworth often exhibits the Dante-Virgil pattern of the learning and the teaching selves (for example, the Matthew poems and *The Excursion*), his feelings toward fathers being as ambivalent as any orthodox Freudian could wish.

26. Geoffrey Hartman, "Wordsworth, *The Borderers*, and 'Intellectual Murder,'" *JEGP*, 62 (1963), 761–68, brilliantly ties together the theme of innocence and experience with that of intellect as against intuitive responsiveness in the play, which he sees as a combination that "fits a myth as old as that of the Garden of Eden, in which knowledge is related to knowledge of self and the death of innocence" (p. 768). Wordsworth's actualization of innocence in the senile in *The Two*

Thieves and in the permanently childlike *Farmer of Tilsbury Vale* clearly supports Professor Hartman's analysis.

27. Almost without exception, the narratives center in the need for unity. In the *Complaint of a Forsaken Indian Woman*, as in most of the poems about forlorn women, a child forms an important tie between the persons and the world, its needs forcing her out of herself to seek meaning and union. The title figure in *The Sailor's Mother*, having lost her child, has a bird to substitute and unite her to life. *The Emigrant Mother*, *Her Eyes Are Wild*, and *The Thorn* present forlorn women tied to life and meaning by babies; in *Vaudracour and Julia* the death of the child causes the hero's dissociation from life, and in *The Idiot Boy* the deprived mother is reunited with her child and saved from mad distress. The story of *Michael* is worth our while, the narrator tells us, because of its unifying effect on him and, he hopes, on his peers. The loss of the boy is very carefully paralleled with the likely loss of a good part of the fields, the implication being the disintegration of harmony in either event, the destruction of the condition of unfallen innocence. The son is sacrificed in the hope of a return to the ideal agricultural order; and the sheepfold is formally a covenant between father and son which becomes a symbolic covenant between the shepherd family and the outer world. In *Peter Bell* on a large scale, and in the lesser *Fidelity*, the vision of a dead man watched over by an animal in a hidden recess has a unifying, restorative effect on the percipient. In *The White Doe* Wordsworth again sings of harmony, in the spirit of Emily but also in the family, in England, and in man. Since Emily is the last survivor of the Nortons, whose division and mutual forgiveness and reunion represent the English nation under Elizabeth, her tranquil restoration has more than personal meaning. *The Excursion* aims more fully to show the restoration of the sorrowing solitary to union and harmony, both in himself and in his quality as symbol of a nation and of mankind; the Wanderer and the Pastor in various places (for example, IV, 1115, 1207 ff.; V, 903–6; IX, 14 ff.) affirm the existence of a divine plan of union in nature and man, and at the end, on the way to the boat for their excursion, the friends pass an arresting vision of union—the ram divided and yet whole, a direct symbol of man and the universe (IX, 439 ff.). *The Prelude* is professedly a study of the elements tending to disharmony within the poet's mind and in its relations to the world around it. In Book XIII, the "Conclusion," which famously opens with the ascent of Snowden and a vision through clouds of the turbulence of the human mind illuminated by the magnificent harmonizing moon of the imagination, a lyric passage in the coda shows Wordsworth as a singing creature rising out of the organic world, himself an archetypal vision (XIII, 377–85).

28. On the use and nature of sound in Wordsworth's poetry, see Langbaum, "Evolution of Soul in Wordsworth's Poetry," p. 272; John S. Martin, "Wordsworth's Echoes," *ELN*, 5 (1968), 186–92; and especially Hartman, *The Unmediated Vision*, p. 43.

29. As uniting elements central to the poet's identity, see *To a Butterfly* and *The Sparrow's Nest. A Farewell* ties together the cottage and Wordsworth and Dorothy and Mary; *A Morning Exercise* sees the lark as linking the high with the low; *To the Daisy* praises the flower for contributing to his unconscious serenity and growth; in *To a Sky-Lark*, the lark's joy heals the spirit of the traveler; in *The Redbreast Chasing the Butterfly*, the poet attempts to unite the creatures to each other; *Glad Sight Whenever New With Old* is directly on the theme of union; *Love Lies Bleeding* and *Companion to the Foregoing* celebrate this flower's superiority to art as a unifying force for men. Like the rainbow, other elements in nature take on the accumulated levels of human meaning, a kind of transcendence of matter, in the process of uniting and integrating the poet. *To the Cuckoo* describes the creature as not a bird but a voice which can restore to Wordsworth the sense of the mystery of his childhood, which like the rainbow affirms his identity through time. An immense tree in *Yew-Trees* is a tie to the past, to English medieval history, and to the supernatural. *The Simplon Pass*, dealing with what physically unites mountain and valley as well as different nations, is a reflection of a mind and opening for man to eternity. *There Was a Boy* and *Three Years She Grew in Sun and Shower* celebrate the unified, integrated self living in nature and united with it by ordinary sounds and sights. The same attitude suffuses *A Slumber Did My Spirit Seal*, where perfect union is achieved by the beloved in death. In *I Wandered Lonely As a Cloud*, clouds, daffodils, lake, breeze, and stars have all been made intensely alive on the poet's level and will remain so all his life, through the agency of the mind and memory. Among the many studies which have noted Wordsworth's concern for unifying symbols, Christopher Salvesen, *The Landscape of Memory* (London: Edward Arnold, 1965), and Newton P. Stallknecht, *Strange Seas of Thought* (Bloomington: University of Indiana Press, 1958), are particularly useful.

30. As various critics have noted: cf. Gérard's Chapter V, "Dark Passages: Wordsworth's *Tintern Abbey*," in his *English Romantic Poetry*, pp. 89–117; James Benziger, *Images of Eternity* (Carbondale: Southern Illinois University Press, 1962), p. 39; Frederick A. Pottle, "Wordsworth's *Lines Composed a Few Miles Above Tintern Abbey*, 72–102," *Explicator*, 16 (March, 1958), No. 36; Robert M. Maniquis, "Comparison, Intensity, and Time in *Tintern Abbey*," *Criticism*, 11 (1969), 358–82.

31. In *To Joanna* Wordsworth repeated central elements in *Tintern Abbey*: a vision of unity in the natural scene of Rotha's banks, in company with Mary Hutchinson's younger sister. In *Water Fowl* the birds become angelic, uniting lake, mountains, and sky; *The Primrose of the Rock* (1831) is one of Wordsworth's later attempts to catch intense response to the vision of unity; so is *Presentiments*, which posits uniting impulses sent from nature and God to give meaning to the world. *To the Clouds* opens with the movement of clouds, which as always implies a union between the start and the destination, a favorite symbol for Wordsworth's vision. Their origin is "a calm descent of sky" suggesting the passage of time and leading to the "abyss" in which the generations swiftly disappear, and they symbolize and connect with the poet's soul; recurring through the ages and through the periods of a single life, the clouds encourage our "credulous desire" to hope that memory can keep the vision "unimpaired," but this is a "vain thought." Among the shorter poems, many attempt to catch the moment of harmony or record its loss: see "Miscellaneous Sonnets" VI, VIII, IX, X, XXX, XXXIII; Pt. II, Sonnets VII, XV, XX, XXXII, XXXVI; Pt. III, Sonnets VII, X, XIV, XVIII, XX, XXII, XXIII, XXIX, XXXII, XLVII. The powerful effect of *To a Highland Girl* is achieved by showing that the girl and her setting are a unified vision; in *Address to Kilchurn Castle*, Wordsworth touches on the tie that ruins or old buildings can make between the generations; in *The Brownie's Cell*, the conclusion compares the cell to Bacchus' wild sanctuary, to emphasize the unity of human myths and aspirations; *Yarrow Visited* provides a scene like *Tintern Abbey's*, which unites the various elements of life, particularly the different ages of man. The most frequent theme in the "Poems to National Independence and Liberty" is human solidarity through the ages and over national boundaries, particularly as concentrated in single heroic spirits or in a significant spot; the short poems of the "Memorials of a Tour on the Continent, 1820," again tend to deal with unifying perceptions: in No. III, *Bruges*, of "The Spirit of Antiquity"; in No. VIII, *In the Cathedral at Cologne*, of man's response to the idea of the divine; in No. XVII, of peasant girls singing on the river; in No. XVIII, of the tie of this world and heaven symbolized in the Engelberg. Similarly, in the rest of this series, in the "Memorials of a Tour in Italy, 1837," in *The River Dudden*, in *Yarrow Revisited and Other Poems*, Wordsworth celebrates the various sorts of visions of unity effected by, among other things, music; Leonardo's "Last Supper"; a solar eclipse; the silence of the peaceful Valley of Dover; his imagination at work on his tour, at Aquapendente; a pine tree; a dove; a cuckoo; the River Dudden; an eagle following a raven; a recollection of the past; the harmony of the times of day and year;

herbs in Roslin Chapel; a robin in *The Trosachs*; the Earl of Breadal-
bane's house and mausoleum.

32. For useful explications of the poem, see Garber, "Point of View and
the Egotistical Sublime"; Gérard, "A Leading from Above: Wordsworth's *Resolution and Independence*," in his *English Romantic Poets*,
pp. 118–35; Anthony E. M. Conran, "The Dialectic of Experience: A
Study of Wordsworth's *Resolution and Independence*," *PMLA*, 75
(1960), 66–74; Alan Grob, "Process and Permanence in *Resolution
and Independence*," *ELH*, 28 (1961), 89–100.

33. Cf. Kenneth MacLean, "Levels of Imagination in Wordsworth's
Prelude (1805)," *PQ*, 38 (1959), 385–400: *The Prelude* "is a story of
an Eden, a fall, and a redemption. Eden of original imagination gives
way to a second condition of imagination, which waits outside the
garden gate" (p. 391); Foakes, *The Romantic Assertion*, says that the
structure of the poem is not a traditional narrative but "a journey as
an image of development; it is a voyage in time and in space, of infinite duration" (p. 60). The poem bends easily to fit the pattern
which Northrop Frye has seen in a great deal of literature, and which
he schematizes in his "The Drunken Boat: The Revolutionary Element in Romanticism," as the vision of "Christian Humanism" in four
levels of being: heaven, unfallen man, physical nature, and sinful, dead
hell; man, having left the second level to live in the third, must strive
to return to the first or he will fall to the fourth (*Romanticism Reconsidered*, p. 4). For the structure of *The Prelude* and for Wordsworth's
form and thought generally, see Hartman, *Wordsworth's Poetry,
1787–1814*, and Lindenberger, *On Wordsworth's Prelude*.

34. Geoffrey H. Hartman, "Wordsworth, Inscriptions and Romantic
Nature Poetry," in *From Sensibility to Romanticism*, ed. Hilles and
Bloom, pp. 389–407, has effectively shown the connection between
Wordsworth's interest in inscriptions as poetry and his tendency to
read mementos as condensed symbols of human events; Ernest Bern-
hardt-Kabisch, "Wordsworth: The Monumental Poet," *PQ*, 44 (1965),
503–18, examines the writings on epitaphs and the inscriptional poems
from a similar viewpoint; James G. Taaffe, "Poet and Lover in Wordsworth's 'Lucy Poems,'" *MLR*, 61 (1966), 175–79, notes Wordsworth's
frequent expression of "the poet's experience of the paradox of loss
and ultimate gain" (p. 175). Alan Grob, "Wordsworth's *Immortality
Ode* and the Search for Identity," *ELH*, 32 (1965), 32–61, sees the
poem as a triumphal record of a conversion, a recovery of rule by the
divine spirit.

35. The "Miscellaneous Sonnets," to pick a group of poems almost at random, continually return to this fear of losing the past. No. III describes the effect on Wordsworth of seeing his Vale again, when he
expected to be ashamed of the pettiness of his childish recollections

but was instead consoled by delight; in No. VI the solace is characteristically in the recollection of a shared scene. No. XXII, *Decay of Piety*, mourns the loss of the trusting fervor of his youth. In No. XXVII, he is reminded of the death of someone he had loved, and for once sees no consolation; in contrast, the next sonnet is a vision of immortality, the consolation for the death, and No. XXIX describes the smile of his dying beloved which consoled him and confirmed his faith. In No. XXXV, he finds in imagination a guarantee of faith, a religious consolation which recurs in his major poems. In another, generally routine series, the "Poems to National Independence and Liberty," No. VI mourns the lost independence of Venice; No. VIII, on the other hand, celebrates the survival after Toussaint l'Ouverture's death of the allied powers of the universe, particularly those in "man's unconquerable mind." No. VIII of Pt. II, written while Wordsworth was busy with his pamphlet on the Convention of Cintra, combines, like Shelley's *Ode to the West Wind*, the idea of dirge and prophecy. In No. XIX of the same part, Wordsworth apostrophizes the brave martyr Schill, providing traditional Christian elegy's consolation of God's favorable judgment in heaven. The pervasive image of *Evening Voluntaries* is of sunset, the pervasive subject exactly the same—the consolation available when so much is lost with the advance of age and the wearing out of nature, mankind, and the sense of imagination. Echoing some of the Intimations Ode's phrasing, No. III of this group says that all is becoming quiet on the water, only the tide remaining: "Stealthy withdrawings, interminglings mild/ Of light with shade in beauty reconciled" (*Poetical Works*, IV, 3). No. IX, *Composed upon an Evening of Extraordinary Splendour and Beauty*—written somewhat earlier than the others (1817)—opens like the Ode with a remnant which relieves of blankness, the afterglow of a living past which is connected with the state before the Fall. As in the Ode, the exhilerating and hopeful beauty comes from the unearthly, "From worlds not quickened by the sun," which he had sensed in childhood but which is now lost in the shades of night. In the next poem, *Composed by the Sea Shore* (1833), the opening yearnings from the past are devastating.

36. *To the Clouds*, for example, is a condensed recapitulation of the themes and movements of the Ode some three years later. The reminder by signs of what is lost has analogues in the *Elegiac Stanzas* (1805); *Once I Could Hail* (1826); *At Home* (1837); *The Cuckoo at Laverna* (1837); and *Sonnet to an Octogenarian* (1846).

INDEX

THE JOHNS HOPKINS PRESS

Designed by Selma Ordewer
Composed in Janson text and display
by Monotype Composition Company
Printed on 60-lb. Perkins and Squier R and
Bound in Columbia Llamique
by The Maple Press Company